Praise for *Serving Up Scripture*

"Bashaw and Higashi are wise and learned guides to the Bible. Even more than that, they're loving and hospitable. Their heart for liberative, life-giving scriptural interpretation shines through in this friendly, accessible book—a gift to readers who have hoped for a more healing path through the Bible but didn't think they could access the necessary tools or skills to find their way there."

—**Jeff Chu**, editor at large for *Travel+Leisure*, teacher in residence at Crosspointe Church in North Carolina, and author of *Good Soil: The Education of an Accidental Farmhand*

"If Guy Fieri took a road trip through biblical scholarship, this would be his Triple D destination—it's got all the FLAVOR! Jennifer Garcia Bashaw and Aaron Higashi have created the ultimate comfort food for anyone who's ever been intimidated by Scripture study. They've managed to make historical criticism feel like a dinner party with your smartest friends, serving up exegetical techniques that are 'money' and hermeneutical approaches that are straight-up 'bananas.' The cooking metaphor isn't just clever—it's transformative, helping you understand that interpretation is an art, a skill you can develop, and a joyful practice rather than a burden. This isn't just about reading ancient texts; it's about reclaiming your own voice in the conversation and finding your own interpretive joint that's off the hook. This book is going to democratize biblical interpretation in the best possible way—taking it from Flavortown to Faithtown!"

—**Tripp Fuller**, host of the *Homebrewed Christianity* podcast and visiting professor of theology and culture at Luther Seminary

"Jennifer Garcia Bashaw and Aaron Higashi's *Serving Up Scripture* is a brilliant guide to the complexities and subjectivities of interpreting the Bible. In a refreshingly accessible way, Bashaw and Higashi pull back the curtain on interpretation to reveal the role of the reader and their social position in guiding the production of meaning with the Bible. Using the analogy of cooking, they place the Bible reader in the role of the chef, who works with a variety of ingredients—the various voices of the biblical texts—to prepare readings that will be meaningful and useful to themselves and to their own audiences. The introductions to the various books of the Bible and the types of questions that can be brought to them are themselves worth the price of admission. *Serving Up Scripture* will be an indispensable guide for those seeking to engage the Bible in more informed, intentional, and productive ways."

—**Dan McClellan**, honorary fellow, Cadbury Centre for the Public Understanding of Religion, University of Birmingham

"With the brilliance of scholars and the warmth of friends, Jennifer Garcia Bashaw and Aaron Higashi invite us to take holy responsibility for how our interpretations play out in God's kingdom, and offer the accessibility and tools to work through our questions with curiosity and care. I cannot wait to shove this book into the hands of everyone I know."

—**Erin Hicks Moon**, author of *I've Got Questions: The Spiritual Practice of Having It Out with God* and cohost of the *Faith Adjacent* podcast

"Scripture says that 'people do not live on bread alone,' but understanding how the meal the Bible offers us is prepared is an essential part of the feast. In *Serving Up Scripture*, Jennifer Garcia Bashaw and Aaron Higashi masterfully expand this meal metaphor to explain the act and art of interpreting Scripture, and our role in that process. This book is helpful, fascinating, and a must-read for anyone who wants to take the Bible more seriously."

—**Josh Scott**, lead pastor of GracePointe Church and author of *Bible Stories for Grown-Ups* and *Parables: Putting Jesus's Stories in Their Place*

"Starting from a comparison between reading the Bible and cooking a meal, Jennifer Garcia Bashaw and Aaron Higashi have produced a lively, accessible, and pragmatic introduction to biblical interpretation. Informed by biblical scholarship, theological reflection, and close attention to both textual details and contemporary experience, this excellent volume offers tools that will allow its readers to participate in biblical interpretation in responsible and creative ways."

—**Ken Stone**, Distinguished Service Professor and professor of Bible, culture, and hermeneutics, Chicago Theological Seminary

"Though it should be obvious, it still needs to be said: The Bible has to be interpreted. The inane little ditty 'God said it, I believe it, that settles it' as an approach to biblical interpretation—an approach many evangelicals have unfortunately inherited—is wholly inadequate. No matter how highly we regard Scripture, *the text still has to be interpreted*. The Bible is indisputably precious, but modern readers need assistance in accessing this ancient treasure. Thankfully, Jennifer Garcia Bashaw and Aaron Higashi are reliable guides in the labyrinth of biblical interpretation. Instead of treating the Bible as a totem before which we merely mutter, 'I believe it,' *Serving Up Scripture* provides the reader with the necessary tools of interpretation, thus unlocking the true treasury of Scripture."

— **Brian Zahnd**, pastor of Word of Life Church in St. Joseph, Missouri, and author of *The Wood Between the Worlds*

SERVING UP SCRIPTURE

Foreword by Peter Enns

SERVING UP SCRIPTURE

How to Interpret the Bible for Yourself and Others

BY JENNIFER GARCIA BASHAW AND AARON HIGASHI

BROADLEAF BOOKS
Minneapolis

SERVING UP SCRIPTURE
How to Interpret the Bible for Yourself and Others

30 29 28 27 26 25 1 2 3 4 5 6 7 8 9

Library of Congress Cataloging-in-Publication Data

Names: Bashaw, Jennifer Garcia, author | Higashi, Aaron author
Title: Serving up scripture : how to interpret the Bible for yourself and others / by Jennifer Garcia Bashaw and Aaron Higashi ; foreword by Pete Enns.
Description: Minneapolis : Broadleaf Books, [2026] | Includes appendices. | Includes bibliographical references.
Identifiers: LCCN 2025022999 (print) | LCCN 2025023000 (ebook) | ISBN 9798889835561 paperback | ISBN 9798889835578 ebook
Subjects: LCSH: Bible--Criticism, interpretation, etc.--Miscellanea | Cooking--Miscellanea
Classification: LCC BS511.3 .B37 2026 (print) | LCC BS511.3 (ebook)
LC record available at https://lccn.loc.gov/2025022999
LC ebook record available at https://lccn.loc.gov/2025023000

Cover image: © Getty Images / E+ Collection / Old Cutting Board by Barcin
Cover design: Broadleaf Books / Alisha Lofgren

Print ISBN: 979-8-8898-3556-1
eBook ISBN: 979-8-8898-3557-8

CONTENTS

Part III
Preparing the Ingredients

Part IV
Feeding People

FOREWORD

A tension exists in American versions of Christianity: What does it mean to be faithful to the ancient Christian tradition while also embracing the various and legitimate challenges to that tradition arising in our current day? If my experience counts for anything, I will say that many pilgrims of faith are seeking to bring these two horizons of past and future into meaningful conversation. Some, of course, may choose to ignore this task, which is their prerogative, but many others are not content to do so. I'm grateful to Jennifer Garcia Bashaw and Aaron Higashi for bringing their insights to bear on this work of interpretation.

The fact that information concerning the Bible's origins and history of interpretation is more readily available in this digital age than previous eras has certainly played a pivotal role in bringing to public scrutiny more conventional and familiar attitudes toward the Bible. This historical consciousness concerning the Bible's origins and its history of interpretation has brought to the forefront, among other things, the complexities of the Bible and has for many problematized what it means to interpret it well. What do we do with a Bible that has two incompatible creation stories, or provides competing views of the history of Israel's monarchies, or contains four Gospels, where each writer was determined to say what he thought, even when that meant putting themselves intentionally at odds with the others? The Bible is not a storybook for children but an anthology of diverse writings that offer diverse perspectives written during the first millennium BCE and, with respect to the Christian Scriptures, spilling over into the first century or two, of the common era.

All this is to say that the popularizing of biblical scholarship in an age of instant information has introduced many to the complexities concerning the nature and interpretation of their sacred book. For good reason, there is a sense of confusion amid the whirlwind. Add to this the related matter of the spread of misinformation—including harmful misinformation—in this age of easy access. The democratization of information and the ease by which it can be accessed has, perhaps ironically, led to the polarization of Scripture on a scale that is unprecedented in human history. Hardliner camps are formed across the ideological spectrum, and too many are content to pick sides quickly.

As a result, interpreting the Bible can be confusing, intimidating, and perhaps for some even futile. *Serving Up Scripture* speaks to this dilemma by taking a step back from the chaos and introducing a bit of calm and order. Bashaw and Higashi help us take a deep breath and walk us through the various issues concerning the nature and interpretation of the Bible. Their aim is to inform and encourage readers of the Bible, which is a rare combination in our present moment. With clarity and sensitivity, they illuminate a path toward interpreting the Bible well, and I am honored to commend their work to you.

Peter Enns, Abram S. Clemens Professor of Biblical Studies, Eastern University, and author of *How the Bible Actually Works*

Introduction

I (JENNIFER) REMEMBER clearly the moment I realized that the Bible could be used to harm rather than help. I was a junior in college and had just decided that I wanted to go to seminary. I had experienced a pull toward the vocation of ministry for several years, but since I had been raised Southern Baptist, it took me awhile to finally say out loud that I felt called to be in church leadership. Southern Baptists, if you don't already know, do not allow women to be leaders in the church.

I was reminded of that prohibition in dramatic fashion when a couple of my college friends sat me down on the porch swing one night to give me a talk about my decision.

Jennifer, we are not sure why you would go to seminary if you can't even be a pastor.

The guys were shaking their heads and furrowing their brows with concern. I gently pushed back, asking them to tell me more about what they meant.

Well, you know that in Ephesians it says that men are the heads of the household, right? How can a woman be the head of a church if she can't even be the head of a family?

Their words landed heavy in my chest, and suddenly I had trouble breathing. They sounded so confident about their interpretation of the Bible on this subject, but what they said felt wrong to me. I shook my head and tried to protest, but nothing came out of my mouth. I knew that there was more to say about women and the family, about women and church leadership, but I didn't know where to start. I didn't know how to counter their vehement argument against my calling.

I spent that night wandering around the campus, distraught and crying. There was a war raging within me. I had always been a people pleaser, and my years in youth group had further shaped me into a compliant, don't-rock-the boat kind of Christian. But that night, something inside of me rebelled. I knew that I felt a calling to go to seminary and give my life to church ministry. And when I thought of all I had learned about Jesus and his life and ministry, my conscience screamed that the protests my friends had raised were wrong. Harmful, even.

I resolved that I would learn more about biblical interpretation, more about the Bible and biblical languages and the cultural and historical background of Scripture, so that the next time someone used the Bible to counter my calling, I would know how to respond. And that's what I did. I went to seminary and then on to a doctoral program in New Testament, and for the past couple of decades, I have taught biblical interpretation in churches and universities and on podcasts and social media. I don't think it's an exaggeration to say that one of my primary missions in life since that porch swing talk has been to counter the harmful use of the Bible through teaching people how to read it well. That is also one of the goals my coauthor Aaron and I have for this book.

Bible Interpretation and You

Maybe, like us, you've seen the Bible used to hurt someone or you have the feeling people are misusing the Bible but can't explain how. Maybe you want to interpret the Bible in new and better ways than you did growing up or you just want to learn more about its history or its contents. Maybe you have a completely different goal. But whatever your reason, if you want to better understand how people interpret the Bible, and especially how *you* can interpret it, then you are reading the right book.

Serving Up Scripture is designed to be a guidebook of sorts for people who want to learn how to read the Bible better. In it, we will lay a solid foundation that introduces budding interpreters to the literature and background of the Bible, help people to understand what interpretation is, and demonstrate how many dynamic and diverse ways there are to interpret Scripture. All of these things are exciting to us. But we understand that not everyone sees biblical interpretation as an accessible subject, and so we have structured this guide around a metaphor that we think is pretty fun: cooking.

Cooking and the Bible

If you think about it, interpreting the Bible is a lot like cooking.

First, when it comes to cooking, the cook matters. The cook's culture, language, country of national origin, race, class, religion, family, and living situation all affect the kinds of meals they're familiar with and the meals they're inclined to cook on any given occasion. What a poor American college student living in a dorm cooks, what a rural farmer cooks, and what a wealthy businessperson on a private plane has cooked for them will no doubt be different. A cook's preferences, expectations, and context influence what they cook.

Similarly, when it comes to biblical interpretation, the interpreter matters. The interpreter's culture, language, country of national origin, race, class, religion, family, and living situation all affect the kinds of interpretations they're familiar with and the interpretations they're inclined to make on any given occasion. The same student, farmer, and businessperson from above will likely interpret the Bible differently, just as they cook differently—because again, an interpreter's preferences, expectations, and context affects what they interpret.

Some people only cook one recipe, or just a small handful of recipes, but some people like to cook as many dishes as they can for the sake of diversifying their palates and exploring what other cultures offer. Variety, they'll say, is the spice of life. The same is true for biblical interpretation. Some people only interpret the Bible in a single way, or in a small handful of ways, but some people like to interpret it in as many ways as they can for the sake of diversifying their literary and theological imaginations.

There are also professional cooks, sometimes called chefs, who have more practice cooking and a greater knowledge of ways to cook than people who aren't professionals. And there are professional Bible interpreters, called Bible scholars, who have more practice interpreting and a greater knowledge of ways to interpret than people who aren't professionals.

A second way that interpreting the Bible is like cooking is that when it comes to cooking, some ingredients are more familiar to us than others. There are some ingredients that we grew up with, others that seem exotic to us, and still others we've never heard of before. Sometimes people are prejudiced against ingredients they don't like or prejudiced against the people who prefer those ingredients. Some ingredients are easy for us to find because supply chains and grocery stores provide them, while other ingredients are virtually beyond our reach. Regardless, the more ingredients we know and the better we know them, the more dishes we can cook.

Interpretation is very much the same. Some interpretations are more familiar to us than others. Many people grow up with certain interpretations, while others can seem exotic to us, and there are for sure interpretations of the Bible we've never heard of before. Sometimes people are prejudiced against particular interpretations they don't like or even prejudiced against the people who make those interpretations. Some interpretations are easy for us to find because schools, churches, Bible studies, and even popular media provide them, while other interpretations are virtually beyond our reach—we lack the experience to even attempt them. Regardless, the more we know about the Bible, the more passages we can fruitfully interpret.

A third similarity between biblical interpretation and cooking has to do with ingredients. When it comes to cooking, two people can take the same basic ingredients and make wildly different dishes with them. Chicken nuggets, chicken tacos, chicken teriyaki, and chicken tikka masala all have the same basic ingredient: chicken. But that chicken is prepared in different ways that reflect the tastes, histories, and the material resources of different groups of people. One person could be totally reliant on chicken nuggets to provide their young and picky children with protein (me, that person is me), while another person may have never heard of chicken nuggets before. Someone could like chicken, generally speaking, but find one particular chicken dish to be disgusting.

Once again, interpretation follows the same principles. Two people can take the same passage in the Bible and interpret that passage in different ways to get radically different meanings. One person could look at Genesis 3 and the story of Adam and Eve and say, "Hey, clearly this story opposes gay marriage, because it's Adam and Eve and not Adam and Steve." Someone else could look at Genesis 3 and say, "Hey, clearly this story opposes straight marriage, because Eve's desire for her husband is a punishment and not an ideal state of affairs." Still other people could look at Genesis 3 and wonder why anyone is talking about marriage at all, since the idea of marriage as an institution is never mentioned in the chapter.

Here is a fourth similarity: When it comes to cooking, we do it for a variety of reasons. We sometimes cook simply to feed ourselves. And we often cook in order to feed the people we're responsible for. At times, we even cook for our larger community: extended family or a church group, say, or maybe we help prepare food at a soup kitchen. Cooking isn't private work, exactly, though we do tend to cook for people we know rather than random strangers on the street. Cooking can be nourishing, and indeed, cooking and eating the right things can help us grow stronger and live longer. Sometimes we eat without cooking at all. We go to someone else's house to eat and they cook for us, or we go out to eat at a restaurant. Eating food this way can be a social experience, an entertaining experience, even a romantic experience.

This is all true of biblical interpretation as well. We interpret for many reasons, to spiritually nourish ourselves, our community, and the people we're responsible for. Interpreting isn't private, per se, but we don't often do it for strangers. Interpreting the Bible well can be healthy for us, giving us joy, peace, truth, conviction, and resilience. Sometimes we listen to other people interpret the Bible for us, and sometimes we seek out new ways of interpreting the Bible just to satisfy our curiosities. Biblical interpretation can be a social experience. If you're a nerd like me, it might even be entertaining. I don't find it to be romantic, but your mileage may vary, and I won't shame you.

What to Expect from This Book

Interpreting the Bible is like cooking in other ways, too, and we'll draw your attention to some of them as the book goes on, but the four ways described above are the four we'll spend the most time on.

In Part I: Setting the Table, we'll talk about what it means to interpret, and then compare interpreters to chefs to explore why an interpreter's social identity matters for the act of interpretation.

In Part II: The Main Ingredients, we'll talk about what the Bible is and isn't, we'll introduce all of the Bible's major sections, and we'll briefly describe major movements in the history of biblical interpretation. The more ingredients you know and the more you know about them, the more dishes you can cook, just as the more you know about the Bible, the more ways you will be able to interpret.

In Part III: Preparing the Ingredients, we'll compare different methods of biblical interpretation just as a chef might compare different ways of preparing food. This section will help explain how and why two different people looking at the same passage can get two different interpretations, and it will give you a variety of easy-to-use interpretive questions you can apply to biblical texts to enliven your interpretations.

Last, in Part IV: Feeding People, we'll compare the reasons people cook to the reasons people interpret, and talk about how you can interpret the Bible in ways that are healthy for both yourself and others.

Throughout the book, you will encounter italicized terms that we want to highlight as important to the interpretive task and which might be new to you. We will also provide discussion questions for each chapter at the end of the book so you can practice what you have learned, review, or think further about the significance of the chapter's content. These questions will be especially helpful if you are reading the book in a group or classroom setting.

A Delicious and Empowering Metaphor

Why compare biblical interpretation to cooking? Partly because it's cute and catchy. Partly because, as you can see above and will continue to see throughout the book, the comparison just works in a number of ways. But perhaps most importantly, the comparison helps us to focus on two values that are core to this book: freedom and empowerment.

When you start to think of biblical interpretation like cooking, you'll start to see how specific to people's backgrounds it is. Interpretations of the Bible you grew up with aren't the only interpretations of the Bible possible, just like the food you grew up with isn't the only food that's out there.

Did you grow up with sexist interpretations of the Bible? Guess what? There are feminist interpretations of the Bible that you can try instead. Did you grow up with homophobic interpretations of the Bible? Guess what? There are queer interpretations of the Bible that you may find more nourishing. Did you grow up with white nationalist interpretations of the Bible? Guess what? There are Black, Latino, Asian, liberationist, and anti-imperial interpretations of the Bible that offer you a healthier choice. Learning about the options available to you can be a powerful catalyst for change and for freeing yourself from the kinds of interpretations you don't want to be repeating anymore.

Cooking is also a skill. Like science, it can be technical. Like art, it can be beautiful. Like when making a craft, you end up with a usable product at the end.

Biblical interpretation is similarly a skill, sometimes like science, sometimes like art, sometimes like a craft. And just like any skill, biblical interpretation is something you can get better at with practice. Maybe you know little to nothing about the Bible and interpretation right now. Wonderful. You'll know a lot by the end of this book, and you'll know even more if you continue to practice what you learn in this book after you're done reading it.

You can enjoy your improvement in the skill of cooking with your senses, and in a way, you can experience your improvement in the skill of biblical interpretation by practicing some self-reflection. Good cooking tastes good. Good biblical interpretation feels good to your heart and your mind. It feels like you're solving a puzzle. It feels like you're taking steps in a journey. It feels like you're drawing nearer to something just beyond the reach of your senses.

And there's one other thing: When you feel yourself getting better at interpreting the Bible, you'll know you have a power no one can ever take away from you. There may have been a time when other people interpreted the Bible for you and you had no choice but to listen. But no more. That power is in your hands now, to do with as you please.

Meet Your Cooking Teachers

We, your authors and guides in this book, are excited to empower you with the knowledge we have gained in our studies and experiences. We are both scholars of the Bible, but we have different expertise and life journeys.

I (Jennifer) have shared a little bit of my story with you already. I grew up Southern Baptist in Texas and eventually followed my call to ministry to an evangelical seminary. Once I realized that it would be easier to teach the Bible as a professor than as a female pastor, I got a doctorate in New Testament.

Today, I am an ordained Baptist minister (not Southern Baptist, obviously), and I teach New Testament and ministry at a Christian university with Baptist roots. I also work at a progressive church in North Carolina as a teacher-in-residence, and I do side gigs with organizations like the Bible for Normal People. My favorite part of the different jobs I do is building bridges between the academic study of the Bible and practical application of the Bible in the church. Very often, people in churches (and beyond) do not have access to formal theological education or the most recent scholarship on the Bible, so I love to provide that by teaching others what I have learned in my study and research.

I (Aaron) studied biblical interpretation and culture at a progressive seminary. Like many people in the United States, I grew up in a broadly evangelical environment. Perhaps unlike most people, I was basically an atheist by the time I started studying the Bible in graduate school. That study was what brought me back to Christian faith, and now I'm a member of the United Methodist Church.

My wife and children are Jewish, and so I have a heart for interfaith dialogue and the stories in the Hebrew Bible. For years I taught Bible, theology, and philosophy at both the university and seminary level, but lately I've been spending more time out of academia, writing biblical commentaries and teaching biblical interpretation to lay audiences on social media. Fortunately, a lot of what biblical scholars know would be useful to everyday people looking to get value out of the Bible, whether intellectually or spiritually. Unfortunately, a lot of what biblical scholars know is kept in the ivory tower of the discipline. I'd like to help change that, and this book is part of that change.

You, our readers, can also be a part of that change. You are now interns in this craft of biblical interpretation, like apprentice chefs learning the culinary arts. And goodness knows we need responsible and equipped interpreters of Scripture as much as we need skilled chefs. So, welcome to our kitchen.

Now, let's get cooking.

Part I

Setting the Table

The late Anthony Bourdain, famous chef, traveling food critic, and *Food Network* darling, once said, "Food is everything we are. It's an extension of nationalist feeling, ethnic feeling, your personal history, your province, your region, your tribe, your grandma. It's inseparable from those from the get-go."

Given a second, many people will agree with this opinion about food. But we'd like to suggest that interpretation can be described using similar language. Interpretation, too, is everything we are. It's also an extension of nationalist and ethnic feeling, of our personal history, of our province, region, tribe, and grandparents. That is to say: We are born into an interpretive world. We've all been interpreting for years before we ever stop and try to define what interpretation is, and when we finally do, we see that so much of how we do it is a product of when, where, and how we were raised.

Part I of this book is dedicated to defining interpretation. Since interpretation is part of who we are, it's also dedicated to exploring who we are as interpreters and how our personal histories affect interpretation.

After all, meals don't begin with food but with a cook. A chef is the one who makes the meal for themselves or others, and they do it on a particular occasion for particular reasons. Feeding my (Aaron's) three young daughters a quick breakfast in the morning before my wife and I catapult them off to school is a very different experience than me cooking a meal for my wife on a date night. You can see the difference in the emotions at play, the lighting, the food choices, the drinks, and the company. Of course, you can also see the difference in how the table is set.

In much the same way, biblical interpretation doesn't begin with the Bible either. Rather, it begins with the interpreter, who comes to the Bible on a particular occasion for particular reasons. Interpreting for my three young daughters as part of reading a bedtime story is a very different experience than interpreting in front of a hundred undergraduates in an introduction to theology course. You can see a difference here, too, and though the ingredients of interpretation might not be familiar to you yet, they will be by the time you finish reading this book.

So, let's set the table for our conversation by talking interpretation and interpreters, and by exploring why the latter matters so much for the former.

CHAPTER 1

What Does It Mean to Interpret?

THERE'S A FAMOUS skit from *Key & Peele* in which Keegan-Michael Key and Jordan Peele play friends who are texting back and forth about going out that night. Key interprets all their texts as aggressively as possible, seeing "You're priceless" as an insult and "Okay, let's go" as an invitation to fight. Meanwhile, Peele interprets the exact same words as friendly. Key's question "Do you even want to hang out?" prompts Peele to think "That's considerate."

How can two friends disagree about the interpretation of the same simple words? In some ways, this question is easy to answer. Tone helps convey the meaning of words, and there's no tone when we text. That's what emojis are for.

But there's also a slightly more complicated, but no less true, answer to this question. Words can mean a lot of different things, and it's our attitudes toward those words that affects how we interpret them. Angry attitudes lead to angry interpretations. Friendly attitudes lead to friendly interpretations.

What's true of simple text messages is even more true of the Bible. To get a better understanding of how we interpret the Bible, then, we need to define "interpret" with more precision and find some way to talk about how our attitudes affect interpretation that allows us to control the process. We'll do both below.

Understanding What It Means to Interpret

Good old Merriam-Webster says that "to interpret" something is to explain it or to tell the meaning of it. Explanations are usually given in response to a question. For example, the question "How do I do X?" prompts an explanation about how to do X. In general terms, meaning is something conveyed, an idea that's communicated, often but not always by language. In this book, we are mainly interested in the Bible, and the Bible conveys ideas through language, so language is the form of communication we'll examine to determine meaning, and the language in question will be biblical passages. Interpretation, then, is going to involve asking and answering questions about the ideas the language in those passages conveys.

What kind of questions are we asking of these passages? Interpretive questions.

An interpretive question is a question that, through its focus or framing, prioritizes one or two of a passage's many contexts over the others. Context in general is all the information that could possibly pertain to the composition and reception (that is, reading and discussing) of a text. Who writes a text, when, how, for whom, on what occasion, in response to what events, in what genre and style, et cetera, are all elements of a text's context. But we can speak about these individual elements more precisely.

For instance, the question "What is this story about?" is an interpretive question that prioritizes a passage's narrative or thematic context over other contexts. It could be answered narratively (that is, in terms of the story or series of events) by saying "These are the characters, and here are the things that happen to them in the book." It could also be answered thematically (that is, in terms of the story's major ideas) by saying "These are the major themes of the book."

Imagine for a moment that someone asks you what *Harry Potter* is about. You might say that narratively, it's about a boy wizard who goes to a magical school and gets caught up in all sorts of fantastical and dangerous shenanigans. Or that thematically, it's about coming of age, good versus evil, and the power of love. In answering these questions, you have interpreted the texts of *Harry Potter.* While the Bible is a very different kind of text than *Harry Potter,* both in terms of its composition and in terms of the stakes surrounding its interpretation, the basic process of asking and answering interpretive questions is the same across many kinds of texts.

Prioritizing Contexts

That's *Harry Potter*. But what about the Bible, which is not a novel written by one author but rather a text made up of many different narratives and literary genres, written by multiple authors? What kinds of contexts should we keep in mind when asking interpretive questions of it?

Every biblical passage has multiple contexts. These include:

- historical contexts that have to do with who wrote it, and to whom, when, where, why, and how it was written;
- literary contexts such as its genre, imagery, structure, word choice, and its relationship to other passages in the Bible both near and far;
- ideological contexts that concern deep-seated, sometimes unconscious beliefs about social life, economics, and cultural identity;
- theological contexts that involve the relationship between our own religious commitments and those we find in the text.

These aren't the only contexts biblical passages have, but they are the ones most commonly discussed in both religious and academic contexts, and they're the ones we'll be talking about in greater length in this book. All of these contexts are important. However, we cannot consider the meaning of a passage in light of all of its contexts at once because then the process of interpretation would become confused and incoherent. Instead, we use interpretive questions to focus on one or two contexts at a time.

Which ones should we focus on? That's up to each of us to decide. Sometimes you will hear people say "You're taking that passage out of context." However, people who say this rarely identify which context you are "taking it out of."

Again, each passage has dozens of contexts, but what such a person often means is that you are not asking the same interpretive questions that they are asking. Because you are not asking the same interpretive questions they are, you are not prioritizing the same contexts that they would like you to prioritize. If you are interested in historical questions and they insist on asking theological questions, then you are both prioritizing different contexts, and to them it might feel like you are taking the passage out of the context they want it to be in.

But truthfully, neither of you are taking the passage out of context. You are simply prioritizing different contexts. There is nothing wrong with prioritizing different contexts than someone else, so long as you understand what you are doing. The Bible does not tell us which interpretive questions to ask it, and there are no correct or incorrect interpretive questions.

Like cooking, biblical interpretation is an art. A skilled chef may make any number of dishes using the same ingredients. The same thing is true of interpretation. The art of biblical interpretation is the art of asking interpretive questions, because when we ask different interpretive questions of the same biblical passage, we get different answers about what the passage means.

Four Ways of Interpreting the First Creation Story

Consider the example of Genesis 1:1–2:3, the first and most famous story of creation, where God makes the universe in seven days. What does the passage mean? There are a lot of ways to answer that question, and the answer each of us arrives at depends on which interpretive questions we ask.

We could begin by asking a simple *theological* question: "What is God like in this passage?" We see a God that creates effortlessly, without opposition, through spoken words. This attests to God's power. We see a God that creates in an orderly and poetic structure, attesting to God's wisdom. We see a God who pronounces creation good, attesting to a God interested in the moral status of what is made. All of this is part of the meaning of the passage.

Or we could ask a *historical* question like "Who was this passage's original audience?" That might be an intimidating question for a layperson to try to answer, but many biblical scholars have noted similarities between Genesis 1 and the writings of Ezekiel. Both, for example, account for some of the few instances of the word "image" in biblical Hebrew, along with Numbers 33, which includes the kinds of lists that priests often record. If we put these things together, we might be looking at a priestly audience around the time of Ezekiel in the middle of the sixth century BCE. This is also part of the passage's meaning.

It might also be worth asking a *literary* question like "How is this creation story similar to and different from other ancient Near Eastern creation stories?" Well, in the Babylonian creation story, the Enuma Elish, the world is created out of primordial waters just like in Genesis 1. But in the Enuma Elish, those waters are personified as a great beast that must be slain to build the world. In contrast, there is no violence in Genesis 1. This is part of the passage's meaning too.

But someone else could ask an *ideological* question like "What ideas of gender do we see expressed in this text?" We see that men and women are created simultaneously as the crown of creation, both made in the image of God, and both given the same set of commands to be fruitful and multiply, to fill the earth and subdue it. There are no gender-based roles or distinctions in the passage. There is no human hierarchy. It is egalitarian. That is an interesting part of the passage's meaning, and it is quite different from what we see in Genesis 2 and following.

The "Real" Meaning of the Passage

Here we have asked four different kinds of interpretive questions, theological, historical, literary, and ideological, each focusing on a different context, and we have gotten four different answers to those questions that contribute to the meaning of the passage.

But which one of these meanings is the *real* meaning of the passage? That's an impossible question to answer because the passage really means *all* these different meanings at the same time. One meaning never excludes the others. Biblical interpretation is not a zero-sum game. We all have freedom as interpreters to choose which interpretive questions we are interested in and to ignore ones we are not interested in. Because of this freedom, every interpretive question is also an interpretive choice.

And since we don't get meaning out of a text without making these interpretive choices, there's no such thing as "just reading a text." Sometimes people will say, "I'm not *interpreting* the Bible, I'm just *reading what it says.*" Such people are mistaken. All reading is interpretation, and all interpretation involves choice.

Either we will be conscious of the interpretive questions we ask, which allows us to take full responsibility for the questions we choose, or we will ask these questions unconsciously and be unable to take responsibility for them. By "taking responsibility," I mean being able to openly admit to our role as an interpreter, being willing to admit that other interpretations are possible but we chose this one, and being willing to accept praise and blame for the positive and negative outcomes of our interpretations.

If a person is not able or willing to take responsibility for their interpretive questions and for the meaning they get from the Bible, then it may be wise for us to be skeptical of their agenda, even if they themselves aren't aware that they have one. (A sign that someone has an agenda is that they clearly want to use the Bible to advance a belief of theirs, but they don't want to admit that there are alternatives; they want to be able to blame the book, and not themselves, if something goes wrong—for example, if someone gets emotionally or physically harmed. This rule of thumb for gauging if someone has an agenda is as true for us as it is for others.)

People who insist they are "simply" reading the text and not interpreting it will imagine that the Bible is speaking its meaning to them and they are passively receiving it. But the Bible has no meaning apart from a reader and their interpretive questions. Bibles don't *mean*, people mean with Bibles.

The fact that interpretive questions make meaning is not unique to the Bible. Even when we read much simpler things, like news articles, novels, or text messages from friends and family, we are still making meaning by asking interpretive questions. Often, we are so used to asking these questions that doing so is unconscious and automatic.

In the case of the news, our main interpretive question is often "What is the article trying to inform me about?" With a novel, we tend to ask questions about plot or about characters and their motivations, like "What's going to happen next?" or "Why is he doing this?" With casual messages from friends and family, we often ask questions about the writer's feelings in ways we would not with other texts, such as "How can I support them?" or "Given our history together, what can I surmise about where this idea may be coming from?"

In situations like these, it's easy to see the role interpretive questions play in the process of making meaning, as well as how different interpretive questions can lead to different kinds of meaning. In the case of the Bible, however, some people insist that biblical passages have only a single *real* meaning. They may even pride themselves on holding this idea. When we get to chapter 3, we'll discuss some reasons why someone might hold onto this idea.

For now, it's important to simply note that no biblical passage can be limited to just one meaning—just as no item of food can be made into only one dish. Bible passages—verses and chapters and books—are ingredients. It is the interpreter who makes meaning out of them. Rather like a chef in a kitchen.

Let's take a look at what we mean.

CHAPTER 2

The Chef Matters

The Interpreter and Their Context

MY (JENNIFER'S) DAD is a careful and predictable cook. Though he makes only half a dozen dishes, he has perfectly calibrated them over the years with the precision of a retired lieutenant colonel. He didn't learn those recipes in the army, though, and he didn't pick them up from a cookbook. In fact, the recipes aren't written down anywhere. They are all dishes he learned to cook from his mother, my grandma, Delia Garcia, and the knowledge of how to make them lives within him.

My siblings and I think there is something special, even magical, about the exact combination of measurements he uses and the order in which he adds the ingredients. That's why every time I make the mouthwatering Mexican rice that I grew up on, the kind my grandma whipped up almost weekly, I call my dad just to make sure I am getting it right. He reminds me that I need to combine *half* a can of tomato paste with a *full* can of RO-TEL and that I shouldn't add that combination to the rice until the onions and green peppers are good and cooked.

Now, my family could certainly write the rice recipe down, but there is a relational element we would lose if we did that. I love the way that hearing my dad's sternly practical instructions over the phone strikes a chord of nostalgia in me. It's how he has always sounded giving instructions. I imagine it is also the way my grandma sounded when she taught him. And I am convinced that the rice turns out much better when my dad's voice is echoing in my head and my grandmother's face is floating through my consciousness while I cook. That's because cooking is not just about sought-after recipes or high-quality ingredients. It's about people and their histories.

The Power of the Chef

When a chef prepares a meal for her guests, much preliminary work has already been done. Before the first burner flicks on, the cook has already carefully selected, purchased, and readied cookware. She has reworked and enhanced tried-and-true recipes over the years. She has gathered and prepared fresh and tasty ingredients, and she has prepped the pans and preheated the ovens. All of this prework affects how the dish will turn out.

The most influential preliminary consideration in a cooking event, however, is perhaps the chef herself. How long has she been cooking? What kind of cuisine does she prefer or have the most skill with? What dishes might she avoid or be apprehensive about because of her bad experiences? When it comes time to cook, a chef's experiences and personal context all matter.

The same is true of a person who interprets the Bible. The context and experiences of the interpreter matter when it comes to interpretation. In the previous chapter, we established that interpretation involves asking and answering questions about the ideas that a text conveys. Why does the interpreter matter? Because she is the one who decides what questions to ask and how to go about answering those questions. It stands to reason, then, that who an interpreter is and where an interpreter comes from greatly impact the interpretive process as well as the end result.

An Interpreter's Context Matters

We already talked a little bit about context when we introduced the concept of biblical interpretation. Context is a lens that can be applied to a wide range of subjects, but it is most often used in the realm of communication. In the case of written language, the contexts of a text can include the historical context in which it was written, the literary format and arrangement, and the cultural background pertinent to the writing. All of these are vital for an interpreter exploring what a passage can mean. But context is also important when it comes to the reader of a text. That context is who they are and where and how they encounter a passage.

Have you ever heard the phrase "Context is key"? Our favorite example of how important context can be comes from a meme. The first picture in the meme shows a kitschy plaque that reads "Life is short; lick the bowl." The second picture zooms out to show the little sign perched not on a shelf in the kitchen but on top of a toilet. Context is key indeed!

The place where one encounters a "lick the bowl" plaque—kitchen or bathroom—certainly influences how the sign will be interpreted, if it might be taken seriously or if it should be dismissed as inapplicable (even harmful) to the situation. Similarly, the place from which a reader encounters a text also impacts interpretation. All of this demonstrates that there is context that is tied to the text, and there is context that is tied to the reader or interpreter. Context matters for pithy proverbs *and* for people.

Let's take, for example, the poetic lines from the Song of Songs:

> *Set me as a seal upon your heart,*
> *as a seal upon your arm,*
> *for love is strong as death,*
> *passion fierce as the grave.*
> *Its flashes are flashes of fire,*
> *a raging flame.*
>
> (Song of Songs 8:6)

Someone who has been taught to read the Song of Songs as an allegory about the love of God for God's people might read this verse as a devotional inspiration and feel a passion for God blazing within them. A different person, one who had studied the phenomenon of ancient love poetry and recognized Song of Songs as such, might read this passage as a testimony to the power of erotic love, and it might incite in them a wave of affection for their spouse. A mourner who heard these words read at a funeral might interpret them from a place of sadness, grieving a love lost. On the other hand, a wedding guest could hear these words as a promise of love's longevity or maybe as a warning about the destructive and fickle strength of love and physical attraction. Someone from a more stoic and pragmatic culture would probably interpret this passage with some restraint and suspicion, while someone from a culture that valued spontaneity and affection would have the opposite inclination.

As we said before, the context of interpreters impacts the way they read a text. In the world of biblical interpretation, the context of the interpreter is also known as her or his *social location*.

What Is Social Location?

Let's look closer at this idea of social location because it will help us understand why people interpret the same Bible in radically different ways. Social location is the collection of human experiences that shapes a person's perspective and provides lenses through which they interpret Scripture (and the world). The experiences and environments that make up one's social location are multifaceted. They include (1) a person's history and customs, cultural influences, and geographical environment *(culture);* (2) a person's learned and inherited set of biases and assumptions, as well as their moral, intellectual, spiritual, and emotional atmosphere *(preconceptions);* and (3) a person's position of power and privilege in society, which takes into account age, gender, race, nationality, social class, marital status, political commitments, language, et cetera *(demographics).*

An interpreter's culture, preconceptions, and demographics all play a part in determining their social location and their interpretive lenses. There is not one reader of Scripture who comes to the text without lenses or without having been molded by their social location—not the two of us as authors, not you as the reader, nor anyone else. In other words, despite some people's claims to the contrary, there is no neutral (or plain sense) reading of the Bible; we all bring our own specific backgrounds, biases, and, yes, baggage of some sort to our interpretation of the text. Our social location is a given. We all have one, and it will influence the way we read the Bible.

Why does this matter? Because sometimes our social location will influence the way we read the Bible in positive ways (like helping us to empathize with a character or situation), and sometimes it will influence us in negative ways (such as by causing us to fill in gaps in a story with erroneous assumptions). Either way, we need to be aware that this is happening. The most dangerous crime we can commit as readers of Scripture is to deny or remain unaware of how our social location affects our interpretation.

Because of this, it is important for us to know and understand what our social location is and begin to recognize the kinds of lenses we wear when we interpret. With that goal in mind, let's investigate further the three aspects of an interpreter's context that we mentioned above: culture, preconceptions, and demographics.

Culture

A person's culture is a complex and multilayered reality; it involves their own family history and customs, the social influences that surround them, and their geographical environment. Let me illustrate how these factors work together by giving you a glimpse into the cultural differences between my husband and I. On the surface, we aren't that different. We are both Americans who spent their childhood years in Texas, we are both from middle-class families that escaped poverty a generation ago, and we were both raised as devout Christians in Baptist environments. Despite these similarities, we have significant differences when it comes to the cultural factors that have shaped us.

I spent much of my adolescence influenced by the Mexican American culture of my dad's family. We are Texas Mexicans (or Texicans, as I like to say); our ancestors have been in Texas since it was Mexico. My Texican family culture instilled several values in me that continue to shape my life. First, we consider extended family as part of our core community (you should see our family reunions!). Second, we never underestimate the joy that great food and drink can bring (again, you should see our family reunions!). Lastly, we value hard work and humility, and we recognize the importance of helping each other succeed and helping those who have less than we do. All of these cultural mores (the often unspoken rules or values that a particular group prioritizes) influence not only how I show up in the world but also how I read the Bible.

My husband, Kerry, has a completely different set of cultural mores. His family has Western European roots, and they highly value their individualism and independence. They trust their nuclear family and spend quality time with them but do not have close relationships with their extended family members. Kerry was raised to prioritize self-control and moderation, and so he has inherited a practicality about food and drink. His family has never enjoyed alcoholic beverages, and, when it comes to food, Kerry likes to say, "Food is fuel" (not "Food is fun," which is my mantra).

It might be helpful to pause for a moment and note how our contemporary cultures compare with ancient Mediterranean and Near East cultures, the cultures that form the background of the New Testament and Old Testament. Both were collectivist cultures organized around the concept of kinship, while Western culture in the United States is more of an individualist culture. Kerry's family reflects individualist values well, and though I have certainly been shaped by those, my Mexican family is more collectivist leaning. Collectivist cultures place a high value on a much larger unit than the nuclear family of the

West. Kinship—who is in your family or tribe and who is not—is a structuring principle of these societies. Collectivist cultures also organize identity around the group rather than the individual. Who we are together is much more important than who I am as an individual. The characteristics of collectivist cultures stand in stark contrast to the individualistic values of American culture, where the individual chooses their vocation and makes important decisions on their own rather than following the family or tribe.

Now, back to my husband and I. Another interesting factor in Kerry's upbringing is that his dad worked for an oil company, and so his family embarked on the adventure of becoming expats in the United Arab Emirates when he was in high school. In the Middle East, Kerry was immersed in an honor/shame culture that revolved around patronage and kinship. Many modern cultures operate on an honor/shame system, but Western societies rarely do. We tend to enforce boundaries through laws and punishments, sometimes mixed in with a healthy dose of guilt.

In the ancient Mediterranean world, however, the concepts of honor and shame served as boundary enforcers, ensuring that future generations continued to adhere to the cultural values central to their society. A person's choices and actions could either earn honor or shame for their family group. The honor of a family unit was so central to their survival in the world that all members would work for more honor while using shame as a strong deterrent against breaking from tradition or acting against the family unit. Both Kerry's exposure to an honor/shame culture and his childhood spent in a law-and-order culture play a role in shaping his social location.

Now let's consider how our cultures—my more collectivist culture and Kerry's individualist culture, with a dash of honor/shame—impact how each of us interprets Scripture. If we both read the wedding at Cana story from John, we would offer unique insights and ask different sorts of questions because of our cultural backgrounds.

Let's look at the passage first and then explore how our cultural lenses might affect our understanding of it:

> On the third day there was a wedding in Cana of Galilee, and the mother of Jesus was there. Jesus and his disciples had also been invited to the wedding. When the wine gave out,

> the mother of Jesus said to him, "They have no wine." And Jesus said to her, "Woman, what concern is that to me and to you? My hour has not yet come." His mother said to the servants, "Do whatever he tells you." Now standing there were six stone water jars for the Jewish rites of purification, each holding twenty or thirty gallons. Jesus said to them, "Fill the jars with water." And they filled them up to the brim. He said to them, "Now draw some out, and take it to the person in charge of the banquet." So they took it. When the person in charge tasted the water that had become wine and did not know where it came from (though the servants who had drawn the water knew), that person called the bridegroom and said to him, "Everyone serves the good wine first and then the inferior wine after the guests have become drunk. But you have kept the good wine until now." Jesus did this, the first of his signs, in Cana of Galilee and revealed his glory, and his disciples believed in him.
>
> John 2:1–11

To begin with, Kerry and I would bring contrasting perspectives regarding the setting of this story—a family wedding. Even if I didn't know anything about ancient Mediterranean weddings, my cultural experience with extended family gatherings overflowing with good food and wine would help me better understand and value the tenor of this wedding party. I might instinctively picture a larger gathering than my husband would, and I might better appreciate the joy associated with such a festive meal, especially one with large quantities of good wine available well into the party. I would probably consider Jesus's mother as the hero of the story because she noticed someone in need and tried to help, an impulse that my family values greatly.

On the other hand, the independence and individualism that Kerry's culture taught him might make him uncomfortable with the idea of this large gathering and with Jesus's mom asking for help. The idea that Jesus changed a bunch of water into huge quantities of wine could provoke some resistance from Kerry's teetotalist family. They might try to explain away the wine, saying it might have been grape juice or something. At the same time, Kerry's experience in a Middle

Eastern honor/shame culture would give him greater insight than me into the social shame that the family would have endured if they had thrown a party without being prepared enough for all the guests.

Can you see now how a person's complex cultural lenses come into play when they read and interpret the Bible? A person's cultural background might help them relate more closely to the text, or it could serve as a set of blinders that cause them to overlook or mistake context clues. That's true for me and Kerry, and it's true for you too. For better or worse, all readers come to the biblical text with a web of cultural values working behind the scenes. Our job, if we want to be responsible interpreters, is to acknowledge these influences so that we are aware when they shape the questions we ask and affect the assumptions we make.

Preconceptions

Working in tandem with culture is a person's *preconceptions*, or the learned biases or assumptions a person has developed because of their family of origin and experiences. Preconceptions—which are shaped by influences that may be categorized as moral, intellectual, spiritual, and emotional—may come from one's culture, but they may also be handed down as teachings or impressions from families, friends, entertainment, or faith communities.

Let's revisit the wedding at Cana story to illustrate how preconceptions play a role in interpretation. Someone who has been raised in a Christian environment, especially one that accepts the miracles and the supernatural accounts in the Bible, would probably have little issue with the claim that Jesus miraculously changed water into wine. They might ask questions like "How did this miracle affect the people at the wedding?" or "How does this miracle compare to some of the other miracles that Jesus did during his life?"

In contrast, a person who does not have a faith background that trained them to accept the miraculous might automatically assume that this episode from Jesus's life is not literal history but a literary creation of the author or authors of John's Gospel. Their intellectual influences would likely be stronger than spiritual ones. They might ask questions like "What do the details of this miracle—the wedding setting, the purification jars of water, the final product of wine—symbolize in this ancient,

Jewish/Christian setting?" or "What message is the author of John trying to convey by starting Jesus's ministry with a miracle at a wedding?"

Of the different types of assumptions or biases we might bring to our reading of Scripture, those influenced by our *emotional environments* might be the most challenging to recognize. Most of us who were shaped by a faith community or educated with scientific principles are aware of those *spiritual* and *intellectual backgrounds*. We likewise probably remember the *moral instructions* our parents or our pastors gave us as we grew up—the early bird catches the worm, honesty is the best policy, respect your elders, things like that. Emotions, however, are trickier. Let me give you a personal example.

In the Cana story, right after Jesus's mother makes him aware of the shortage of wine, Jesus says this to her: "Woman, what concern is that to me and to you? My hour has not yet come." For much of my life, this line has made me extremely uncomfortable. The reasons for my discomfort have not always been clear to me, but I think I understand them better now.

After years of considering my feelings on this, I have come to realize that I have a lot of emotional baggage surrounding the word "woman," especially when it is used by a man to address a woman. This baggage comes from an amalgamation of personal experiences and cultural encounters, from movie lines to comedians' jokes to real family dynamics I've witnessed. As a result, when I hear a man address someone not by her name but by the term "woman," I assume that it is disrespectful or belittling—for example, as in: "Woman, get me a beer!," "Woman, why are you bothering me?," or "Woman, what did you do this time?"

All the emotions evoked by my experiences with this term have influenced the way I read Jesus's address of his mother. However, my reactions are not specifically driven by the text itself. The fact is, although there are valid reasons to read this as a gentle rebuke by Jesus concerning the timing of his ministry, it is unlikely that Jesus (or the author of John) used this term to express disrespect toward his mother. The negative tenor I associate with the word "woman" here comes not from Jesus's ancient context but from my own context and from my emotions surrounding the term.

In the example above, my emotions moved me further away from the literary meaning of the text. But the opposite can also occur:

Emotions can also bring us closer to the literary meaning of the text. The effect varies from person to person and situation to situation.

As humans, our experiences and our emotions are always at work to help us make sense of things around us. This is not a bad thing; it is inevitable and can be helpful at times. However, this does mean that we all have biases and assumptions, not just about people and events but about the stories and teachings we read in the Bible.

If we remain unaware of the way our experiences and emotions come into play, or if we deny that we have assumptions and biases, then we will certainly end up reading things into Scripture. That can be damaging if we are teaching others or using Scripture to shape our lives and our character. Fortunately, we are here to help you recognize and better understand your preconceptions. At the end of the book, you'll find some discussion questions that will guide you to explore your social location better, and in the next chapter, we will address how we can navigate our biases when it comes to interpreting the Bible.

Demographics

Working together with culture and preconceptions to shape a person's interpretive perspective are their *demographics*. In this book, when we use the term "demographics," we are referring to a range of personal details like age or generation, gender, race, nationality, social class, marital status, political association, language, and more. While "culture" refers to where a person comes from, and preconceptions are how people's experiences have shaped their beliefs or assumptions, demographics include the forces and communities that continue to exert influence on individuals within the diverse (and sometimes divided) society we all live in.

Let's consider how all of this shapes biblical interpretation. The passage we will use to illustrate the impact of demographics on interpretation is not an easy one. We want to be clear: We are not going to do a full interpretive workup on these verses. It's important to note that this passage from the apostle Paul's letter to the Romans has a very specific historical, political, and literary context that makes it complicated on many levels. It also has been used throughout history to control and cause great harm to certain people groups, to justify a wide range of political actions, and (more benignly) to inspire patriotism and good citizenship. But for now, we're simply going to focus on the fact that the demographics of any person reading this passage will greatly affect the way they approach or apply it.

> Let every person be subject to the governing authorities, for there is no authority except from God, and those authorities that exist have been instituted by God. Therefore whoever resists authority resists what God has appointed, and those who resist will incur judgment. For rulers are not a terror to good conduct but to bad. Do you wish to have no fear of the authority? Then do what is good, and you will receive its approval, for it is God's agent for your good. But if you do what is wrong, you should be afraid, for the authority does not bear the sword in vain! It is the agent of God to execute wrath on the wrongdoer. Therefore one must be subject, not only because of wrath but also because of conscience. For the same reason you also pay taxes, for the authorities are God's agents, busy with this very thing. Pay to all what is due them: taxes to whom taxes are due, revenue to whom revenue is due, respect to whom respect is due, honor to whom honor is due.
>
> Romans 13:1–7

One of the key concepts in this passage is authority: who has authority, where authority comes from, what people can do with authority, and how people might respond to authority. But depending on a reader's demographics, the *idea* of an authority or authorities could elicit very different responses. Consider this: What ideas about authority might a white, middle-class veteran from the baby boomer generation have in mind as he reads this? Or a millennial woman from New York City whose parents were deported by the American government? What about a wealthy Christian congressman who exploits tax loopholes as a regular practice? Or an underemployed libertarian from the rural Midwest? Or a Black mother whose son was shot by police officers who were never brought to justice?

We cannot answer for any of these hypothetical people, but with a little empathetic imagination, we can certainly see that they would each bring their own nuanced evaluation and ideological commitments to a text like Romans 13. People at different points across the *socioeconomic spectrum* would ask the text different questions too. For example, someone who has lived under a totalitarian regime might ask, "When Paul writes that rulers aren't a terror to good conduct but to bad, does that include dictators who cause the good to suffer?" A Revolutionary War reenactor with deep-seated patriotism might ask, "Paul doesn't mean we must submit to all authorities, right? What about the Boston Tea Party? Surely that was justified?" Our complex identities often dictate what perspective we take when we read the Bible and can cause us to mold a text to fit with our own priorities instead of seeking to understand it in its contexts.

In addition to previously held ideas and socioeconomics, there is one more vital aspect of demographics in social location that we should be aware of when we are interpreting the Bible, and that is the influence that *privilege*—and the power that comes with it—has on our understanding of Scripture. Every one of us needs to be cognizant of what kind of privilege we have and how it might muddy our understanding of the biblical writers and their messages. That's because if we aren't aware of our privilege, we might assume that the original authors and audiences are just like us. This will then lead us to misunderstand their circumstances and perspectives, which could cause us to seriously misinterpret the text.

Some pieces of our social identities may give us privilege while others do not. For example, I (Jennifer) am straight, cisgender, and able-bodied. Although I am half-Mexican, I pass as white because my features lean toward European rather than Indigenous. I am also middle-class and very educated. Each of those social realities afford me some semblance of power and ease in my context. However, I am also a woman, and I come from a minority culture in America, so I do not have as much privilege as a dominant-culture male would have.

I (Aaron) am a straight, cisgender, and able-bodied man of mixed race, half-white, one-fourth Black, and one-fourth Japanese. I'd have to go without sun for quite a while, and then be surrounded by a lot of white friends with Starbucks in hand, to pass as white though. Despite this, I haven't encountered much in the way of racism. I'm middle-class and very fortunate to have a spouse who makes decent money; otherwise, I wouldn't have been able to afford to get a PhD. As far as privilege goes, I have a lot.

If the two of us train ourselves to be aware of these privileges, then we will be more likely to catch some of the assumptions we might make while reading literature written from the perspective of a minority group in the ancient Mediterranean world. When we read Romans 13, we might be tempted to peer through our own middle-class American lenses—and miss the fact that paying taxes in the Roman Empire was not a matter of losing a little bit of a paycheck to help pay for public schools and other services. In fact, Rome's collection of taxes was an extremely unjust practice that lined the pockets of the wealthy and often pushed people groups in the empire (farmers, merchants, fisherman, etc.) into extreme poverty.

The truth is, taxes are not a big inconvenience for either of us, but they were for many of the first Christians. If we lose sight of our privilege, it could cause us to make some wrong assumptions about the economic factors that exist in the background of this passage.

Understanding Our Own Social Location: The Chef Matters

We started this chapter by talking about how the context and experiences of a chef matter when it comes time to cook. We then demonstrated how the same is true with interpreters and texts. Understanding our personal social location as readers of the Bible is a necessary step in the process of biblical interpretation. It helps us approach the texts we interpret with awareness about the place from which we read—our cultural history, preconceptions, and demographic influences.

That awareness will serve to expose our interpretive obstacles and control our biases. When we understand how our cultural values influence our perspective, we can be more open to decipher the cultural differences between the world of the Bible and our own. When we acknowledge that we all come to the text with preconceptions, we can make sure these don't skew our reading of the stories and teachings of Scripture.

Finally, when we recognize our own societal privilege as well as our social commitments, the elements we read into a text and the aspects we ignore become clearer. All of these acknowledgments make us better interpreters.

CHAPTER 3

Navigating Biases

DECIDING WHAT TO eat at a buffet can be difficult. There are so many choices, and your stomach is only so big. You might be interested in trying something new. You may also be tempted to fall back on familiar favorites while also avoiding anything you've eaten too recently. After all, you can't have pizza two days in a row. Or can you? I (Aaron) can.

Even though there are so many options at a buffet, you probably won't find yourself consciously drawing up a list of pros and cons for every choice. Rather, you'll cut out most choices right away, narrow it down to a few options, and go with your gut. Most people will do the same thing. How do we go about simplifying our choices like this? By using our biases.

A bias is a tendency to favor certain choices even before fully considering all of our options. Some of our biases are conscious. For example, you probably know and can say out loud what your favorite kind of movie is. Other biases are unconscious. It might be more difficult, for instance, to articulate how you respond to stress or heartbreak or to interpersonal challenges.

We all have biases when it comes to food—and thank God we do. These biases help us navigate choices and keep us from having to expend a lot of unnecessary energy in situations like the one described above. But so often we also have biases about the Bible and what we should do with it. These biases can be helpful too—or not. The one thing that biases can't be, though, is escaped.

Can We Escape Our Biases?

In her book *Introduction to the Bible,* biblical scholar Christine Hayes says of the Bible, "Everyone has opinions about this text," and in *Introduction to the Hebrew Bible,* biblical scholar John J. Collins notes that "people are surprisingly uninformed about this text." This is a true but unfortunate pair of observations. What is unfortunate about this combination? Let's take a closer look.

On the one hand, people often have strong—and differing—opinions about the Bible. People hate the Bible, and people love the Bible. People think the Bible is a hideous and barbaric relic of the Iron Age, and people think the Bible is the word of God, divinely inspired and inerrant in everything it teaches. People think the Bible is a tool for a declining majority to wield in the imposition of their political agenda. People think the Bible is the foundation for their lives and the only possible chance they have of overcoming death.

Even if a person's opinions about the Bible aren't strong ones, Western culture virtually assures that those living in it have a passing familiarity with some of the Bible's stories and characters. People have often heard of Adam and Eve, of Moses, of David and Goliath, of Jesus and Paul. Books, film, music, and art reference these characters and their stories. They are part of sayings and figures of speech. They are common metaphors and illustrations. And, of course, billions of people are adherents to religions who read stories of these characters and look to their lives for spiritual significance.

For better or worse, the Bible is a big deal. And yet, people in general know very little about the facts of the biblical text. According to a Pew Research Center, a 2019 survey of more than ten thousand people found that on average people got 4.2 out of seven Bible questions correct when asked. That's 60 percent, or a D- in grading terms. That's as bad as a person can possibly be without getting an F.

It's important to note that none of these questions required a detailed knowledge of biblical texts. Indeed, some of them could be answered without reading the Bible at all, just through familiarity with other media. If more difficult questions were asked, questions on which serious historical or theological issues depend, the answers would no doubt be even worse.

So, on the one hand, many people have passionate opinions about the Bible; on the other hand, people know hardly anything about the Bible. This can be a dangerous combination. It's very difficult for people to resist taking action when they're passionate about something, and it's very difficult to make good choices when they're ignorant about something. (We—Jennifer and Aaron—have certainly experienced this in our own lives. Perhaps you have too.)

Put those two factors together, and we human beings end up doing a lot of dumb things. All this to say, even if a person were to sit down to try to read and interpret the Bible for the first time in their adult lives, they would not be doing it as a blank slate. They've heard things about the Bible, felt things about the Bible, seen the Bible used this way or that. Put plainly: They're biased.

Sitting down to read and interpret a passage yourself, you might think, "But I've never really read this text before, so how could I be biased in how I interpret it?" But it's true—you are biased.

How can this be? Let's use food to illustrate.

Coming to the Bible with Bias

Think about the first time you ever tried to make some food. It might have been as a child with family or friends. It might have been as a teenager when you were alone in the house for a day. It might have been as a young adult, out on your own.

Regardless of when it happened, the first time you made food was certainly not the first time you *had* food. By the time that day arrives for each of us, we've already been eating food for years; so we already have certain tastes, preferences, and expectations about food. No one ever makes food without biases, sometimes a lifetime of them. The same is true of the Bible. We're born into an environment in which the Bible is already being read, preached, discussed, politicized, and made into art, such that we inherit a history of the Bible's use even if we never read it for ourselves growing up.

So, just as it's uncontroversial to say that a person's culture, preconceptions, and demographics affect the foods they make and eat, it should be uncontroversial to say that—as we noted in chapter 1—a person's culture, preconceptions, and demographics affect the way they interpret the Bible. Even without much direct experience of the Bible, you can easily find yourself thinking some passages have "obvious" meanings, just like there are "obvious" ingredients in your favorite food. You might get the sense that someone else is doing something wrong when they interpret a passage differently, just like it can feel like someone is doing something wrong when they add a new side to a meal you often enjoy. You'll find some interpretive questions are comfortable to ask and answer, while others feel strange to you, much like the way that, when you're having a bad day, certain comfort foods come to mind while others don't. Why do you feel all these things? It's because, whether you know it or not, you're biased.

Are Biases Always Bad?

The word "bias" is often perceived as having a negative connotation. When we say a person is biased, that statement is often part of an accusation that they've mishandled some facts or misconstrued a story to favor their own beliefs. That sense of the word "bias" is important, but the word can also have a more neutral meaning. Everyone is biased in the more basic sense that we all see the world around us through our own lenses, which are in turn colored by our personal experiences and understanding. And while we can listen to other people and empathize with them, we can never truly see the world through their lenses like they do.

Yet biases can have a positive impact on our lives too. You might think, "Well, if I can just get rid of my biases, then I won't have to look at the world through my own lenses, and I'll see the world as it really is." But that's not the case. If we were to get rid of our biases completely (which is impossible), and therefore get rid of our lenses completely, we wouldn't see anything at all; like a nearsighted person, we need our lenses to navigate the world. Biases and the lenses they create are tools that we use to help us make meaning out of the world and the texts we read. In this sense, they are empowering.

Let us illustrate what we mean by that. Imagine that you're hungry and blessed enough to be staring at a kitchen full of ingredients. In this case, your biases are helpful. Your preferences for certain foods help you decide what to make. Your past experience making food helps you make it again. And your tastes help you to feel satisfied with the food once you've eaten it.

The same idea holds true for the Bible. When you interpret the Bible, your biases are actually beneficial. They help you choose what to read and how. They help you ask and answer interpretive questions you pose to the text. And they help you feel satisfied with your interpretation once you've made it. Once we recognize this beneficial role of biases, the question of what to do with our biases begins to clarify. Our goal should not be to purge ourselves of our biases, which is, again, impossible. Instead we should handle our biases in responsible and constructive ways.

Let's look at some ways we can do exactly that.

Ways to Handle Our Biases

There are helpful and unhelpful ways to manage our biases. Some are best avoided, and at least one is worth pursuing. Let's begin with what we should avoid.

Failing to Recognize Our Biases

Perhaps the worst way to handle our biases is to fail to recognize they exist at all. This failure is commonly expressed in a variety of ways. People might say, "I'm not *interpreting* the text; I'm just reading what it says." Or they might say, "That's not my view; that's the view given in the text," or, similarly, "That's not my view; that's God's view." More simply, a person might say, "The Bible says X," as if inanimate objects speak.

In each of these instances, the person is denying their own biases by denying their subjective role in the process of interpretation. The person is holding up a book and acting like they're not involved in the process of drawing meaning from it. But remember, interpretation is the result of asking interpretive questions, and our biases (culture, preconceptions, demographics) are what give us the initial motivation to ask and answer these interpretive questions. No biases, no interpretation.

As a result, each of the above hypothetical statements is false. The person isn't just reading the text, they're interpreting it just like everyone else. The view being expressed is not the view of the text, it's the view of the person who is interpreting the text. The Bible doesn't say X, the person is using the Bible to say X.

Why would a person deny their own biases? It could just be a matter of innocent ignorance. A person might not know that biases exist that would influence their interpretation of the Bible. Perhaps they've never thought about it, no one's ever told them, and they've never read a handy book like this one. Or maybe they have been trained to deny their biases. They've grown up in a context or have been educated in a context where denials of biases are commonplace, and so, in fact, the denial of bias has become their bias.

Or, perhaps more alarmingly, they're denying their biases for the sake of power. Because of the prominence of the Bible in Western culture and in Christian/Christian-adjacent spaces, there's a certain social power in the idea of saying objectively correct things about the Bible. It's much easier to convince people that your interpretation is objectively correct if you deny any subjective role in coming to that interpretation. You'll often find a denial of a person's biases paired with the idea that there's only one correct interpretation of any given passage in the Bible.

Consider the 1982 "Chicago Statement on Biblical Hermeneutics," an influential document for how Evangelicals in the United States and elsewhere understand the Bible. Article VII of the statement says that the meaning of "each biblical text is single, definite, and fixed." And article IX denies "that the message of Scripture derives from, or is dictated by, the interpreter's understanding." Article XIX later adds, "Any preunderstandings [that is, biases] which the interpreter brings to Scripture should be in harmony with scriptural teaching and subject to correction by it."

Taken together, these statements advance the idea that there's one meaning of any given passage in the Bible, and a person's biases aren't welcome unless they're somehow synonymous with that one meaning. Someone who believes this idea isn't going to admit to any biases they have, because according to article IX, their biases can't play any positive role in understanding the text, and according to article XIX, we ought to get rid of our biases as soon as possible anyway. The only role left for biases here is to distract from the one true meaning of a passage, and so admitting to having biases is tantamount to admitting to error.

Failure to recognize our biases, however, can result in several problems. The first is that if we don't recognize our biases, then a significant part of the interpretive process is invisible to us. That part of the process is still happening—our biases are still directing us to certain interpretive questions over others—but it's happening unconsciously. When it's unconscious, we can't explain why we're asking the interpretive questions that we're asking, we can't explain why other people are asking different interpretive questions, and the only way we can show other people how to interpret is by insisting that ours is the one true way to do it.

Imagine baking cookies for someone and them asking you, "Why did you add chocolate chips?" Now picture yourself saying, "Because that's the only way *real* cookies are made" rather than, "Because I like chocolate chips and thought you might like them too." Imagine someone writing a document that says, "Any cookie preferences that a baker brings to the cookie making should be in harmony with chocolate chip cookies and subject to correction by it." This is what the "Chicago Statement" is instructing people to do.

A second problem that comes from failing to recognize our biases is that this failure makes it impossible to take responsibility for our interpretations. To take responsibility for something, we have to be able to admit our role in it. Since our role in interpretation is affected by our biases, we can't fully admit our role without also admitting our biases. When we leave out our biases, we're really leaving out ourselves, since our biases come from our identities and experiences.

There's a famous scene from the television show *The West Wing* that helps illustrate a failure to take responsibility for our role as interpreters. In the scene, a conservative talk show host named Dr. Jenna Jacobs argues with President Bartlet about biblical interpretation. The president says sarcastically, "I like your show. I like how you call homosexuality an abomination." Jacobs replies, "I don't say homosexuality is an abomination, Mr. President. The Bible does."

The president's statement places responsibility on Jacobs for characterizing homosexuality as an abomination, while Jacobs's statement denies any responsibility. By doing this, she washes her hands of any harm that comes to people as a result of the claim that she made—or the biblical interpretation that she presented—on her show.

Generally speaking, if someone refuses to take responsibility for the outcome of their actions, this is seen as immature or outright immoral. If you rear-end someone and blame your car, or hang up on someone and blame your phone, or gossip about someone and blame the friend you told, people will rightly think you're trying to avoid responsibility. And certainly, if someone refused to take responsibility for the ingredients that ended up in the food they've prepared for you, you'd likely decline to eat it. Indeed, when restaurants and other food providers don't take enough responsibility for the quality of their food, they're subject to legal action. The Bible is a powerful thing, and we should treat anyone with skepticism if they refuse to take responsibility for their interpretations of it.

A third problem that comes from not recognizing our biases is that this failure makes us powerless to change them. As will be discussed in more detail below, biases are not static things but can and do change over time. But if a person insists that they have no biases, then they're also not in a position to interact with them in a conscious and meaningful way.

Such a person can't say, "This bias of mine is helpful in this situation" or "This bias of mine is making this situation more difficult." When a person doesn't recognize their biases, their biases will still change over time, just as they would if they did recognize them. The difference is, they won't be able to intentionally shape the way their biases change.

Presuming Our Biases Are Correct

A second unhelpful and even damaging way of handling our biases is to presume that our biases are the correct biases and different biases—other people's biases—are incorrect. Sometimes this presumption is fairly innocent in nature. All of us are, of course, most comfortable with our own biases. Other biases, especially ones arising from cultures and demographics very different from our own, can cause us to feel discomfort. And if we feel like our biases have helped us get at the truth in the past, then it's not a big leap for us to believe different biases won't get us there now or in the future.

But other biases aren't necessarily wrong even if they do make us uncomfortable. Once again, food is a helpful analogy. The food we grow up eating is often the food we're most comfortable with and most enjoy eating. That doesn't mean other foods are wrong or bad even if we don't like them. Indeed, many people, as they grow up, enjoy eating a variety of foods from backgrounds very different from their own. In Western culture a certain social prestige is commonly associated with eating the delicacies of other cultures. Conversely, people who eat only a very narrow range of foods are frequently derided as picky.

People are, of course, entitled to their preferences, and perhaps we shouldn't assign too much prestige to people with diverse tastes and deride people with narrow tastes. Regardless, when close mindedness about different foods becomes prejudice against people who create and enjoy other foods, then we have a more serious problem. And that brings us to our next point.

One of the worst manifestations of the assumption that our biases are correct and other people's biases are incorrect is what happens when people invent explanations for *why* other people's biases are incorrect.

If our explanation was simply that their biases are different because of differences in their demographics and preconceptions, et cetera, then we'd be unlikely to think our biases are more correct than theirs. We'd realize how both sets of biases are equally arbitrary.

Historically, however, Christians have often said that other people have different biases because they are sinful and/or they haven't been given the right biases by the grace of the Holy Spirit. This can easily become an argument like, "I'm the right kind of Christian and so I can read the Bible correctly. You're the wrong kind of Christian, so you can't."

This stance is especially pernicious when we reflect on the fact that biases are related to demographics and identity. So when two people have different biases based on social identity, and one of those people explains this difference by saying the other person isn't the right kind of Christian, what you can end up with is theological xenophobia: "They have the wrong biases because they're sinful. They just so happen to be of a different gender, different race, different culture, et cetera. Only people with my biases are the right kind of Christian, and they just so happen to have the same identity as me."

This manifestation of bias is one of the worst kinds because it can lead to racism, misogyny, xenophobia, colonialism, imperialism, and other forms of violent oppression. *After all*, we may come to think, *those biases over* there *are incorrect* because *they come from cultures other than our own, which is the true culture with the correct biases.*

Recognizing and Naming Our Biases

The opposite of failing to recognize our biases, or pretending they are something they're not, is to recognize them and think of them accurately. Once we learn what our biases are, we should make a practice of calling them to mind, saying them out loud, and attempting to connect them to our interpretive questions whenever possible.

We can use a simple formula: "I'm interpreting this passage this way because of X," where X is the bias that's most motivating us. Alternatively, we can try: "As a person with X experience or background, I interpret the passage this way." We can also ask other interpreters why they're interpreting texts in the way that they are: "Why do you connect with this passage in this way?," "What about your experience leads you to interpret this passage in this way?," and "Why do you think this question is the most important question for you?"

Hearing other people explain the connection between their interpretations and their own biases can be a helpful way for us to practice doing the same. While it's likely that some of our biases will remain unconscious regardless of how much we try to recognize them, the more we actively practice accounting for our biases, the easier it will become.

Part II

The Main Ingredients

In December 2024, I (Aaron) went with my family on a trip to Thailand. We ate at street markets, mall food courts, and fancy restaurants, in far flung mountain villages and at hotel buffets. My family had to spend a lot of time staring at menus or walking circles around markets just to get a sense of all the different foods on offer. I was born and raised in the southwestern United States, so there were a lot of new dishes for me to try. I'd had American versions of some of the foods, and some I'd never heard of before. My kids had heard of even fewer. We always managed to find something delicious, but because of our lack of familiarity with the foods, we had to put in more time and effort than we would have at home.

It would be uncontroversial to say you're not familiar with every kind of food in the world. Don't worry. Neither are we—neither is anyone, for that matter. Depending on where you've lived and how you've grouped up with others, you'll have become familiar with a certain number of foods before you started making food for yourself. This might seem like a basic point to make, but it's an important one, because the same is true of the Bible.

As we've implied in part I, where you live and the groups you're a part of make you familiar with a certain amount of the Bible. But no one is familiar with all of the Bible, not even biblical scholars. Even if a person had the entire Bible memorized, there are still things they wouldn't know about the historical, literary, and religious contexts that lay behind the Bible. There's always room to learn more.

That's why part II of this book exists. Think of it like a tour of a foreign food market. The purpose of part II is to introduce you to the Bible from an academic perspective. If you don't know anything about the Bible, this might be the first time you're exposed to some of the Bible's content. If you know a few things about the Bible that you picked up from your religious community, this might be the first time you've been exposed to the Bible's content outside the lens of faith. Sometimes we'll be summarizing famous biblical stories. Sometimes we'll be giving you new ways to think of them. There's a lot of information in the chapters that follow, and you might want to take your time working your way through it. Like a foreign market, you might have to put in more time and effort than you would have at home to find something delicious.

Trying to teach you how to interpret the Bible without teaching you something about the Bible's contents would be like trying to teach you how to cook only those dishes with which you're already familiar. We want to make as much of the Bible as accessible to you as possible, so that, going forward, you feel confident interpreting as much of it as possible.

CHAPTER 4

The Bible in General

MY (AARON'S) KIDS are just old enough to start making breakfast for themselves in the morning. In our house, a few cupboards and shelves are set aside specifically for the kids' stuff: their bowls, plates, cups, and utensils, along with their cereals, breads, snacks, pre-cut vegetables, fruits, cheeses, et cetera. So, when my kids go to make themselves breakfast, they go to specific places in the kitchen to do it. Those places are a little different from the places I go in the kitchen when I make breakfast, lunch, and dinner for the whole family. We're all coming to the kitchen for different things.

If an interpreter is like a cook, then what is the Bible? You might guess that since the Bible is the thing we're interpreting, then the Bible is like food. But that's not quite the case. Rather, the Bible is the thing that holds all the food we'll cook. The Bible is a kitchen, a pantry, a deep freezer in the garage, an outdoor herb garden, and a decorative wine rack in the dining room. It's the space we enter when we go to interpret. And it turns out that this is a large and somewhat confusing space. Just like it would be helpful to know a little bit about a kitchen and what is and isn't in it before you try making anything, it's helpful to know a little about the Bible before we sit down to try to interpret any passage in it.

What Do We Mean by "the Bible"?

Most people in Western culture have at least a passing familiarity with the Bible. But not everyone has the same understanding of what it is. So, let's start out with some basic definitions.

We'll begin with the name itself. Again, Merriam-Webster is a helpful starting point, saying that a bible is the sacred scriptures of a religion. As simple as this definition is, it conceals a lot of complexity.

First, we can note that bibles are bibles of a religion. That is to say, the status of a bible is dependent on the religious community that uses it. There are no bibles existing objectively out there in the universe, somehow independent of religious communities. All bibles exist because religious communities compose, preserve, and utilize them, and they would cease to exist if that wasn't the case.

Second, we should note that "religion," in the singular, is hiding a little bit here. Protestant Christians and Catholic Christians broadly belong to the same religion, but they have different bibles with different numbers of books in them, as do Ethiopic Christians, as did Christians living sixteen hundred years ago, as did the very first Christians who were the disciples of Jesus. So it's less that bibles are the sacred scriptures of a religion and more that bibles are the sacred scriptures of more specific religious communities.

Third, we can ask a little more about what sacred scripture is. We're not talking about any kind of texts that make up a bible, but rather texts that communicate something special about the divine, however different religious communities define that. Sacred scripture is set apart from other texts because religious communities believe it tells them something about God that they otherwise couldn't know, and so they hold it in especially high regard. The term "divine inspiration" is often attached to scripture, implying that God took an active role in the composition of this text. It says true things about God because God revealed those true things to the texts' authors in some way.

Fourth, we should emphasize that we're talking about "sacred scriptures," plural. No bible I can think of is only a single text, but rather a collection of originally independent texts that have been brought together by a religious community to serve as its Bible.

Fifth and finally, we should also emphasize, as Marc Brettler does in the New Oxford Annotated Bible, that bibles are canons. A *canon* is defined by being a closed and unchangeable standard for a community. People cannot add or subtract texts from a bible on a whim. In fact, to attempt to add or subtract texts from a religious community's bible would likely result in a person falling outside that religious community. Therefore, because bibles are canons, they also serve to mark the boundaries around a religious community. People are in the community if they accept the community's bible and the canonical texts it contains and people are out of the community if they don't. While there is often more to a person's admission or rejection from a given community, bibles and their canonical status contributes to this distinction.

To rephrase *Merriam-Webster's* definition then, a bible is a fixed collection of originally independent texts held by a religious community in uniquely high regard because they preserve truths about God.

People usually don't say "a bible" though. We say "the Bible," with the definite article and a capital *B*. And that's because, within our individual communities, we tend to assume which bible we're talking about, and also that it's the only bible worth discussing. The expression "the Bible," then, is quite local to people and their experience. This means that a Jewish person, a Catholic person, and a Protestant person can all sit at the same table and talk about "the Bible" while referring to three substantially different canonical collections of scripture, all of which in turn reflect different perspectives.

The Bible's Many Voices

When considering the Bible, it's important to keep in mind that it is a *multivocal* text. To be multivocal simply means that something is composed of many different voices or perspectives. The books that make up the Bible, and the texts that were edited together to make up the books of the Bible, were written in different times, in different places, by different people, in different genres, with different theologies. These differences are easy to recognize when you know to look for them. The voice of a tenth-century BCE court history, for instance, is different from the voice of a sixth-century BCE piece of wisdom literature, which is also different from the voice of a late first-century CE gospel. Just as a quilt is made of many different sections, or an anthology is made of many different essays, the Bible is a collection of independent things.

What does this look like in practice? One easy example of the Bible's multivocality is its two different histories of the rise and fall of the ancient Israelite monarchy, one in the books of Samuel and Kings, and one in Chronicles. Both histories cover roughly the same period and share many stories in common, with some passages even mirroring each other word for word, but they are written by very different people with different perspectives, and so they amount to very distinct voices.

In Samuel and Kings, for example, David rises to power through mercenary work (1 Samuel 27), bribery (1 Samuel 30:26–31), and assassination (2 Samuel 3:22–39), but in Chronicles, all of these stories are omitted, and David becomes king peacefully through the charismatic consensus of every person in the land (1 Chronicles 11:1–3). In Samuel and Kings, prophets like Samuel, Elijah, and Elisha appear frequently, taking on the roles of kingmaker, miracle worker, and rebel against the kingdom. But in Chronicles, Samuel's role is drastically reduced, and Elijah and Elisha's are all but eliminated. In Samuel and Kings, God often punishes later generations for the sins of earlier ones (e.g., 2 Kings 23:26–27), but in Chronicles that does not happen, and people are frequently warned before they do something that will result in immediate punishment (e.g., 2 Chronicles 35:20–24). The Bible could have included only a single history of this monarchy, but it has two: two histories with two very different voices.

Another clear example of the Bible's multivocality are the different stories of Jesus's life, death, and resurrection in the four Gospels. Mark and John say nothing about Jesus as a child, while Matthew and Luke provide conflicting accounts of Jesus's birth (Matthew 1:18–25 vs. Luke 2:1–21) with different genealogies (Matthew 1:1–17 vs. Luke 3:23–38). In Mark, Matthew, and Luke, Jesus drives the money changers out of the temple near the end of his life (in Mark 11, Matthew 21, and Luke 19), but in John the incident happens near the beginning of his ministry (in John 2). In all four Gospels, a different woman comes to either wash or perfume Jesus, but all the details are different on each occasion, resulting in very different perspectives on the scene (Mark 14:1–11, Matthew 26:6–13, Luke 7:36–50, John 12:1–8). In Mark and Luke, the disciples who come to visit Jesus's tomb do not see him there, but in Matthew and John, two different groups of disciples see the resurrected Jesus (Matthew 28:1–10 vs. John 20:11–18).

The Bible could have had only a single Gospel, but it has four: four Gospels with four very different voices.

A Collection of Independent Voices

How did this come about? Why is the Bible a multivocal text?

One key reason for the Bible's multivocality is very simple: No text in the Bible was originally written with the purpose of being *in* a Bible. The prophet Isaiah did not write his oracles and then think to himself, "Surely, centuries from now, people will place my writings beside some guy named Jeremiah and some other guy named Ezekiel, and together we will make up the major prophets of a thirty-nine-book collection called the Hebrew Bible!"

It is true that biblical texts occasionally demonstrate an awareness of previous texts that also were later included in the Bible, as is the case with the writers of Chronicles being aware of Samuel and Kings, and Matthew and Luke being aware of Mark. But as was clear in the examples above, this awareness does not mean the authors wrote the texts in full or even partial agreement with the previous texts. Even if a biblical author hoped their text would be preserved for future generations, there was no way they could have predicted the many varied canonical collections Jewish people and Christians would put together over the centuries. As a result, the original context of *every* text in the Bible is one that is independent of the Bible itself.

That independence has wide-reaching implications. For example, because the Bible is a collection of texts that were not written to work together, the Bible is prone to narrative repetition, theological tension, and outright contradiction. Let's look at some of these.

Narrative Repetition

In the Pentateuch there are two stories of creation (Genesis 1:1–2:3 vs. Genesis 2:4–25), two flood stories (alternating throughout Genesis 6–9), two stories of the covenant with Abraham (Genesis 15 vs. Genesis 17), three sister wife stories (Genesis 12:10–20 vs. Genesis 20 vs. Genesis 26:1–11), two stories of Joseph being sold into slavery in Egypt (alternating throughout Genesis 37:12–36), and two stories of the revelation of the divine name to Moses (Exodus 3:1–15 vs. Exodus 6:2–8). Many of the plagues are repeated twice, there is one prose account and one poetic account of the crossing of the Red Sea that do not agree (Exodus 14:15–31 vs. Exodus 15:1–18), and there are three sets of the Ten Commandments that also do not agree (Exodus 20:1–17 vs. Exodus 34:10–28 vs. Deuteronomy 5:1–21). Stories beyond the Pentateuch are not immune to this phenomenon. There are three stories of Saul becoming king (1 Samuel 9:1–10:2 vs. 1 Samuel 10:17–24 vs. 1 Samuel 11:5–15) and two stories of David coming into Saul's service (1 Samuel 16:14–23 vs. 1 Samuel 17), any one of which would be sufficient.

Theological Tension

Next let's consider some theological tensions between the Bible's different voices. Biblical scholars have long noted that Genesis 1:1–2:3

and Genesis 2:4 appear to have different authors, in part because their theology is so markedly different. In Genesis 1:1–2:3, God is the transcendent creator of the universe who instantly, effortlessly, and with much foresight speaks all things into being and then is able to rest when the work is complete.

In Genesis 2:4 and following, however, God is the immanent and embodied creator of some parts of the world, who is surprised when Adam is lonely, surprised again when animals do not satisfy that loneliness, and then surprised yet again when everything goes wrong in the following chapter for easily preventable reasons. This God, unlike God in Genesis 1:1–2–3, creates in a laborious process of adjustment and compromise.

Even God's most iconic attributes are at times subject to this tension. Let's look at some.

In some passages of the Bible, God appears to be all knowing, but in Genesis 11:5 and the Tower of Babel story, God only notices the tower's construction belatedly.

In some passages God appears to be all powerful, but in Judges 1:19 and 2 Kings 3:27, God lacks the power to secure military victories for Israel.

In some passages God appears to be all good, but in some God is portrayed as condoning slavery (Exodus 21:1–11), genocide (1 Samuel 15:3), and mass sexual assault (Numbers 31:18).

There are moral and religious tensions in the text as well. For instance, Exodus 20:5 and Numbers 14:18 both insist that God punishes children for the sins of their parents, but Jeremiah 31:29 and Ezekiel 18:30 insist that God does no such thing. In Ezra 11, marriages to foreigners are condemned, but in Ruth 4, they are celebrated. In Deuteronomy 12, there is only a single legitimate place to offer sacrifices, but Samuel (1 Samuel 7:9), Saul (1 Samuel 13:9), David (1 Samuel 24:25), and Solomon (1 Kings 3:4) seem to disagree. Deuteronomy 20 presents an elaborate vision of holy war, while John 18:36 presents a more pacifist alternative. Paul believes sex work to be an exceptionally egregious sin in 1 Corinthians 6:18, but the story of Tamar in Genesis 38 makes her into a hero.

We can add to these broader thematic tensions as well. In Proverbs, wisdom is both readily available (Proverbs 1:20–21) and desirable (Proverbs 3:13–18). But in Job, while wisdom is desirable

(Job 9:4), it is so unavailable that not even primordial beings know where it can be found (Job 28:20–22). In Ecclesiastes, wisdom is available (Ecclesiastes 1:12–17), but its desirability is constantly being undercut (Ecclesiastes 1:18).

Such tensions don't involve only peripheral or inessential issues. Some in fact even concern salvation. The text in Hebrews 9:22 insists that forgiveness requires the shedding of blood, but in Matthew 9:2, Jesus forgives the sins of several men because of their unspoken faith. Ephesians 2:8–9 insists that salvation is by faith and not by works, but James 2:17 says that faith without works is dead. Paul says in Romans 10:9 that if you declare Jesus is Lord then you will be saved, but Jesus says in Matthew 7:21 that not everyone who calls him Lord will be saved.

Outright Contradiction

In addition to repetition and tension, outright contradiction also appears in the text. In Genesis 1, the order of creation is vegetation, animals, then human beings, but in Genesis 2, the order is Adam, then vegetation, then animals, then Eve. In Genesis 37:28b and 36, Joseph is taken by Midianites and sold into slavery in Egypt, but in Genesis 37:27–28a and 39:1, Joseph is sold to Ishmaelites and taken to Egypt. In Exodus 12:9, the Israelites are supposed to roast the Passover lamb over a fire and not boil it in water, but in Deuteronomy 16:7, the Israelites are supposed to boil it in water.

There are also many contradictions in the history of the monarchy. In 1 Samuel 16:10–11, David is the eighth son of Jesse, but in 1 Chronicles 2:15, he is the seventh. In 1 Samuel 17, David kills Goliath, but in 2 Samuel 21:19, Elhanan kills Goliath. In 1 Samuel 28:6, Saul inquires of God before battle, but in 1 Chronicles 10:14, Saul does not.

Contradictions appear in the New Testament too. In Matthew 27:5, Judas dies by hanging himself after returning the money he was paid to betray Jesus, but in Acts 1:18, Judas buys a field with the money and then dies by falling and bursting open. In Mark 16:8, Jesus's women disciples run away from his tomb and never tell anyone what they saw there, but in Luke 24:9–12, Jesus's women disciples leave the tomb and immediately tell the apostles what they saw.

Narrative repetition, theological tension, and outright contradiction are all features we would expect to see in the Bible if it were a multivocal text, and features we would not expect to see if the Bible was a univocal text with only a single voice. And yet, because of how uncomfortable the Bible's multivocality can make some people, it's not uncommon to see people argue the Bible is a univocal text instead.

The Argument for a Single Voice

The opposite of seeing the Bible as multivocal is to see the Bible as univocal. To be univocal means that the Bible is ultimately the product of a single voice. Since the term "univocal" is a bit technical, you're not likely to find everyday religious folks saying, "I believe the Bible is a univocal text." Instead, they'll more commonly refer to doctrines that are based on the Bible's univocality. Doctrines like biblical inerrancy, meaning the Bible has no errors or contradictions, and biblical infallibility, meaning the Bible cannot fail in matters of faith and practice, are based on the Bible's univocality. Sometimes, believing the Bible is directly inspired by God is also based on the Bible's univocality.

People who believe the Bible is univocal do not necessarily deny that it was written in different times and places or by different people in different genres. Rather they affirm that even within this diversity, there is a single throughline that unites the texts and ensures their stories and their theologies agree.

If this were true—if the Bible was univocal—then the tenth-century BCE court history, sixth-century BCE wisdom literature, and first CE century gospel could offer alternative and complementary perspectives on the same timeless truths, but they could not disagree or be so different that readers couldn't find some way to make them fit together. This, however, is not the case.

So why do some people believe that it is?

This position does not originate in the text itself. People do not determine that the Bible is a univocal text after a thorough investigation of the Bible's actual content. No such investigation would lead to that conclusion.

Instead, they presuppose the Bible is a univocal text because they believe the Bible is ultimately authored by God and that God is the singular voice behind it all. For people with this belief, denial of the Bible's univocality—which is also an affirmation of its multivocality—is also a denial of the Bible's inspiration by God, and thereby a denial of the Bible's value, reliability, and truth. Viewed from this perspective, the stakes of surrounding a belief in the Bible's univocality can be quite high.

But there are two significant problems with believing the Bible is a univocal text. The first is that it's simply false, as the above examples show, and having false beliefs about the Bible does not aid in its interpretation. The second is that it can lead people to treat different biblical passages as though they are interchangeable in meaning.

Noodles and Chicken

Let's return to the metaphor of cooking.

Imagine someone said they were going to make you chicken tacos, but lo and behold, they were out of chicken, and so they decided to substitute steak. You might like that substitution, you might not, but most people would agree it's a substitution that makes sense. They're trading out one animal protein for another.

But imagine they were out of chicken and decided to substitute tofu. You might be okay with that, but since it's not an animal protein, it's a bigger substitution than steak would have been. But hey, it could work.

Now imagine they were out of chicken and decided to substitute noodles. What is going on? Is it still a taco, or is it some strange food abomination never before seen in culinary history?

Imagine you asked this person why they decided to substitute noodles for chicken and they said, "Noodles and chicken are basically the same thing." What would you say? Hopefully, you'd disagree. Steak and chicken are both animal proteins. Tofu is a common substitute for animal proteins. But noodles? No one with any appreciable culinary skill would say that noodles and chicken are basically the same thing because the differences between them are both obvious and significant.

And yet, when it comes to the Bible, we make this same mistake all the time, substituting one thing for another when we interpret.

Let's see how.

A Need for Harmony?

Consider this example (which just happens to also involve food). In Genesis 2:17, God explains the consequences of eating from the tree of the knowledge of good and evil to Adam, saying, "On the day you eat from it, you will surely die." But when we turn to Genesis 3:6, where Adam eats from the tree, he does not die that day. Indeed, we see in Genesis 5:5 that Adam lived 930 years, far beyond the day he ate from the tree.

So, does this mean that God lied about the consequences of eating from the tree? In attempting to answer this question, a person might cite 1 Samuel 15:29, in which Samuel says that God does not lie. They might further appeal to 2 Peter 3:8 which says that for God, "one day is as a thousand years." If these later passages were applied to the interpretation of Genesis 2:17 and Genesis 5:5, then God cannot lie, and the only reason it looked like God lied is because when God said "on the day" in Genesis 2:17, God really meant up to one thousand years. Since Adam died before reaching one thousand years of age, God was still telling the truth, just in an unexpected and poetic way.

But can these later passages be applied to the interpretation of earlier ones in this way? If the Bible is a univocal text with a single, unifying and consistent voice behind it, then they could be. But if the Bible is a multivocal text, then the answer is no, they are almost certainly not applicable in this way.

If the Bible is a multivocal text, then the answer to the question "Does God lie in Genesis 2:17?" cannot be found by looking at other passages by different voices with different theologies. After all, centuries separate the composition of Genesis 2, 1 Samuel 15, and 2 Peter 3, and each could be written by different people in service of the needs of very different audiences. If the Bible is a multivocal text, then it's entirely possible for some passages to state that God lies while other passages affirm that God cannot.

This is an important point to acknowledge. That's because treating the Bible as a univocal text not only flies in the face of the facts, it causes people to ignore the unique differences that exist between the various contexts and content of diverse biblical passages. That is to say, treating the Bible as a univocal text and substituting the meaning of one text for the meaning of another text is like the friend who substitutes noodles for chicken in a taco and pretends that they're basically the same. Cooking doesn't work this way because there are real differences in taste, texture, and modes of preparation between ingredients like chicken and noodles. Biblical interpretation does not work this way, either, because there are real differences in historical, literary, and ideological contexts between biblical passages like Genesis 2 and 2 Peter 3.

This is not to say that different biblical passages are always useless in helping us to understand others, just as it's not the case that different ingredients can never be substituted for one another. However, an interpreter has to know what they are doing, the same way a cook does. Just as a chef must logically offer a protein substitution, an interpreter must use evidence to argue for the similarities between two texts. Put simply, we can use one text to help us understand another only when there is actual evidence that the texts are composed in similar historical, literary, and ideological contexts (i.e., that they have a similar voice). And even then, we should be modest and qualify our interpretation by saying something like "This other verse *might* be helpful here."

We've now determined that the Bible is a multivocal text, not a univocal one, and that in order to interpret the Bible well, we have to respect the individual qualities of the many voices that have contributed to its composition, all of which were written apart from the Bible itself. It's important to remember that we should expect to encounter theological diversity in the text, along with the repetition, tension, and outright contradiction this leads to. We should not rush to force a crude harmonization on this diversity and thereby destroy one of the most unique features of the Bible. The Bible felt no need to impose this harmony on itself. For us to do it, then, even in service to the Bible, is profoundly unbiblical.

Now that we understand all of this about multivocality, though, we may find ourselves asking a new question about it.

What Is the Point of Multivocality?

Given all this talk about repetition and contradictions, it would be easy to assume that the multivocality of the Bible is bad. After all, the Bible's multivocality entails that the text is very complex, probably the most complex text that you will ever interact with. This complexity makes interpretation more difficult than it otherwise would be. It also can (and sometimes should) undermine our confidence in the text's historical reliability and theological truth. After all, if the Bible contradicts itself about what happened long ago or about God's attributes, then we have less reason to think the Bible is always correct. So, if the cons of the Bible's multivocality are clear, what are the pros?

First and quickly, we should point out that even if the Bible's multivocality offered no benefit at all, the fact of it would still be true, and so we'd have to deal with multivocality if we were approaching the Bible honestly. We can't reject a truth merely because it inconveniences us.

But secondly and importantly, there *are* advantages to the Bible's multivocality. Let's look at three of them.

The first advantage of the Bible's multivocality is that the unreliability of some parts of the Bible have no effect on the reliability of other parts. For example, Exodus 12:37 claims that upward of two million people—including women, children, the elderly, and six hundred thousand fighting men—set out from Egypt during the exodus. The book of Joshua claims that in a single generation, an invading army of Israelites conquered the land of Canaan, eliminating more than thirty kings and burning cities to the ground left and right. 1 Kings 10 claims that King Solomon was the wealthiest king on earth and gives extravagant descriptions of his possessions. All three of these claims are historically false. (Ancient Egypt could barely sustain a population of two million people, and there's no archaeological evidence of that many people traipsing through the wilderness for forty years or settling in Canaan afterwords. Most of the cities mentioned in Joshua were unoccupied at the times the Bible variously reports the conquest happened, and the Bible can't keep its story straight on when those times were. And we have zero archaeological evidence of Solomon's massive wealth, nor does that amount of wealth make sense in its historical context.)

If the Bible were a univocal text, from a single source, cast in a single voice, with a single overarching agenda, then the fact that these claims are false would have a significant impact on the historical reliability of everything else in the Bible. A person would be justified in thinking, "If the Bible gets so many things wrong, maybe it gets everything wrong" or "if I can't trust the Bible here, then I can't trust the Bible anywhere."

But as we've already determined, the Bible isn't a univocal text. Just as one person getting a fact wrong has no effect on whether someone else is right, one passage in the Bible getting something wrong has no effect on whether another passage is right. The Bible's multivocality requires us to consider its narratives, its wisdom, and its theology on a case-by-case basis.

A second and more nuanced advantage of the Bible's multivocality is that multivocality empowers us to resist harmful interpretations by giving us biblical counterexamples. For example, the Bible includes verses that can be used to justify slavery (Ephesians 6:5), sexism

(1 Timothy 2:11–15), and nationalism (Romans 13:1–7), but the Bible also includes verses that can be used to support abolition (Philemon 1:16), egalitarianism (Galatians 3:28), and pacifism (John 18:36). Harm done to others with Bible-driven justification gives us a motivation to undermine bad interpretations, and the Bible's multivocality provides us with the resources.

A final, personal advantage of the Bible's multivocality is that it makes it easier for the reader to find themselves in the text. The Bible offers a diverse set of passages or ingredients to enjoy, which make it possible for people with many different needs and many different tastes to come away satisfied. The pessimism of Ecclesiastes and the heartbrokenness of Lamentations and the yearning of the Song of Songs might all prove valuable to one person in various seasons of their lives, or they may prove valuable to range of different people in the identical season of life. The quick and unembellished narrative of Mark might appeal to some, while the more theologically reflective narrative of John might appeal to someone else.

In this and other ways, it offers something to us all.

Conclusion

Because the Bible has so many different things to say, it can be heard by so many different people, and it only has so many different things to say because so many different people across time and space have contributed to it. The Bible only exists at all because for three thousand years, people have found parts of it useful and worth preserving for future generations. When you read the Bible, you join a transhistorical, transcultural conversation, and through your interpretations of the text, you contribute to that conversation. Life doesn't offer many opportunities like that, but a multivocal Bible does. There is space for you in the Bible, regardless of who you are, where you come from, or where you're going.

A univocal text could only tell you to think. A multivocal text invites you to think alongside its many voices.

A univocal text positions you as a passive audience member. A multivocal text adds you to the choir.

A univocal text can't speak to the diversity of human life. A multivocal text is in fact born from that diversity.

A univocal text can't provide diverse ingredients for you to cook. A multivocal text says, "Welcome to the kitchen."

CHAPTER 5

The Pentateuch

THE TERM "PENTATEUCH" means "five scrolls" in Greek, and it's the term most commonly used for the first five books of the Bible: Genesis, Exodus, Leviticus, Numbers, and Deuteronomy. The Hebrew word for these texts is *Torah*, which means "guidance," because the bulk of the texts concern guidance given by God to the ancient people of Israel, largely in the forms of laws and instructions. Both Jewish and Christian traditions have long held that Moses wrote the Pentateuch. Most biblical scholars today, however, recognize that these texts were composed over centuries, sometime between the tenth and fifth centuries BCE, by at least three different authors with very different theologies and understandings of ancient Israel's history.

While it's intuitive to think the biblical texts were written in the order that the appear—for example, to think Genesis was written before Exodus, which was written before Leviticus, and so on—this is not necessarily the case anywhere in the Bible. Indeed, the books of the Pentateuch, and many other books in the Bible, are made up of smaller units that were edited together to form the complete books we have today, and these smaller units were at times composed centuries apart.

Beginning at the Beginning

The first book of the Bible is called Genesis in English. The word "genesis" means "the beginning of something," and it's an appropriate title for a book that opens with the creation of the world. In Hebrew, the book is titled *B'reshit*, which is the first word of the first verse of the book and is famously translated as "in the beginning."

Genesis 1–2:3 lays out God's creation of the world in a seven-day schema. On days one, two, and three, God creates spaces that are then populated with inhabitants on days four, five, and six. Days one and four see the creation of light, its separation from darkness, and then the population of that light and darkness with the sun, moon, and stars. Days two and five see the creation of the sky and the sea, followed by the population of those spaces with flying and swimming animals. Then days three and six see the creation of land and land animals, culminating in the creation of human beings. On the seventh day, God rests and sanctifies the day, creating a sacred moment in time and one of the most important Jewish holidays: Shabbat or the sabbath.

It can be difficult to fully appreciate the seven-day schema of creation in Genesis 1 when we're reading the text in the modern world, where the sciences all attest to an earth that formed over billions of years. Many people in fact feel uncomfortable with this apparent contradiction. Maybe you're one of those people, or have been in the past.

Indeed, there are many Bible readers who, out of a sense of loyalty to a literal-historical understanding of Genesis 1, feel compelled to deny the conclusions of modern sciences. But this feeling is unnecessary because Genesis 1–2:3 does not claim to be a literal-historical text. Rather, it's a part of a common genre of ancient religious literature known as the creation myth, which is not intended to be a historical representation of events. (We'll give you some tips for interpreting myths later in the chapter.) In the case of the Bible, it's a good thing it's not, because in literal-historical terms, things just don't add up.

Tips for Interpreting Prose

Much of the Pentateuch and the rest of the Hebrew Bible is made of prose narratives—that is, stories that are written in plain, literal language that reflects how people naturally speak. You might think that, because it's plain and literal, it's also effortless to interpret well. Sometimes it is, but sometimes that very simplicity of the text is its greatest challenge. Let's look at three tips that are useful when interpreting prose.

1. Prioritize Immediate Context

Words in biblical languages are no different from words in any other language and can have multiple meanings depending on the context. When we're trying to determine what a word means in any given place in the Bible, the most important context is always the immediate context: the other words, sentences and paragraphs immediately before and after a word we're curious about. The further away a word appears from the same word in a different passage, the less relevant it is for figuring out what that word means.

For example, the meaning of the word "covenant" in Genesis 9:11 is identical to its meaning in Genesis 9:12 and many other parts of Genesis, where it refers generically to a mutually obligating agreement between God and humanity. But it's less similar to the meaning of "covenant" in Joshua 7:11, for example, where it more specifically refers to the laws in Deuteronomy, or in 2 Samuel 3:13, where it's specifically a political treaty between men. Similarly, the greater the historical distance between two usages of a word, the less likely they are to have similar meanings, because meanings naturally change over time to accommodate new social circumstances.

Christian readers in particular struggle with this fact, often succumbing to the urge to use the meaning of a word as it appears in the New Testament to inform the meaning of a word in the Hebrew Bible, or to use things Jesus said and did to interpret the Hebrew Bible despite both the historical distance in time and the literary difference in genre between them. Many modern readers display a tendency to assume that words in the Bible have the same sense they do today. Both of these tendencies are weaker approaches to interpretation because they prioritize distant contexts.

The better approach is this: Anytime we're trying to understand a key term or concept, we should look for other examples nearby first. In the hierarchy of contextual interpretation, immediate context, not some later dogmatic context, is king.

2. Don't Be Misled by Chapters, Verses, and Headings

It's important to remember that chapters, verses, and those helpful headings in your Bible aren't part of the original texts themselves but have all been added centuries or millennia after the text's composition. That doesn't mean that they don't serve a purpose. These things can be useful in making the text easier to navigate. However, they can also unintentionally mislead a reader into thinking an idea stops where a verse or chapter does. (For example, Genesis 2 begins before the seventh day of creation is complete, detaching it from the rest of the days. Chapters inconsistently separate Jesus's baptism from his temptation in the wilderness. In Mark, they're together, but in Matthew they're apart for no apparent reason. Romans 1 stops before the grand reveal in Romans 2:1 that everything Paul has just said hasn't been his view necessarily, but rather a view he's adopted for the rhetorical purpose of getting his reader to condemn themselves for hypocrisy.)

Even worse, sometimes translations will use headings to try to get you to interpret a text in a specific way. For example, the New International Version's heading before Genesis chapter 3 is "The Fall," a phrase that is less about the actual text and more about a particular theological doctrine that Christians have adopted about Genesis 3.

These are just a few examples of how chapters, verses, and headings in the Bible can sway one's understanding. As you can see, it's wise to not base your interpretations on any of these features of the text.

3. Be Mindful of Gapped Narratives

A common feature of prose narratives in the Hebrew Bible, which differentiate them from more modern prose narratives, such as the ones we find in novels, is how "gapped" the narratives are. That is to say, biblical prose narratives often lack much descriptive detail, especially as it relates to the interior lives of characters, including their thoughts, feelings, and intentions.

On the plus side, this lack of detail invites us to fill in those gaps with imagined details and intentions of our own. This is likely part of the reason why the Bible has been such an influential text: People across time, and from all over the world, have been able to read themselves into it.

On the negative side, however, gapped narratives can lead us to overwhelm the text with our own ideas, so much so that we forget what the text actually says and only recall the things we imagine about the text.

Keeping in mind that biblical prose is filled with gapped narratives is important when we're interpreting the Bible. If we want to interpret in healthy ways, we should work to carefully maintain the difference between the text and our ideas about the text.

The Order of Creation

When we turn to Genesis 2:4 and the verses that follow, we encounter something a reader might not expect: a desolate world. Genesis 2:5 tells us there's no vegetation and no people to work the ground, which is surprising, since the picture we're left with at the end of Genesis 1 is a world full of both.

But that's just the beginning. The further we get into Genesis 2, the more apparent the stark contrast with Genesis 1 becomes. In Genesis 1, God is a transcendent being who creates the world through acts of speech in a structured process where each step is already anticipating the next. In Genesis 1, God is so successful in creating the world that each day is called good, and God can rest at the end, certain that everything is working as intended.

In Genesis 2, we see something different. In this passage, God is a human-like being who creates by forming things with God's own hands and breathing life into them. The process in Genesis 2 is fraught with setbacks, where God discovers man's loneliness isn't good. God proceeds to make animals to try to fix that loneliness, and then makes Eve because the animals don't suffice.

In addition to the chapters' portrayals of God, the stories flatly contradict each other in their orders of creation. In Genesis 1, vegetation is created before animals, then animals are created before men and women, who are made at the same time. But in Genesis 2:4 and following, Adam is created before any vegetation, then animals are created before Eve.

If these stories were in different texts, a reader would probably assume that they're the creation myths of two different cultures. But both stories are in the Bible, back-to-back. Why include both?

Over the past two hundred and fifty years, what the majority of biblical scholars have come to believe is that these two creation myths in Genesis 1–2:3 and Genesis 2:4 and following were originally composed independently of each other and then edited together later by a third party, who desired to preserve the stories that were both important to their contemporary community. This theory helps explain why the two creation myths have such different ideas of how God creates and why the stories contradict each other, but it also helps us explain other instances of contradictions that appear throughout the Pentateuch. The multiple authorship of biblical texts is an idea we'll return to frequently in this book.

In many ways, the Bible does us a favor by beginning with two contradictory stories. In so doing, the Bible signals to us at the outset what this text actually is: a diverse collection of religious traditions that have been brought together by different communities of faith over a long period of time. Put another way, the Bible tells us in the first two chapters that it is a multivocal text. When you read the Bible, you're reading an anthology of ancient religious literature—not a textbook, not an instructional manual, not a love letter from God, and not a complete work of systematic theology.

Now, just because it's an anthology of ancient religious literature doesn't mean it can't be inspired by God, or say true things about God, or be helpful in trying to understand God. Its being an anthology just means that whatever is in it that is true, inspired, or helpful will come through in many, sometimes conflicting, voices.

With that in mind, we can see the story that begins in Genesis 2:4 as an alternative creation myth to the one in Genesis 1–2:3, with its own distinct purpose.

The Creation Myths

The story of Adam and Eve is iconic in Western culture. It's a story about the loss of innocence, widely understood to depict humanity as first existing in an unashamed state in a paradise of ease, only to be tempted into disobedience with forbidden knowledge, which then burdens them with self-consciousness and death.

Later Christian tradition has often associated the serpent in the garden with Satan, the great deceiver and antagonist to God, but the text of Genesis 3 never identifies the serpent as anything more than a serpent, and, strictly speaking, in the story the serpent never lies. The serpent asks a question, "Did God say, 'You shall not eat from any tree in the garden'?", and then correctly notes that the consequences of eating from the tree of the knowledge of good and evil (Genesis 3:1–4) are not in fact death. If anyone lies in the story, it's God, who told Adam that if he eats from the fruit of the tree of the knowledge of good and evil, then on that day he'll surely die (Genesis 2:17), which turns out not to be the case. God could be lying for the same reason parents often lie to kids, exaggerating consequences in the hope that it will deter them, only to tone down the actual consequences in the end. Or God could be lying in this story because, in a similar ancient Southwest Asian myth,

"Adapa and the South Wind," the deity Ea also lies to a man about the consequences of eating magical food.

The other (non-death) consequences of Adam and Eve's disobedience give us insight into the world of the author of this passage. You may notice that all of their consequences are things that continue to affect us today and affected us even more three thousand years ago: serpents do crawl on their bellies (3:14), there is an imperfect relationship between humans and animals (3:15), childbirth is painful and patriarchy is real (3:16), work is difficult (3:17–18), and people do die (3:19). Since these consequences are bad, if we reverse them, we gain some insight into what the author thought was good. Wouldn't it be good if, for example, humans and animals lived in harmony, childbirth were painless, the genders were more egalitarian, work were easier and more satisfying, and people didn't die?

Genesis 4–11 contains still more myths. Central among them are two versions of the flood story that have been tightly edited together from Genesis 6–9. Biblical scholars have been able to unravel these originally independent stories by beginning with their contradictions, like in how many animals are to be brought on the ark, and then dividing up the remaining verses where they match in narrative, theme, and theology. For example, if Noah brought only a single pair of animals on the ark (6:19–20) and offered sacrifices to God afterward (8:20), then that would result in the death of the animal species, and Noah may as well had never saved them to begin with. But if Noah brought seven pairs of clean animals on the ark (7:2), animals specifically for sacrifice, then there's no problem with him offering sacrifices to God afterward (8:20).

If we continue in this way, we get two versions of the story. In one version of the story, God decides to wipe out humanity because every inclination of our hearts is evil (Genesis 6:5), but Noah finds favor in God's eyes (6:8), so Noah brings seven pairs of clean animals and one pair of unclean animals (7:2) onto the ark to survive a forty day flood (7:4) and offers sacrifices to God afterward (8:20), whereupon God promises to never do it again (8:21).

In the other version of the story, God decides to wipe out humanity because the earth is full of violence (6:11), but Noah is a righteous man who walks with God (6:9), so Noah brings two of every kind of animal (6:19–20) onto the ark to survive a 150-day flood (7:24) and makes a covenant—that is, enters into an agreement—with God afterward (9:8–10), whereupon God promises to never do it again (9:11–17).

The biblical versions of the flood story are not the only stories of their kind. Ancient Southwest Asian flood stories also depict God's decision to wipe out life. But the biblical stories depict this decision as a moral judgment of humanity, while the story known as the "Mesopotamian Epic of Atrahasis" paints the decision as the result of humanity having become too noisy.

When viewed as pieces of literal history, the collective flood stories are horrific, given the mass loss of life and how unbelievable it is that infants and children could warrant drowning before a reasonable age of moral accountability. But when we consider the biblical stories as a play on a familiar cultural myth, we can see them instead as an interesting attempt to imagine God as less capricious than the deities of surrounding peoples. We can see a God who brought the flood as a result of people's actions, rather than on a whim.

Tips for Interpreting Myths

Generally, myths are stories that are set in or around the primordial past—that is, around the beginning of time. These stories have etiological functions that serve to explain features of the world, they're either not literally true or can be appreciated without their literal truth, and they give a people a shared sense of identity and purpose. Many of the Bible's most popular myths are found in Genesis chapters 1–11—the story of creation, Cain and Abel, the flood, the tower of Babel—but there are instances of mythic language elsewhere, like in Psalm 74:13–14, where God kills a sea monster before the creation of the world

Reading and making sense of myths, like reading and making sense of other texts in the Bible, requires that we engage in the act of interpretation. Here are some general rules to keep in mind when interpreting myths.

1. Don't Force Myths to Be More than They Are

Many Bible readers feel compelled to believe that if something is in the Bible, then it is literally and historically true. Yet the evidence at the disposal of biblical scholars indicates quite clearly that not everything in the Bible is true in these ways. This is the case for most of the Pentateuch and the next several books after it, and it's especially the case for the myths in Genesis. Still, people will attempt to force these stories to be true by disregarding evidence. When we do that, however, we end up building our worldviews on unsustainable foundations. Exposure to facts, critical reflection, or interacting with people of different views becomes something to avoid, lest it shake those already shaky foundations, and the mildest push can result in a complete loss of faith.

None of this is necessary. Myths are myths, and we get the most out of them when we treat them like myths. It's the same principle that applies to anything else. Comedy isn't funny when it's viewed as if it's a documentary. Horror isn't scary when it's viewed as whimsical fantasy. Georgia peaches aren't delicious when they're covered in enchilada sauce. Sushi doesn't make a great candy.

A good principle to keep in mind? Don't force these texts to be something other than what was intended. Simply enjoy them for what they are.

2. Consider the Etiology

Myths are primarily etiological in nature. That is to say, they are stories that explain why the world of the author works the way it does. Such stories are often set far in the past because that's when the social world came into existence.

Genesis 1, for example, tells us that humanity is the crown of creation, having been made in the image of God and thereby suitable to represent the deity in the world. The idea that a human is made in the image of God is one that's only attributed to kings in Egypt and Southwest Asia. The Bible democratizes that claim, endowing humanity in general with intrinsic value.

The Genesis 1 story also culminates in the creation of a sacred moment of time, Shabbat, the sabbath, a prominent and distinctive holiday practiced in Jewish communities throughout history. The story tells us where the holiday comes from. And Genesis 2–3 tells us that humanity's foundational problem is that we want to know more than we ought, and that ideally, we shouldn't have to suffer and die in labor or suffer and work ourselves to death to put food on the table.

Both of these passages answer existential questions about what humanity is like, who God is like in creating us, and why life is the way it is. Answering these questions is what myths are all about.

3. Compare and Contrast with Other Myths

Once we correctly identify something in the Bible as a myth, we can compare and contrast it to other ancient Southwest Asian myths to learn more about the context in which an author was writing and what they intended to convey.

For example, we might observe that there's only a single deity doing anything in Genesis 1. We might further observe that this contrasts sharply with most other creation myths in which a whole host of deities participate in creation. In Genesis 1, God and God alone performs creative actions in this story. That's not to say that God is the *only* deity in this story. In Genesis 1:26, God says, "Let *us* make humans in *our* image, according to *our* likeness." The plural pronouns here refer to the divine council, a common feature of ancient Southwest Asian pantheons, where the high god is surrounded by a gathering of divine advisers, messengers, rivals, consorts, children, and other more minor divinities, in a similar way to how a human ruler would be surrounded by human versions of the same. We see this divine council in action in 1 Kings 22:19 and following, Psalm 82, and Job 1. These other deities, though, play no active role in creation here.

The Sagas

From Genesis 12 and on, we move away from creation myths with a global scope and toward a different type of literature that biblical scholars sometimes refer to as "sagas." Starting in Genesis 12, these sagas focus on the relational drama of four generations of a single family and include more personal encounters between characters and God. The primary purpose of these saga texts isn't to record a straightforward account of history but rather to preserve important ancestral traditions that will help people centuries later grapple with questions of identity and kinship. "Where do we come from?" and "Who are we related to?" are the major questions being answered with these stories.

Two themes run throughout these sagas and the remainder of the book of Genesis.

The first theme is covenant. Although we saw a covenant between Noah and God in Genesis 9, the covenants between God and Abraham in Genesis 15 and 17 will be referred to repeatedly in later books. A covenant is a mutually binding contract usually between two parties with very different amounts of social status, and they're one of the main ways that God relates to humanity in the Bible.

In Genesis 15 and 17, God promises Abraham innumerable descendants and the land of Canaan in exchange for his faithfulness. Many of the stories that follow describe threats to God's fulfillment of these promises, and these threats create the stories' narrative suspense.

One of these recurring threats is also our second recurring theme in Genesis and the sagas: that of reproductive difficulties. Sarah, Abraham's first wife, struggles to conceive (Genesis 16:1) and so gives her slave, Hagar, to Abraham to have children (16:4). Rebekah struggles to conceive in the next generation (25:21), and both Rachel and Leah take turns struggling to conceive in the generation after that and also give their respective slaves to their husband Jacob to have children (29:30–30:24). Rivalries ensue between the favored wives and their slaves or between the children of these different women, constantly calling Abraham's line into question.

Related to these issues are threats to matriarchs themselves. On three instances, Genesis 12:10–20, Genesis 20, and Genesis 26:6–11, Abraham or Isaac passes off his wife as his sister out of fear that some violence will be done to him on account of her beautiful appearance. In each instance, only divine intervention or coincidence allows the patriarch and his wife to escape without him dead and her permanently added to the harem of some foreign king.

One story in this section is of particular note because it serves the etiological function of explaining where the name "Israel" comes from. We find it in Genesis 32. Jacob, anxiety-ridden as he sits on the verge of confronting his brother after having stolen his birthright and run away, wrestles with a mysterious man in the middle of the night (32:24). As a result of this encounter, Jacob's name is changed to Israel, and the narrator explains the name by saying, "For you have striven with God and with humans and have prevailed." The word "Israel" then means "to strive with God," and it becomes the name not only of a single character but of the nation that descends from him.

It's also an accurate description of what the Bible is: a millennium-long attempt by countless voices to strive with God together.

From Egypt to Sinai

After Genesis, we move on to the book of Exodus, in whose opening chapters we learn that the first part of God's promise to Abraham has indeed been fulfilled, as the Israelites have become a numerous people (Exodus 1:7). But just as Genesis depicted complications to the fulfillment of the first part of the promise, Exodus depicts complications to the fulfillment of the second part. The Israelites are still in Egypt rather than Canaan. Worse, they have been enslaved and can't leave (1:8–14).

Enter the Pentateuch's main character: Moses. Moses is born to Hebrew slaves and miraculously spared from execution in infancy by being placed in a basket and sent down a river. Moses is adopted into Pharaoh's household and lives a life of privilege until he kills an Egyptian slaver and runs away from Egypt to avoid punishment. In the wilderness, he marries into the family of a Midianite priest and encounters God in a burning bush; then he's chosen to return to Egypt and free the Hebrew people from slavery.

The next chapters describe a supernatural contest between God and Pharaoh for the fate of the enslaved Hebrew people. God empowers Moses and Aaron to perform an escalating series of plagues that result in the destruction of Egyptian lives and resources, culminating in the death of every firstborn child in Egypt. This is explained as poetic justice in Exodus 4:22: "You shall say to Pharaoh, 'Thus says the Lord: Israel is my firstborn son.' I said to you, 'Let my son go that he may serve me.' But you refused to let him go; now I will kill your firstborn son."

When the Pharaoh's firstborn child is dead, he relents and allows the Israelites to leave Egypt. But he changes his mind and pursues them, only for Moses to part the Red Sea so he and his people can escape, whereupon Pharaoh is caught in the collapsing sea and his army is destroyed.

This brings us to Exodus 15:1–18, the Song of the Sea, widely regarded by biblical scholars as the single oldest passage in the entire Bible because of its archaic language, older depiction of God as a warrior who fights with the sea, and similarities to other old poetry in the region of Canaan. The song memorializes God's victory over Pharaoh at the sea. In Exodus 15:3, God is celebrated as an *ish milchama*, a man of war. God defeats Pharaoh with a "blast from his nostrils" (15:8). "Who is like you among the gods?" asks Exodus 15:11. The text tells us the purpose of God's victory is to bring his people to his sanctuary (15:17), not just to Canaan in fulfillment of God's promise to Abraham but to a sacred place where God can be properly worshipped.

This is one of our first indications in the narrative that what is at stake here is not just the movement of a people from one place to another but rather the gathering of a people to a place for a specific reason. That reason is revealed in Exodus 19:6, where God informs the Israelites that they are to be a "priestly kingdom and a holy nation." Without understanding this, the rest of the story in Exodus, and indeed the next three books, doesn't make much sense. If God only needed to get people to a spot, that could be done quickly. But preparing the people to take on a sacred occupation—well, that's going to take some time.

The exodus is one of the most referenced events in the Hebrew Bible, and it goes down in both Jewish and Christian tradition as an iconic example of God's power to act definitively in history on behalf of the oppressed. It's behind the Jewish holiday of Passover, and therefore behind the story of the Last Supper in the New Testament and the institution of the eucharist or communion.

Law and Identity

After the Israelites successfully escape Egypt, they're brought to the foot of Mount Sinai, whose location is debated today, where they have a series of intense religious experiences and encounters with God. Many of these experiences have to do with them receiving laws and instructions. Almost the entire rest of the book of Exodus, all of Leviticus, big parts of Numbers, and most of Deuteronomy are dedicated to the content of these laws and instructions.

There's not much "story" to these texts. God gives the Israelites the opportunity to enter Canaan, but they're too scared to do it, so God compels them to wander in the wilderness for forty years until the generation that was afraid dies out. Wandering in the wilderness results in repeated episodes of the Israelites complaining and God either miraculously accommodating their complaints or drastically punishing them for the same.

Other than these episodes, though, the text focuses on the aforementioned laws and instructions. This brings us back to the sacred occupation for which the Israelites are being prepared. Exodus 25–31 and 35–40, plus Leviticus 1–16, are dedicated to the construction and ritual maintenance of the tabernacle, along with the requirements and responsibilities of the priests who attend the tabernacle. The tabernacle (the *mishkan*, literally "dwelling" in Hebrew) is a mobile tent sanctuary complex that houses the special presence of God. While God is understood to be spiritual and omnipresent in some biblical passages, God is also understood to be especially present and thereby accessible in other places, and the tabernacle is chief among these places until the construction of the temple in Jerusalem. Having access to God allows the Israelites to celebrate holidays, inquire of God through divination, and perform sacrifices for the forgiveness of sins.

The Forgiveness of Sins

An important element of maintaining the tabernacle, and humanity's access to God through it, is ritual purity, a concept that is often misunderstood today. Today, people tend to think of purity in moral terms, and purity culture in American evangelical spaces has further tended to see it in explicitly sexual terms. But in the Bible, ritual purity has neither of these connotations.

Rather, "ritual purity" is simply the term used for readiness to engage in ritual activity. It's sort of like metaphysical cleanliness—like washing up before eating a meal, except for the spirit. But this does not mean that ritual purity points to a lack of goodness. Just because you'd wash your hands before eating or take a shower before an important meeting doesn't mean being dirty is evil. Healthy things can get a person dirty, and healthy and even obligatory things can make a person ritually impure.

In addition to instructions, there are also collections of laws in the Pentateuch relating to the civil life of the people of Israel. The first collection we encounter is the Ten Commandments in Exodus 20. The first five commandments are primarily related to people's relationship with God, while the second five are primarily related to people's relationship with each other. The first four are unique to ancient Israel, worshipping

Yahweh alone, a ban on sacred images, and the celebration of Shabbat in particular. The second five are fairly generic prohibitions that you'd find in most other cultures at the time and since.

A note about the first of these commandments: "You shall have no other gods before me" (Exodus 20:3) does not mean there are no other gods besides Yahweh the God of Israel, merely that any other gods there should not be worshipped. Ancient Israel and the greater region of Canaan were full of people who were polytheists and worshipped many gods. Biblical authors sometimes disagreed with this, but their perspective was a minority position, which explains why the prophets we'll encounter later have to continually remind people not to worship other gods. It wasn't the people's default worldview.

The larger legal collections in the next books are called the covenant code (Exodus 21–23), which features routine examples of case law; the holiness code (Leviticus 17–26), which requires the entire community to maintain a standard of holiness, meaning to be set apart from other nations and their practices; and the Deuteronomic code (Deuteronomy 12–26), which is highly idealized and features unique laws about kings, false prophets, and war. Many of the specific laws in these codes are similar to laws found in other ancient Southwest Asian law codes. For example, Exodus 21:18–19's law concerning quarreling men and 21:28–29's law concerning an ox who gores a person are both found nearly word for word in the Code of Hammurabi. And of course, nearly every law code, ancient or modern, has laws against basic offenses like murder and theft.

But some of the laws we see in these biblical codes are quite unique for ancient Southwest Asia. Some of these laws concern matters of individual conscience, such as Leviticus 19:18, which requires a person to love their neighbor, and Exodus 23:5, which requires a person to relieve the burdens of animals owned by people who hate you. Neither law could be arbitrated in court since they rely on how people subjectively feel about one another. Some laws mandate a concern for the poor and the foreigner, like Leviticus 19:9–10. Some laws, like the law against adultery in Deuteronomy 22:22, appear in other, non-biblical law codes, but those codes allow for people to pay their way out of the situation, whereas in the Bible they do not. Several laws have "motive clauses" attached to them, which require people to do things for specific reasons, usually related to the ancient Israelites' experience as slaves or foreigners

(Exodus 22:20, Leviticus 19:33–34, or Deuteronomy 24:17–22 are good examples).

Even a casual read through these legal texts can cause a person discomfort because ancient values so often conflict with our more modern ones. This is especially true when it comes to how these texts deal with slavery and women. The institution of slavery in several forms is permitted in each of these three major law codes: Exodus 21:1–11, Leviticus 25:44–45, and Deuteronomy 15:12–18 (and indeed in each of the three major New Testament household codes: Ephesians 6:5–9, Colossians 3:22–4:1, and 1 Peter 2:18–25). There is also no explicit condemnation of slavery as an institution anywhere in the Bible, despite it being an unqualified evil. It's true that abolitionists appealed to passages in the Bible as a justification for freeing slaves. George Cheever cited texts in both the Hebrew Bible and New Testament for the cause of abolition in his book *God Against Slavery* (1857). But it's also true that enslavers like Richard Furman, in his widely read 1822 letter to the governor of South Carolina, appealed to passages in the Bible as a justification for the continuation of slavery.

There are some biblical laws that slightly improve the conditions of slaves over what was common in surrounding cultures. Laws limit violence against slaves (Exodus 21:26–27), require slaves to be avenged (Exodus 21:20), entitle slaves to rest (Exodus 20:10), and free fugitive slaves (Deuteronomy 23:16–17). But *better slavery* is still slavery.

Laws concerning women leave much to be desired. Only men can initiate divorce (Deuteronomy 24:1–4). Laws against rape have significant gaps and may even require rape victims to marry their rapist (Deuteronomy 22:25–29). Premarital sex is a capital offense, but only for women (Deuteronomy 22:13–21). Since women can't inherit, if a woman's husband dies before they have a son, she has to marry his brother in the hopes of having a son to get economic security for herself (Deuteronomy 25:5–6). The Bible has stories of exceptional women in positions of power, and many more women who through cunning or desperation are able to subvert harmful gender expectations, but this is not the norm, nor is it reflected in these laws.

In conclusion, while legal texts can be some of the most boring material for modern audiences to read, they were critical to ancient Israel's self-conception as a nation of priests with the unique responsibility of maintaining holiness and housing God's presence on earth.

Tips for Interpreting Laws

Often, if people know anything about the beginning of the Bible, they know there are laws in it. Moses's reception of the Ten Commandments on Mount Sinai is one of the most famous episodes in the entire Bible. There are indeed lots of laws in Scripture—hundreds, the exact number depending on how you count them. Most laws are contained in the three legal collections discussed in this chapter: Exodus 21–23, Leviticus 17–26, and Deuteronomy 12–26. Any thorough reading of the Pentateuch will involve navigating these laws.

Because so many of them are written for a very specific time and place, the language and ideas of the laws can be difficult to make sense of, and even if we can make sense of them, they might still seem *weird*. A certain amount of weirdness is fine. That's what gives the laws their flavor. But with some tips, perhaps we can make them a little less weird. Let's look at three tips for interpreting laws.

1. Don't Divide the Laws

When reading the laws in the Hebrew Bible, many Christians divide them into categories: civil law, ceremonial/cultic law, and moral law. Such Christians often go on to say that moral laws are the only kind still applicable today, while the others were specific to ancient Israel. This approach is both mistaken and confused.

It's mistaken because the texts themselves never distinguish between the laws like this. From a biblical perspective, these categories don't exist. Indeed, one of the most distinctive features of the laws in the Hebrew Bible is that the civil is the cultic, the cultic is the moral, the moral is the civil. Or put another way: All laws are simultaneously civil, religious, and moral in nature. That's what you get when you have a people that conceives of itself as a nation of priests governed by God and obligated by religious covenant to act morally.

This approach of dividing up the laws into categories is confused because it assumes that the goal of interpreting these texts is to sort through them and find the bits we still need to be following today, which is not the case. Of course, a reader is more than welcome to take that goal upon themselves. But they certainly don't have to. Take you, for example. You can read these texts for their literary, theological, or historical value, or, frankly, skip them all together if you feel so inclined. No text can ever force you to read it as being applicable to you, and anytime someone argues that you ought to follow one of these laws, you can simply decline to read it like they do.

That said, there are some differences between the laws we find throughout the Pentateuch. Some are casuistic or case law and usually take the form of "if X happens, then Y is the consequence or penalty." Others are apodictic, meaning that they're stated as absolutes, as in the case of the commandment "do not commit adultery." Laws that take these forms are mixed together with other laws that appear as statements of value, advice and explanations, motive clauses, commands of conscience, exhortations to remember God, short narratives, lists and calendars, and a whole host of other nonlegal material.

This variety and these differences could make these texts difficult to apply in actual legal practice. But it turns out that this isn't a problem because—surprise—legal practice is not really what these laws are for. Which brings us to our second tip for interpreting biblical law.

2. Understand That Laws Weren't Meant to Be Enforced

When we read these extensive sets of laws in the Pentateuch, it's pretty natural to assume that they are similar to laws today, which exist to be widely enforced. But interestingly, this appears not to be the case. In fact, these biblical laws are never appealed to in any text that experts believe was written prior to the Babylonian exile in 586 BCE. The characters in these texts don't seem to know the laws even exist, let alone make any effort to follow them when the occasion arises.

For example, 1 Samuel 28 acts as though Saul was the one who outlawed the use of magic in the country and that he did it recently, rather than it being something Moses outlawed centuries before in Exodus 22:18. And even though David rapes and commits adultery with Bathsheba (2 Samuel 11–12), no one in that narrative suggests that the laws against either of those things should apply to him. In another example, Saul, David, and Solomon all build altars and offer sacrifices at places other than the tabernacle or temple—which is expressly forbidden in Pentateuchal law—with no consequences. And in Jeremiah 34:12–16, the prophet Jeremiah talks about the release of debt slaves in language that's similar to but not identical with the laws in Deuteronomy 15:12, indicating that while he's aware of a similar tradition, he's not familiar with an actual written and enforceable law.

This lack of enforcement of the law isn't specific to Israel or the Bible. As biblical scholar Robert Gnuse points out in his book *Trajectories of Justice*, even when we find records of legal rulings in places like Babylon, famous law codes like the Code of Hammurabi aren't cited.

Why write laws and then neither cite nor enforce them? Because in the case of biblical laws, the laws aren't primarily legal. They're primarily theological. They're meant to convey, in a genre not familiar to us, an idealized picture of God's will for the people of Israel. As a result, the point isn't really to follow them but to use them as a vehicle for creatively imagining what God is like. What kind of god is God? The kind of god who would command us to live in these ways.

3. Keep in Mind That the Bible Reworks its Own Laws

Although the Bible directly attributes many of the laws in the Pentateuch to God's spoken and even written word, it does not hesitate to rework or contradict its laws from one book to the next.

For example, Exodus 21:7 does not permit women debt slaves to be freed, but the later Deuteronomy 15:12 does. Exodus 22:16–17 has a law that states a man must marry an unpledged woman whom he seduces, but this rule gets reinterpreted into a law about rape in the later Deuteronomy 22:28–29. The commandment in Exodus 20:8–11 says that people should rest on the sabbath, citing God's rest on the seventh day of creation as a reason. The later Deuteronomy 5:12–15, however, cites the exodus as the reason that people should rest.

Because of changes like these, imagining these laws to be absolute, divine dictations makes little sense. It makes more sense to see them as part of an ongoing act of theological imagination that successive generations continue to contribute to with their interpretive efforts.

Conclusion

Though the material in the Pentateuch isn't necessarily the oldest material in the Hebrew Bible, it reflects biblical authors' vision of humanity's oldest ways of relating to God. It answers questions of origins, of purpose, and of human nature. As a result, the Pentateuch will always sit close to the heart of religions that read the Bible. When you interpret the Pentateuch, you're also invited to imagine what human purpose is and what the ideal relationship between God and human beings is like. Perhaps you will give many of the same answers as the writers of Scripture. Perhaps you will give all new ones.

Despite asking and answering so many big questions, the narrative of the Pentateuch ends on something of an unresolved cliff-hanger. The people of Israel are poised to enter the land of Canaan, and God's promises to the patriarchs are on the verge of being fulfilled, but we don't get to see what happens until we turn to the Hebrew Bible's next section. After Moses the lawgiver, we turn the page to centuries dominated by prophets.

CHAPTER 6

The Prophets

In a Hebrew Bible, the section following the Torah (or Pentateuch) is called the *Nevi'im*, or Prophets. The first books of the Nevi'im are Joshua, Judges, 1 and 2 Samuel, 1 and 2 Kings, and the Talmud, a collection of Jewish commentary, designates these books as the Former Prophets. This can be a bit tricky to make sense of, since these biblical books are not named after prophetic figures like others are. But there are prophetic figures in the stories. Joshua himself is considered a prophet in Jewish tradition. Deborah is a prophetess in the book of Judges. Samuel, Nathan, Gad, Elijah, and Elisha are also prophetic figures who appear in these books.

After the Former Prophets are the Latter Prophets, which are in turn divided into the three Major Prophets—the books of Isaiah, Jeremiah, and Ezekiel—and the twelve Minor Prophets—the books of Hosea, Joel, Amos, Obadiah, Jonah, Micah, Nahum, Habakkuk, Zephaniah, Haggai, Zechariah, and Malachi. The major/minor distinction does not refer to the importance of the prophetic figures in the books, but rather to the size of the books themselves. The Major Prophets are some of the longer books in the Hebrew Bible, while the Minor Prophets are among the shortest.

There are some important things that we should keep in mind while interpreting the Prophets. But before we talk about them, let's review the books themselves so that we can better understand these books that make up more of our main ingredients.

Conquest and Chaos

The book of Deuteronomy, which is also the last book in the Pentateuch, ends with the death of Moses and the transfer of the leadership of the people of Israel to Joshua. At that point in the narrative, the Israelites are just on the eastern side of the Jordan River, ready to cross over west into Canaan and lay claim to the land God originally promised to Abraham back in Genesis.

However, the Israelites face a new problem that stands in the way of that promise's fulfillment: The land is occupied. Perhaps unsurprisingly, Canaanites already live in Canaan. The book of Deuteronomy hints at the solution to this problem: "utter destruction" (Deuteronomy 7:2). The book of Joshua, then, provides a narrative of the war Joshua wages against the native Canaanites, culminating in the Israelites' occupation of the land.

In Joshua 3, the Israelites cross the Jordan River in an episode similar to the parting of the Red Sea. In Joshua 6, the Israelites capture Jericho with help from both God and a prostitute named Rahab, then in Joshua 10 and 11, the Israelites defeat two alliances of Canaanite kings. After that, the land of Canaan is distributed among the twelve tribes of Israel with extensive descriptive detail in chapters 13–21. Joshua's conquest is presented in the text as a rapid and sweeping success.

Wrestling with Charam

We put the words "utter destruction" in quotations above because they are the translation of a Hebrew term that is specific and important. The verb in that phrase is *charam*, a word that is sometimes used to convey that something is banned, dedicated for destruction, or utterly destroyed. *Charam* is a form of ritualized warfare that was practiced by Israelites and their neighbors. In *charam*, an entire enemy population was annihilated in a collective act of human, animal, and agricultural sacrifice to the victorious army's deity. This type of warfare is distinct from more conventional warfare of the time, in which slaves were taken, animals were captured, and agricultural products and infrastructure were maintained. The idea behind *charam* is that a war was so serious, it shouldn't be profited from, with all the "goods" that would normally be acquired during war offered up as a sacrifice. When *charam* is practiced against a people group, it's genocide, and the act explicitly involves the killing of noncombatants and children (Joshua 6:21, 1 Samuel 15:3).

Unfortunately, Joshua and the Israelites practice this devotion to destruction throughout the book of Joshua. Fortunately, the book of Joshua is entirely fictional. Biblical scholars have known for almost seventy years now that there's no archaeological evidence for the conquest of Canaan, with many of the cities mentioned in Joshua 12, including

Jericho, being unoccupied or unfortified when the conquest was supposed to have taken place, in the late thirteenth or early twelfth century BCE.

If the story is so awful, then why invent it? To answer this question, we must first know a little about the circumstances in which the text was written.

Searching for a Better Story

Many biblical scholars today believe that Joshua was mostly composed in the sixth century BCE during the Babylon exile. This would have been after 586 BCE, when the Babylonians invaded the Kingdom of Judah, and after they'd destroyed the temple and deported many of the scribes, priests, and other members of the intellectual class to the interior of the Babylonian Empire.

It was common at the time for people to believe that if one nation conquered another, it was because the conquering nation's god was more powerful than the conquered nation's god. But the authors of the Former Prophets, sitting in exile in Babylon, couldn't accept this explanation and came up with a new one. This new reason was rooted in the theology of Deuteronomy (see the curses in Deuteronomy 28:36 and 30:18) and is showcased in the book of 2 Kings (2 Kings 17:7–23 and 24:1–4).

In the text, the Israelites' occupation of the land of Canaan is said to be contingent on their proper worship of God. When people in general and kings in particular started worshipping other gods, God chose to bring in the Babylonians to punish the Israelites. Basically, the writers of 2 Kings blamed the people of Israel rather than God for their conquest.

Now, if God is the kind of deity who invites a foreign people to punish a native people for their idolatrous worship, then to be consistent, one must also conclude that this is how the Israelites acquired the land of Canaan. The story is very similar to the story in the book of 2 Kings. But this time, in Joshua, the Canaanites are the native idolaters and the Israelites are the foreign people brought in by God to punish them. Read in this way, the Joshua story is less a glorification of a past victory over the Canaanites and more a theological explanation of a present defeat by the Babylonians.

Regardless of why it was written, it's very easy to read Joshua as the most militaristic and jingoistic book in the Bible, its verses openly advocating for holy war and the genocide of a land's native population. It's very easy to read the book that way because *it is* that way in several places, and conscientious readers should recognize how dangerous those ideas have been both historically and in the present. That said, there are also easy-to-overlook places in the text where Joshua reveals a more self-critical perspective.

One of these places is Joshua 5:13–15, where an angel called "the commander of the army of the Lord" appears to Joshua, and Joshua asks the angel whose side the angel is on. Since Joshua has already been told in the opening verses of chapter 1 that God is going to give him victory everywhere he sets foot, we readers expect the angel to say it's on Joshua's side. But instead, the angel says it's on no one's side. That certainly appears to be the case, as eventually God brings the Babylonian army against Israel, as dramatized in both Jeremiah 21 and Ezekiel 21.

A Dark Foreshadowing

The end of Joshua and the beginning of the next book, Judges, should be one of the most optimistic places in the whole Bible. After centuries of threats and complications, the promise originally given to Abraham has finally been fulfilled. Israel is a great people, and they're in the land of Canaan. But Judges 1 informs us that not all the Canaanites have been defeated, and in Judges 2, the angel that had been helping the Israelites abandons them because they've made covenants with the remaining Canaanites.

The rest of Judges 2 describes a cycle of sin and redemption that defines the rest of the book, in which the Israelites worship other gods, causing God to bring in a foreign people to oppress them, at which point the Israelites cry out to God for help, and God responds by sending a charismatic leader called a "judge" to defeat the foreign people and give the Israelites peace for a time. The process then repeats with new idolatries, over and over again.

Some of the most iconic characters and most shockingly evil stories in the Hebrew Bible are found in the book of Judges. Judges 4–5 is home to Deborah, a woman prophet and judge who rallies the armies of Israel against the Canaanites, and Jael, who assassinates a Canaanite general with cunning manipulation. Judges 6 is home to the skeptical

Gideon, who tests God. And Judges 13–16 tells the famous story of Samson and Delilah.

But Judges is also home to the horrible and absurd human sacrifice of Jephthah's daughter in Judges 11, the gruesome gang rape of an unnamed concubine in Judges 19, and the even more gruesome mass rape of the virgins of Shiloh in Judges 21.

Even the narrator is disturbed by these stories, as we see in Judges 21:25: "In those days, there was no king in Israel, and all the people did what was right in their own eyes." This refrain seems to attribute the widespread evils in the land to the lack of a king, and in so doing, foreshadows the direction God and history will go in next.

The Rise and Fall of the Monarchy

The opening chapters of 1 Samuel read a lot like Judges. Like Samson in Judges 13, Samuel is only born after his formerly infertile mother makes a vow to dedicate him to God's service (1:11), and like Ehud, Deborah, Gideon, and Jephthah, Samuel is raised up to subdue a foreign enemy (the Philistines this time) after God permits the Philistines to oppress the Israelites because of their idolatry (1 Samuel 7:2b–4). Samuel even gets the conventional send-off for a judge in 1 Samuel 7, describing the time he spends judging Israel after his success in battle (1 Samuel 7:15–17).

But 1 Samuel 8 makes a hard pivot into a different kind of story. The elders of Israel come to Samuel, point out that his own sons are corrupt and can't lead after him, and demand to have a king like all the other nations (1 Samuel 8:4–5). When Samuel confers with God, God says that in asking for a human king, the elders have rejected God as their king (8:7). After enumerating the ways a king will oppress their people (8:10–18), Samuel and God agree to give the people a king (8:22).

If you were to read only 1 Samuel 8, you'd likely walk away thinking that having a king is a terrible idea; after all, it involves a de facto rejection of God's leadership, and it compromises the unique identity of Israel by making them like all the other nations. In 1 Samuel 12:19, Samuel explicitly says that asking for a king is a sin. And yet, several other passages seem to sound more positive about having a king. In 1 Samuel 9–10, for example, God commissions Samuel to anoint Saul as the first king of Israel, and God gives Saul a new heart, presumably one well adapted for kingship, as though kingship were a good idea. And in 1 Samuel 11, God empowers Saul with his spirit to fight a battle against the Philistines, after which all the Israelites are so enthusiastic about Saul they make him king on the spot—again, as though that's a good idea.

Many biblical scholars have noticed these stories' back-and-forth opinions about whether or not it's a good idea for Israel to have a king. This observation has led some biblical scholars to conclude that these stories, like those stories in the Pentateuch that conflicted or appeared redundant, were also written independently of each other and then edited together later. That explains why we learn three times between 1 Samuel 9 and 11 that Saul is made the first king of Israel, when one time would be sufficient. It also explains the conflicting details involved in the introduction of the next character: David.

Differing Stories of David

Despite being handpicked by God, Saul turns out not to be a very good king, and by 1 Samuel 16, God directs Samuel to anoint a successor. In 1 Samuel 16, David is introduced as the youngest of Jesse's eight sons, but in this chapter, he's an adult. In 1 Samuel 16:18, he's described as a "man of valor and a warrior." When he's brought into Saul's household to play soothing music for him, he's made Saul's armor-bearer, and Saul is said to love him (16:21).

This picture of David contrasts sharply with the David we see in the next chapter, perhaps one of the most well-known stories in the Hebrew Bible, the story of David and Goliath. In 1 Samuel 17, David is not a member of Saul's household, and he is not his armor-bearer but rather a young boy bringing supplies to Saul's army (17:17–18). When David volunteers to fight Goliath, Saul says no because he's just a boy and not a warrior like Goliath (17:33). This contradicts his being called one in the previous chapter. When David persists, he's permitted to fight Goliath, but he's not allowed to wear Saul's armor because he's not used to it (17:38–39); this is another incongruity, as he's called an armor-bearer in the previous chapter. And when David kills Goliath, Saul has to ask who David's family is (17:55–58). This, too, is inconsistent, as he knows this full well in the previous chapter. All of this seems to further indicate that these stories began as independent traditions about how David entered into Saul's service and were edited together later.

David's rise to power is quick and bloody. He becomes famous for his martial exploits (1 Samuel 18:6–7), marries into Saul's household (18:20–29), wins the affection of Jonathan—Saul's oldest son and heir apparent (18:1–4)—then flees the kingdom when Saul gets jealous and tries to kill him (20:42). In the wilderness, David gathers a band of fighting men (22:2), runs a protection racket (25:2–8), becomes a Philistine mercenary (27:1–2), acquires enough wealth to bribe Judah's elders (30:26–31), and becomes king over southern Judah when Saul and Jonathan are killed by the very Philistines for which David is working (2 Samuel 2:1–4). Then after the fortuitous assassination of Saul's old general (3:26–27) and last able-bodied son (4:5–8), David becomes king over all of Israel (5:1–5).

The highlight of David's reign occurs early on, when the prophet Nathan comes to him and reveals an unprecedented promise that God is making to him. God says in 2 Samuel 7:16, "Your house and your kingdom shall be made sure forever before me; your throne shall be established forever." Though the promise is technically broken in 586 BCE, when the Babylonians destroyed Jerusalem and deposed the last Davidic king, the idea that there must be a descendant of David on the throne in Jerusalem forever becomes the basis of many Jewish hopes for renewed political sovereignty in times of foreign oppression and one of the cornerstones of messianic prophecy that the New Testament understands Jesus to have fulfilled.

The remainder of David's reign is marked by immorality and civil war, and he dies without having named a successor, leaving his remaining sons to fight over the throne. Solomon emerges from this conflict as the next king, notable for his wisdom (1 Kings 3:9), wealth and fame (1 Kings 4:20–34), and his construction of the temple in Jerusalem (1 Kings 5–6). Solomon is ultimately undermined by his permissiveness for idolatry (1 Kings 11:1–13) and manages to raise a son so inept that northern Israel and southern Judah break apart and become two separate kingdoms (1 Kings 12:12–19).

No More Kings

The rest of 1 and 2 Kings falls into a predictable pattern. Northern kings of Israel are decried for their idolatry, while southern kings are often struggling against the whims of greater kingdoms. In 722 BCE or

2 Kings 17, Sargon of Assyria destroys Samaria, the capital of northern Israel, and in 586 BCE or 2 Kings 25, Nebuchadnezzar of Babylon destroys Jerusalem, the capital of southern Judah.

Second Kings attempts to end on a positive note, saying that Jehoiachin, the last of David's line, is permitted to dine in the king of Babylon's presence (2 Kings 25:27–30), indicating a potential hope for the survival of the Davidic promise. But no descendant of David will sit on the throne again.

Tips for Interpreting Legends

As we've shown in this chapter, many of the stories in Joshua, Judges, and 1 and 2 Samuel aren't historical in a straightforward sense. Rather, they're combinations of oral legends passed down through the generations and propaganda meant to justify who ended up with power. If we read these stories to figure out what happened in history, we can often miss the point. It's important then to keep certain considerations in mind when reading. Here are some tips that can help us to interpret legends.

1. Be Mindful of the Difference Between Legends and History

The first thing we should do when interpreting legends is to be mindful of the difference between legendary and historical writing. History is what actually happened. And while legends often include genuine historical elements, such as realistic settings, characters, and events, the specific narrative that ties these elements together didn't actually happen. For example, David probably existed, the Israelites did war against the Philistines, and the sling was indeed a potent ranged weapon that was used three thousand years ago. But did little David kill Goliath? That story might be legend, not history.

One way we know stories are legendary is because they contain details no historian could know. History is told through the use of publicly available information, stuff that a historian could know by reading records or by having personally witnessed the events themselves. Many of the stories found in the prophets, though, are not told this way. They're told through the point of view of an omniscient narrator: one who sees everything, including things that happen in private or in people's minds. These narrative additions make the story more compelling, just like in a modern novel, but they also signal that at least some artistic license has been taken by the author.

Another sign that many of the events described throughout this section are legendary and not historical in nature is that there is archaeological evidence that contradicts them. The conquest of Canaan, for example, definitely didn't happen as described in the book of Joshua. We know this because archaeologists have found that many of the cities Joshua was said to have destroyed either weren't destroyed at all or didn't even exist at the time Joshua was supposed to have destroyed them.

Other events described are so personal in nature, no one could ever find any kind of extra-biblical evidence to confirm them. Examples of this category include Rahab and the spies' private conversation in Joshua 2 and Jonathan and David's private conversation in 1 Samuel 20.

When we have stories that evidence can't confirm written by a narrator who is inventing details, "legend" is the appropriate description to use.

2. Understand How the Past Is Made Usable

You may wonder: If a legend isn't the same thing as history, then what's the point of it? In large part, legends exist to make the past usable to different groups in the present by empowering them to find their identity in a shared story. Legends are about people and they play a vital role in maintaining kinship relations in the ancient world. Whereas a myth explains why the world is the way that it is and the fundamentals of the human condition, legends explain who *we* are in that world. Where do *we* come from? What are *we* doing here? What separates *us* from *them*?

Consider the oath found in Deuteronomy 26:5–10, and imagine a few generations of people reciting it. Following this practice, this group of people would have had—in a relatively short amount of time—a brand new cultural identity. If you asked anyone in ancient Israel who they were or where they came from, they'd all be on the same page, they'd all give the same answer.

Notice all the first-person language that appears in the oath despite the fact that it refers to events that were supposed to have happened centuries ago: "The Egyptians treated *us* harshly," "*We* cried out to the Lord," "The Lord brought *us* out of Egypt," et cetera. These statements were, strictly speaking, false for every single person who recited them. They were false even for the people in the story in Deuteronomy, who were the generation *after* the one that came out of Egypt. But that doesn't matter. A legendary story creates the people who tell it.

That's why, when reading legends, it's important to ask what kind of people a story helps create. Finding the answer to that question will be a lot more interesting and helpful for understanding the author's goals than asking "Did this really happen?"

The Prophets

The Hebrew word for prophet is *navi*, meaning one who proclaims something, and the prophets in the Hebrew Bible are in the business of proclaiming things on behalf of God. Prophesying, as in predicting the future, isn't necessarily the central purpose of the prophets. Rather, these individuals were primarily concerned with disclosing the heart of God to an audience in times of social unrest and calling on that audience to respond with social justice, faithfulness, and repentance. Let's look at some examples.

Eighth-Century Prophets

Prophets and prophecy were common in ancient Southwest Asia, and many kings would consult with their deities about important matters of state through court prophets, as King Ahab does in 1 Kings 22:6. The prophets in the Hebrew Bible are not these kinds of prophets though. Instead, they're something called "apostolic prophets"; that is, individual prophets who have been called by God to speak into specific historical situations. Indeed, several texts describe what's known as the "call narratives" of the prophets. These are the stories of these prophets' experience of God and how they come to be commissioned to speak on God's behalf.

The earliest prophets (both books and people) in the Hebrew Bible are Amos, Hosea, Micah, and Isaiah. All of these figures are active in the middle of the eighth century BCE, when the Neo-Assyrian Empire poses a threat to both the kingdoms of northern Israel and southern Judah.

Amos is perhaps best known for his calls to social justice, which include castigating wealthy women for their excess (Amos 4:1–5), elites for their exploitation of the poor (Amos 5:10–17), and the powerful for their complacency (Amos 6:1–7). Amos proclaims, "Let justice roll down like water and righteousness like an ever-flowing stream" (Amos 5:25).

Hosea, by contrast, is less interested in social justice and more concerned with idolatry. Indeed, he invents a new way of thinking about idolatry, comparing Israel's idolatrous worship of other gods to an adulterous wife's affections for another man. In this metaphor, God is the aggrieved husband figure who must win his wife back after a period of separation and humiliation (Hosea 2:14–15).

The book of Micah features one of the clearest articulations of the so-called prophetic critique, which is the idea that ritual religious observance is worthless and moral action is what's valuable instead. Micah 6:6–8 says, "With what shall I come before the Lord and bow myself before God on high? Shall I come before him with burnt offerings, with calves a year old? Will the Lord be pleased with thousands of rams, with ten thousands of rivers of oil? Shall I give my firstborn for my transgression, the fruit of my body for the sin of my soul? He has told you, O mortal, what is good, and what does the Lord require of you but to do justice and to love kindness and to walk humbly with your God?"

The book of Isaiah features a similar idea. After telling people to stop praying, sacrificing, and celebrating holidays because it's pointless, God says in Isaiah 1:17, "Learn to do right; seek justice. Defend the oppressed. Take up the cause of the fatherless; plead the case of the widow."

Isaiah is one of the most well-known of the Hebrew Bible's prophets, both because his book is the longest of the prophets, and because his words have played such a significant role in the life of both the synagogue and the church.

In Jewish tradition, Isaiah is second only to Moses in terms of prominence among the prophets, and he's especially appreciated for his eloquence and consistent messages of consolation. Nevertheless, there's an interesting Jewish tradition that says that Isaiah was executed for having claimed to see God (a claim we find in Isaiah 6), since God had earlier said to Moses that it's impossible to see God and live (Exodus 33:20).

In the New Testament, Isaiah is cited more than any other book in the Hebrew Bible, and Jesus is understood to be a fulfillment of several of Isaiah's prophecies. Isaiah 7:14's apparent reference to a virgin birth, Isaiah 9:6's reference to a child who will somehow be a wonderful counselor, a mighty god, an everlasting father, and a prince of peace at the same time, and Isaiah 53's graphic descriptions of the suffering servant have fueled Christian imagination and theology ever since.

Seventh- to Fifth-Century Prophets

Perhaps one of the most important things to know about the book of Isaiah is that it's not a single work written by a single author. Biblical scholars routinely divide the book into three sections: First Isaiah, chapters 1 to 39, which focuses on the prophetic career of Isaiah and the events leading up to the invasion by Assyria in 701 BCE; Second Isaiah, chapters 40 to 55, which is set right after the Babylonian exile in 538 BCE and focuses on encouraging the exiles to return to Jerusalem and to adopt a strict monotheism; and Third Isaiah, chapters 56 to 66, which is set after the construction of the Second Temple in Jerusalem in 522 BCE and focuses on how the community ought to engage with temple worship far into the future.

At the outset of the seventh century, a new set of prophets rise up to deliver messages concerning the threat of the Babylonian Empire. Nahum celebrates the destruction of the Assyrian capital of Nineveh at the hands of the Babylonians in 615 BCE, while Zephaniah warns of even more destruction to come if the kingdom of southern Judah doesn't repent.

Jeremiah and Ezekiel both witness the destruction of Jerusalem in 586 BCE by the Babylonian Empire, Jeremiah's career beginning before in Jerusalem, and Ezekiel's career beginning after in Babylon.

The book of Jeremiah is full of visceral descriptions of both the prophet Jeremiah's and God's feelings concerning the unfaithfulness of the Israelites. Unlike the book of Isaiah, in which judgment and calls to repentance are followed by statements of consolation, when Jeremiah calls his audience to repentance, those calls are often followed by lines that convey hopelessness. Jeremiah's more pessimistic attitude might be a result of having begun his career during the reign of Josiah (640–609 BCE), which was a relative high point in history as far as biblical authors are concerned, only to live to see the destruction of Jerusalem within a generation after Josiah's death.

Ezekiel, the only prophet who wrote in Babylon in the middle of the exile, is known for his oddities. He experiences strange and detailed visions of God's throne surrounded by divine creatures made of multiple faces, wings, wheels, and eyes (Ezekiel 1). He undertakes even stranger symbolic actions, lying on his side for prolonged periods and eating food cooked over dung (Ezekiel 4). In contrast to something like Exodus 34:7, where parents' guilt is visited upon successive generations, Ezekiel emphasizes personal responsibility (Ezekiel 18). Many scholars have speculated that the traumatic experience of Babylonian exile affected both his theology and his personal psychology.

Two other prophets also appear to be responding to the exile. Habakkuk asks perennial questions about where God is during times of suffering and when God's justice will be done, while Obadiah mourns what he believes to be the betrayal of the neighboring Edomites, who were supposed to be close kin to the Israelites but celebrated the destruction of Jerusalem by Babylon.

The last group of prophets show up in the postexilic period, 539 BCE and later, a time when biblical theology shifts away from emphasizing God's special relationship with a king to God's special relationship with the rebuilt Second Temple in Jerusalem.

Haggai works to encourage the reconstruction of the temple, while Zechariah narrates God's choice of a high priest. Joel, unlike many other prophets, doesn't criticize the value of temple worship, and Malachi castigates the priesthood for their opportunistic divorces and tightfisted tithing. Last, Jonah is a short piece of satire, using hyperbole and irony to mock the ethnocentrism of Israelite prophets who have come before.

Tips for Interpreting Oracles

The prophets are some of the most emotive figures in the Bible, and the books that bear their names are some of the most literarily sophisticated. The prophets were also responding to some of the most psychologically devastating events in the history of the world. Add all this together and you get books that pour out the deepest human feelings in the boldest language. It's easy to lose your footing when you read the prophets. Here are a few tips to consider when you're making your way through.

1. Consider the Power of Provocation

Many people naturally presume that the primary function of prophets is to prophesy, and that texts that bear a prophet's name should be consulted for their predictions of the future. But while prophets do occasionally refer to future states of the world, both actual and hypothetical, the primary function of prophetic literature is actually to provoke an audience into a sudden awareness of God's interior life. Prophets act and speak so that audiences might know what God is thinking and feeling. When reading prophetic literature, it's often helpful to ask "What would the audience be provoked to think about?"

Prophetic texts use a variety of different genres of literature to provoke their audiences in this way.

One such genre is known as "oracles against the nations." These are prophetic condemnations of foreign nations that use hyperbolic language and personification to identify the evils of foreign nations, usually their proclivity for pride, social injustice, and gratuitous violence. Examples can be found in Amos 1:3–2:16 and Isaiah 13–23, passages that describes God's judgment against several nations. Such oracles play to an audience's xenophobia, baiting them into condemning other people groups only to suddenly condemn the audience themselves for the same things, thereby leaving the audience without excuse.

Another provocative, and occasionally problematic, way of provoking the audience of a prophetic text is with a marriage metaphor, sometimes called "bridal theology," in which God is compared to a jilted husband and Israel to an adulterous wife. Famous examples can be found in Hosea 2 and Ezekiel 16. Comparing the mainly male and married audience to an adulterous woman in a sexist context like ancient Southwest Asia, where these texts were written, would be a serious insult that grabs a reader's attention. The metaphor becomes problematic when it depicts God, as a husband figure, hurting, shaming, or exposing the wife to sexual violence as a result of her adultery. It depicts a relationship that isn't loving on either side, even if these metaphors often end with peace and reconciliation.

Whether a prophet is condemning an institution, predicting doom, confronting the powerful, or undertaking dramatic symbolic actions to publicize their message, their intention is to provoke an audience.

2. Listen to the Prophet's Sensitivities

So all of this is done to provoke. But why provoke an audience in the first place? To induce change. According to the Jewish scholar Abraham Joshua Heschel, one of the defining features of prophets is their "breathless impatience with injustice." Evils in the world that others consider minor greatly disturb the prophets, so much so that they can't help but speak at length about them. Moved by their sensitivity, they demand change in God's name.

Jeremiah 18 spells out the goal of many prophets. God says,

> "At one moment I may declare concerning a nation or a kingdom that I will pluck up and break down and destroy it, but if that nation, concerning which I have spoken, turns from its evil, I will change my mind about the disaster that I intended to bring on it. And at another moment I may declare concerning a nation or a kingdom that I will build and plant it, but if it does evil in my sight, not listening to my voice, then I will change my mind about the good that I had intended to do to it."

Their goal, then, is to bring about change. Consequently, the prophets we see in Joshua through 2 Kings, and in the major and minor prophets, aren't so much attempting to accurately predict things that will happen but rather to extrapolate what will happen given people's current behavior and God's feelings about that behavior. If the behavior changes, so too will the people's future.

Keeping all this in mind, as we read the prophets, we can ask, "What is this prophet sensitive to and why?" If we have a desire to apply prophetic texts to our own lives, it then becomes easy to ask the follow-up questions "How can I become more sensitive to these same issues? And how can I, using whatever voice I have, provoke audiences to induce change?"

Conclusion

The Prophets are about character and emotion, about big personalities and the even bigger things they say. It's easy to walk away from stories in the Prophets remembering more about how they made you feel than about the specific events that transpired. That's fine. The texts were written to engage your imagination, not only about the past but about the future as well. Indeed, it's the power of the prophets to shape our view of what's to come that has inspired so many religious communities down through the centuries. The New Testament wouldn't exist, for example, if it weren't for the prophets and their yearning for what God might do next. You can interpret the texts to help inspire your imagination for a better world too.

As powerful as the words of the prophets are, they don't have the final say when it comes to the Hebrew Bible. There's still one more section of the text. While the Pentateuch was dominated by Moses, and the prophets were dominated by their namesakes, the third and final section isn't dominated by any one kind of figure. Rather, it's defined by its great diversity of figures and its even greater diversity of genres in which those figures have their stories. The Hebrew Bible ends with every kind of writing imaginable.

CHAPTER 7

The Writings

THE FINAL SECTION of the Hebrew Bible is called the *Ketuvim*, or Writings, and is a miscellaneous collection of literature that joined the canon relatively late in the life of the Bible's development. Its contents don't even appear to have been fixed by the composition of Luke 24:44, a verse that uses the term "the psalms" as a stand-in for all the books that are included after the Pentateuch and the Prophets.

The Writings is home to great works of poetry, like Psalms, Lamentations, and the Song of Songs; wisdom literature like Proverbs, Job, and Ecclesiastes; revisions of history like Ezra, Nehemiah, and 1 and 2 Chronicles; short stories such as Ruth and Esther; and the prophetic book of Daniel, the best example of apocalyptic literature in the Hebrew Bible, which will be explained later.

Let's look a little closer at each of these.

Poetry

Although poetry can be found dotted throughout many books of the Hebrew Bible, there are three books that are specifically dedicated to the genre. These are the Psalms, Lamentations, and the Song of Songs.

Psalms is the single largest book in the Bible, coming in at 150 chapters, and it features a diverse array of poems. Many appear to be composed specifically for the purpose of being performed with song and musical accompaniment, but regardless of whether they were ever performed or what they sounded like when performed, their literary merits can be appreciated in their written forms today. And what a wonderous variety of written forms we have: There are as many literary styles, themes, and subjects in the Psalms as there are in the rest of the Hebrew Bible combined.

For example, Psalms 1, 14, and 37 offer advice not unlike the kind you'd find in the wisdom literature. Psalms 2, 18, and 45 celebrate God's relationship to a king. Psalm 22 is recited by Jesus on the cross as though it were a hymn of personal piety, and Psalm 23 has long been used as a communal hymn.

Psalms 78, 80, 99, and 114 are more historical in nature, referring to the exodus in different, sometimes contradictory ways, while Psalm 82 contains old, polytheistic theology. In another example of contradiction, Psalm 74 recounts God's mythic battle with the sea monster Leviathan, which is a recurring theme in Canaanite, Babylonian, and Egyptian religions, while Psalm 104 depicts Leviathan frolicking in the sea.

For every occasion, there is a psalm. Whether you are happy or sad, wrathful or forgiving, skeptical or pious, in the mood for history or myth, the past or the future, there's a psalm or two that speaks to that feeling.

Nearly half the Psalms are attributed to David, even ones that reference events that occurred long after David's life and so couldn't have been composed by him. The recounting of events that happened later in history are a good indication that this attribution should be seen as spiritual rather than literal. The number of psalms attributed to David even changes over time. The Greek translation of the Hebrew Bible, the Septuagint, attributes more to David than the Hebrew version, indicating that people who preserved these texts over the centuries took it upon themselves to make attributions where they felt was appropriate. The Psalms are attributed to David less because we know with certainty that he composed them, and more because he is the inspired figure most associated with music in the Hebrew Bible, and he is seen as a kind of patron saint of music.

Lamentations is a series of poems that collectively mourn the destruction of Jerusalem at the hands of the Babylonians in 586 BCE. Chapters 1, 2, and 4 are acrostics, each with twenty-two lines, each line beginning with one of the twenty-two letters of the Hebrew alphabet in order. This style of poetry symbolically represents completeness, as if by using every letter of the alphabet, the author has exhausted everything that can be said about the topic. Chapter 3, in the middle of the collection, is still an acrostic, but on a greater scale, having three lines for each letter for a total of sixty-six. And chapter 5 has twenty-two lines, but not in alphabetical order, almost as if grief has overtaken the author and they can no longer keep their own meter.

There are only two books in the Bible that don't mention God. One of them is the Song of Songs. (The other is Esther.) The Song of Songs is a piece of erotic poetry that describes the desire between a young man and woman in detailed but euphemistic language. Both Jewish and Christian traditions have long read the text as an extended and rather involved allegory about the relationship between either God and Israel or God and the church.

This explanation might have made the text more palatable over the centuries to the many audiences who came to the text in search of a theologically edifying message. However, this explanation also obscures the simplicity of the text, which is about sex: young, unmarried, impassioned sex. The fact that such a text is in the Bible is a testament to the breadth of its multivocality. In a canon that generally ignores women's agency in general and sexual agency in particular, Song of Songs is truly a standout piece of literature.

Revisions of History

In the Christian Old Testament, 1 and 2 Chronicles come immediately after 1 and 2 Kings, and since many of the stories in 1 and 2 Chronicles are copied, sometimes word for word, from Samuel and Kings, many people skip these books when reading the Bible. That's unfortunate, as those two books actually do some of the most radical things in the Bible.

First and Second Chronicles are retellings of the rise and fall of ancient Israel's monarchy. Composed more than one hundred and fifty years after 1 and 2 Kings, they reflect a much later author's perspective and theology. The author removes from the story almost every reference to prophetic figures (Samuel, Nathan, Elijah, Elisha, etc.) and private communication by God to individuals, gets rid of God's tendency to punish later generations for earlier generation's sins, and abandons most of the history of northern Israel.

In this retelling, David is also changed a lot. All the violence, ambition, and political maneuvering that went into David's rise to power is erased in 1 Chronicles, and he peacefully becomes king over Israel in just three verses in 1 Chronicles 11:1–3. There's no mention of his rape of Bathsheba or his civil wars, and unlike in 1 Kings, where Solomon has to rely on assassination to take the throne after David, David clearly establishes Solomon to be his successor in 2 Chronicles.

One Chronicles further transforms David into a spiritual architect of the temple. David writes up plans for the temple, its attendants, and its articles (1 Chronicles 28:11–18), readies all the personnel (1 Chronicles 28:19–21), personally provides the gold and precious materials for the temple's construction (1 Chronicles 29:1–5) and inspires others to do the same (1 Chronicles 29:6–9), and even establishes a first liturgy (1 Chronicles 29:10–20) for the temple service. In the fourth century BCE, when the author of 1 and 2 Chronicles is writing, Israel has had a king of its own, and the temple is the most visible reminder of the people's connection with God. Changing David into a figure associated with the temple makes him more valuable to a later audience.

Chronicles is a dramatic reminder that the Bible is far more interested in explaining the theological significance of history in ways that are helpful for its different audiences than it is in writing an accurate and contradiction-free account of history.

The last historical books we'll consider here are Ezra and Nehemiah. Composed in bits and pieces between the fifth and fourth centuries BCE, these stories focus on Ezra, a scribe and teacher of Pentateuchal texts, and Nehemiah, a governor, as they attempt to rebuild not only the physical structure of Jerusalem but also the identity of the people who occupy the city.

Ezra narrates the circumstances leading up to the construction of the Second Temple in Jerusalem, something that couldn't have happened without the explicit sponsorship of the then-ruling Persian empire, and tells a heartbreaking story where Ezra forces more than one hundred couples to get divorced in an effort to preserve his sense of Judean ethnicity (Ezra 10).

Nehemiah narrates the building of a defensive wall around Jerusalem (Nehemiah 2–4), another thing that couldn't have happened without Persian permission (Nehemiah 2:5), and then describes an instance where Ezra publicly reads the Torah, the first five books of the Bible, out loud to a gathered group of people, whereupon they all swear themselves to abide by its laws (Nehemiah 8–9).

Short Stories

Books like Ruth and Esther are difficult to classify. In the Hebrew Bible, Ruth is placed near the end, alongside other texts that have come to be associated with specific Jewish holidays. But in the Christian Old Testament, Ruth is treated as a historical book and placed between Judges and 1 Samuel, due in no small part to its opening line, which refers to the time of the judges, and its conclusion, which reveals that Ruth is an ancestor of King David.

Ruth has all the hallmarks of a short piece of fiction. It has an omniscient narrator who has access to people's private conversations. It has characters with silly symbolic names related to their role in the story, like Mahlon and Kilyon (Ruth 1:2), whose names mean "sickness" and "wasting." And the book of Ruth has the optimistic tone of a morality tale, in which tragedy and desperation can be overcome by the kindness of strangers.

After the deaths of their husbands (Ruth 1:5), Ruth, a Moabite, and her mother-in-law Naomi, an Israelite, lose their economic security and are forced to rely on gleaning the fields of the wealthy Boaz to survive (Ruth 2:1–3). At Naomi's prompting (Ruth 3:1–5), Ruth sleeps with Boaz. The scene is filled with ambiguity and innuendo. The word "sex" is never mentioned. Indeed, there is no biblical Hebrew word for sex, only euphemisms. Ruth "uncovers Boaz's feet," (Ruth 4:7) and lies at Boaz's feet until morning covered by his cloak (Ruth 4:14). Feet (*reg'laim* in Hebrew) are often a euphemism for the genitals in biblical Hebrew. To cover one's feet means to relieve oneself on a couple occasions (Judges 3:24, 1 Samuel 24:3). To wash one's feet means to have sex (2 Samuel 11:8). God threatens to emasculate disobedient Israelites by metaphorically shaving their "feet" (Isaiah 7:20). Add to this Boaz's drunken state (Ruth 3:7) and Ruth's stealthy departure (Ruth 3:14), and you begin to see a complicated and somewhat dubious scene of seduction. Regardless of what happens on the threshing floor between the two, Ruth manages to secure a marriage to Boaz that's celebrated by the community (Ruth 4:11–12).

Many biblical scholars have argued that Ruth was written around the same time as Ezra, timing that indicates it provided a dissenting voice to what happens in that book. In Ezra, marriages to foreigners are forcibly torn apart in order to preserve the community. But in Ruth, a marriage to a foreigner results in the birth of the most famous person in Israelite history: David.

The book of Esther has the same short fiction features as Ruth. It also has another feature that is shared by only one other book in the Bible: God is never mentioned in Esther. Esther is instead a very human story of people trying to survive as an ethnic minority in diaspora without compromising their identity.

In a story set in the fifth century BCE in the heart of the Persian Empire, the character of Esther is advised by her uncle to enter the Persian king's harem, where she's able to use her influence to thwart a plot to kill Jews throughout the empire. The book of Esther also has comedic elements: The Persian king is idiotic, and coincidences drive much of the plot. These elements are why Esther is celebrated in Jewish communities today with the holiday of Purim, a festival full of costumes and campy retellings of Esther's story. But the book also has a considerable amount of violence in its penultimate chapter, in which Jewish people throughout the empire get revenge on those who plotted against them.

The combination of comedy and violence might read strangely to some of us today, but for an oppressed population who has often had to navigate the arbitrariness of an empire ruling over them, Esther can be an uplifting story.

Daniel

The final book we'll consider here is the book of Daniel, which is one of the most unique books of the Hebrew Bible in terms of genre and structure. Daniel chapters 1–6 are set in the midst of the Babylonian exile in the mid-sixth century BCE. These stories follow Daniel and his friends, Jews who have been adopted into privileged positions in the Babylonian royal court, and who, through a combination of wit, resilience, and divine intervention, navigate the challenges of being a religious minority that refuses to fully assimilate to the dominant culture.

In this way, the chapters Daniel 1–6 are similar to the Joseph stories in Genesis 39–50 and to the book of Esther. Both of those stories also focus on Jewish characters raised to high stature who work to benefit their people in hostile social and political environments. Like Joseph, Daniel is an interpreter of a king's dreams. Like Esther, Daniel refuses to bow before anyone but his own God.

Daniel chapters 7–12 are radically different, though. These chapters are examples of apocalyptic literature, a rarely occurring genre in the Hebrew Bible otherwise only found in Zechariah 9–13 and Isaiah 24–27. Revelation is the most famous biblical example of apocalyptic literature and it will be discussed later. Apocalyptic literature offers a behind-the-scenes look at history, often involving visions of heaven, divine beings, and highly symbolic scenes that represent God's true plan for history. But the most definitive element of apocalyptic literature are descriptions of postmortem judgment, where, after death, people are rewarded or punished according to God's will. In Daniel, this is clearest in 12:2–3, which says: "Many of those who sleep in the dust of the earth shall awake, some to everlasting life and some to shame and everlasting contempt. Those who are wise shall shine like the brightness of the sky, and those who lead the many to righteousness, like the stars forever and ever."

Daniel's apocalyptic chapters heavily influenced the theology of the New Testament, and the Olivet Discourse in Mark 13, Matthew 24–25, and Luke 21 in particular, with the image of the Son of Man coming on the clouds to herald the end of days, like in Daniel 7:13–14.

Something many biblical scholars believe, which the average reader might not, is that the book of Daniel is actually the youngest book in the Hebrew Bible and was not completed until around 165 BCE, long after the sixth-century BCE Babylonian exile, in which the first chapters are set. Scholars believe this is for several reasons. First, the book of Daniel has several historical inaccuracies that someone writing close to the Babylonian exile wouldn't be likely to make. For example, the book of Daniel depicts Belshazzar as the last king of Babylon (Daniel 5:30), when the last king was in fact Nabonidus, Belshazzar's father. The book also names Darius the Mede as the one who conquered Babylon (Daniel 5:31), when it was in fact Cyrus the Great.

The apparent prophecies in Daniel 10–11 symbolically referring to the rise and fall of kingdoms are all accurate up to the reign of a man called a "contemptible person" (Daniel 11:21). This king's career matches that of the historical Antiochus IV Epiphanes, who ruthlessly persecuted the Jews and desecrated the Second Temple, as described in Daniel 11:31. But then suddenly the prophecies become inaccurate and assert that Antiochus IV will die outside Jerusalem (Daniel 11:45). Antiochus did die, of course, in 164 BCE, but he died in the heart of his fading empire, not anywhere near Jerusalem.

When biblical scholars see such a dramatic shift from accurate descriptions of ostensibly future events to inaccurate descriptions, they deduce that the author lived when the shift occurred. The author of Daniel 7–12, writing just before Antiochus IV's death, wasn't prophesying so much as describing the past in symbolic terms in a way that made sense of the course of history for his contemporary audience living under persecution. Suffering is easier to bear if people can believe God is still ultimately in control, and apocalyptic literature provides this kind of comfort.

Tips for Interpreting Poetry

The revisions of history, short stories, and the first six chapters of Daniel discussed above are similar in genre to earlier books of the Hebrew Bible. Check the Tips for Interpreting Prose from chapter 5 and the Tips for Interpreting Legends from chapter 6 to help with those. Here, we'll focus on reading poetry, which will also help for the latter chapters of Daniel.

The Hebrew Bible abounds in figurative language, from the personification of worshipping stars (Job 38:7) to devastating similes of loss (Psalm 22:14). Poetry in different forms makes up a large percentage of the Hebrew Bible. While the Bible's prose narratives are frequently told to children, made the subject of Bible studies, and preached from the pulpit, it's the Bible's poetry that's often made into hymns and prayers. Poetry is then the heart of many religious faiths that make use of the Bible and the vehicle by which countless people give expression to their religious feelings. The power of poetry to speak to us on the basis of our shared humanity is incredible and worth appreciating. Here are some tips to get the most out of it.

1. Expand Your Questions

The Hebrew Bible's poetry is some of its most enduring literature. While questions of historical accuracy or the strangeness of different cultures can make it difficult for readers to engage emotionally with other, narrative sections of the biblical text, poetry often has the power to cut through these obstacles right to our hearts.

Contemporary Bible readers tend to ask devotional questions of poetry, like "What does this tell us about God, Jesus, salvation, and my place in the world?" There's nothing wrong with posing these questions to poetic texts (or any other kind of biblical texts). However, when reading poetry, we can also ask about the emotions these poems are meant to evoke and consider how a community reciting these poems together might share in that experience.

For example, Psalm 139 is a psalm of lament in which a single individual addresses God and mourns the desperation of their situation.

Psalm 44 is also a psalm of lament, but most of it addresses God from the perspective of a "we" and an "us" rather than an "I." It's intended to be used by a community in their expression of collective mourning.

Psalm 7 is a psalm of thanksgiving that lavishes praise on God for intervening in the individual psalmist's life against their enemies. Psalm 95 has many similarities to Psalm 7, but is again communal, and lavishes praise on God for being king over that community.

Other psalms are less about a specific emotion and more about the celebration of a particular piece of theology. Psalm 8 celebrates creation. Psalm 82 celebrates God's sovereignty over other deities. Psalm 106 recalls the exodus in poetic fashion.

A lay reader of these psalms might not ever find a precise answer to the question "How did an ancient community use these psalms in their religious life?" But simply being aware of that question and keeping it in mind can expand the reasons why we read the psalms and sensitize us to the concerns of the texts' original authors.

2. Dig into Parallelism

One of the most iconic features of Hebrew poetry is parallelism, in which couplets or triplets of lines refer to related subjects and verbs.

In each case, the first line of these parallel constructions sets the basic meaning, and then successive lines play with that basic meaning, often making it more dramatic and concrete, but sometimes subverting these expectations with a new twist.

For example, in Psalm 2:1–3 we have the following:

Why do the nations conspire
and the peoples plot in vain?
The kings of the earth set themselves,
and the rulers take counsel together,
against the Lord and his anointed, saying,
"Let us burst their bonds apart
and cast their cords from us."

"Nations conspiring" and "people plotting" are parallel subjects and verbs; the second line dramatizes the first by revealing the effectiveness of this conspiring and plotting as "in vain." "Kings setting themselves" and "rulers taking counsel" are parallel subjects and verbs. But the third line contrasts the former kings and rulers with "the Lord and his anointed," subverting the reader's expectations. "Bursting bonds" and "cutting cords" again parallel each other; the second line personalizes the meaning by specifying who is bound—that is, us.

Once you start to notice parallelism like this, you'll see it everywhere in Hebrew poetry, and because you see it in Hebrew poetry, you may even start to see it in the speeches or descriptive language of narrative prose too.

All this to say, Hebrew poetry shouldn't be understood on the level of individual lines but rather in the parallel constructions it chooses to express itself. The interpretive question "What does this couplet mean?" is more informed and specific to this genre of literature than "What does this one line mean?" or "What does this one verse mean?"

Wisdom Literature

Three books in the canonical Hebrew Bible are considered works of wisdom literature: Proverbs, Job, and Ecclesiastes. In these books, "wisdom" is not aged experience or knowledge of scholarly tomes but rather the practical skill of life. In the wisdom literature, wise people are wise because they can discern, in natural and social patterns, what's necessary for successful living, whereas foolish people disregard these patterns to their own ruin. The definition of "wisdom" is very similar in all three books, but Proverbs, Job, and Ecclesiastes disagree about the desirability and accessibility of wisdom.

In Proverbs, which is a collection of short wisdom sayings frequently cast as advice from father to son, wisdom is portrayed as both desirable and accessible. Wisdom is more valuable than wealth and protects us from danger (Proverbs 3:14–15, 21–26), and wisdom widely advertises itself, personified as a woman who shouts at passersby from a city street corner (Proverbs 1:20–33).

In Job, by contrast, wisdom is desirable but not accessible. After a bet between God and Satan about whether or not Job's perfect piety is genuine or the result of all his good fortune, Job loses everything and spends the rest of the book debating his friends about whether or not he deserved it. Every character in Job believes themselves to be wise and appeals to basic tenets of the wisdom tradition, conveying that wisdom is desirable. But a poem in Job 28 affirms that only God knows where wisdom is. The fact that the characters in Job don't know why he's suffering, but the reader does, adds to this impression that wisdom is forever beyond our reach.

Ecclesiastes differs still further, affirming that wisdom is accessible but not desirable: "For in much wisdom is much vexation" (Ecclesiastes 1:18). In a similar vein, Ecclesiastes 12:12b almost undermines the whole book: "Of making many books there is no end, and much study is weariness for the flesh."

Tips for Interpreting Wisdom Sayings

Perhaps nothing is as quotable in the Hebrew Bible as its wisdom literature, which often comes in the form of concise and memorable little sayings ready to be deployed whenever the occasion calls. Whether warnings for fools or guidelines for the wise, wisdom sayings require us to be attentive to what works practically in day-to-day life. While other kinds of biblical literature are concerned with abstract and spiritual concepts, wisdom sayings tend to focus more on the concrete challenges of life. *What do I say? What do I do? What do I spend my time on? What should I pursue?* The wise are the ones who know these things, and with some tips, you can know them too.

1. Think About Timing

Wisdom sayings are fundamentally oral in nature. By that we mean that, while people might at times read them or read *about* them, they were meant to be used spontaneously in conversation, in moments where they apply. Imagine someone writing down the famous English saying "A stitch in time saves nine." That saying doesn't do anyone any good written down. However, when someone who knows the saying recognizes a situation in which the saying is applicable, they can repeat it and act on it. The same is true for many of the sayings in Proverbs and Ecclesiastes.

This is also why these sayings occasionally contradict, like Proverbs 26:4 and 26:5, which offer opposite advice about how to deal with foolish people. A wise person is a person who knows which wisdom saying to apply at which time. Sometimes you *do* need to answer a fool according to their folly, and sometimes you don't. In the same way, a wise person would know in a given situation whether to apply the saying "A stitch in time saves nine" or "If it ain't broke, don't fix it," even though these sayings offer opposing advice. "There's a time for everything," Ecclesiastes 3:1 tells us, and that includes a time for each of these wisdom sayings.

For this reason, when we're interpreting wisdom sayings, we should be asking ourselves which of these sayings could be useful, rather than regarding any one of them, or all of them, as absolute truths.

2. Imagine a Debate

The three canonical books of wisdom literature in the Hebrew Bible, Proverbs, Job, and Ecclesiastes, perhaps more than other texts in other genres, are actively involved in debating one another. As described earlier in the chapter, each text has a very different idea of the desirability and accessibility of wisdom, and each one dramatizes these competing ideas with their narratives.

Given this, one set of interpretive questions we can ask about these texts concerns the pros and cons of their positions: How desirable is wisdom? How accessible is it? Which text makes the best case for its answers to these questions? Which makes the worst?

Since the texts themselves are debating, we are invited to debate along with them.

Conclusion

While the multivocality of the Bible is noticeable in several places, once you know what to look for, it's especially noticeable in the great diversity of contrasting and debating literature we see in the Writings. They say variety is the spice of life, and if that's true, then the Writings are the spice of the Hebrew Bible.

In Jewish tradition, the Hebrew Bible ends with 2 Chronicles, when the Jewish people were allowed to return to Jerusalem from Babylonian captivity in 538 BCE. In Christian tradition, the Old Testament instead ends with the book of Malachi, which anticipates a messenger to prepare the way (Malachi 3:1) and the figure of Elijah to herald the day of the

Lord (Malachi 4:5), images the Gospels associate with John the Baptist. Both endings to the Hebrew Bible or Old Testament look forward to the future and what God will do next for humanity, and so in their own ways, both texts end on an optimistic note.

The willingness to be receptive to what God is doing despite the trials and tribulations we face, is one of the greatest and most unifying virtues of the entire Bible. Just like eating a big meal can signal that someone is on the mend, or sharing a meal together can signal reconciliation, being ready to turn the page of the Bible to what's next is a healthy thing. Right now, we're turning the page to the New Testament.

CHAPTER 8

The Gospels and Acts

LIKE THE OLD Testament, the New Testament is not one book written from beginning to end by one author. It is a collection of twenty-seven different books written by various authors over about a sixty- or seventy-year period. The books themselves are diverse, both in their genre (or literary style) and in their content. The New Testament contains literary styles such as gospels, letters, theological history, sermons (homilies), and apocalyptic literature, just to mention a few.

In the next three chapters, we are going to become more familiar with those literary styles, summarize the content found in the New Testament, and give some relevant historical background to the whole shebang. This is not an exhaustive introduction to the New Testament (although those are great, and if you want to read one, you'll find some in our resources at the end of the book); it is a beginner's guide to interpreting New Testament literature.

Think of it like a cookbook that introduces the varied cuisines and their common ingredients. Different cuisines—like Mexican, Indian, Italian, or Mediterranean—have their own foundational tastes, textures, and ingredients. It is as important for a well-rounded chef to be familiar with the characteristics of cuisines as it is for a biblical interpreter to be familiar with the different literature and contexts of Scripture.

Our goal in these chapters, then, is to introduce budding interpreters to the diverse writings in the New Testament and provide some pertinent historical and cultural background to those writings and their authors. Along the way, we will give some tips about how to responsibly interpret the different genres (or cuisines!) found in the New Testament.

The Gospels

The genre of the Gospels is different from any type of writing we have in modern literature. It shares the most characteristics with ancient biographies, a popular style of writing used by Roman historians in the first and second centuries CE to memorialize famous leaders. Like these ancient historians, the Gospel writers chose key episodes from their subject's (Jesus's) life in order to portray the central pieces of his character. They organized Jesus's words and actions more thematically than chronologically; this was for the benefit of their audiences, who would expect such arrangement. Their narratives also highlight Jesus's death instead of his childhood, because in antiquity people believed how a person died revealed much about that person's character.

Matthew, Mark, Luke, and John are the four canonical Gospels: the main sources we have that tell us about the life and ministry of Jesus. The books are attributed to these apostles, though as we will see, their true authorship is not known with any certainty. In this chapter, however, we will generally use these four names to refer to these books' authors, whoever they may be.

Jesus was born sometime between 6 BCE and 1 CE and died around 30 CE; that means his life in Galilee and death in Jerusalem occurred under the violent reign of the Roman Empire. It is important to keep this in mind when reading the Gospels. That's because most of the people Jesus interacted with during his ministry were people in poverty affected in dire ways by the structure and rule of the empire. The authors of the Gospels, probably written between 60 and 100 CE, faced a similar situation in different parts of the empire.

Good News

The Greek word for gospel is *euangelion*, and it literally means "good news." Normally, when one spoke of "good news" in the Roman Empire, it was political propaganda. Heralds would use the term to spread a positive picture of Caesar or to announce Rome's superiority and dominance.

When the Gospel writers use the term, however, they are not referring to Rome or the emperor; on the contrary, they use it to refer to the peaceful reign of God initiated by Jesus. The angel announcing Jesus's birth says, "I bring the *good news* of great joy that is for all people" (Luke 2:10). Mark places it in the first verse of his Gospel as a way to introduce Jesus's life and ministry: "[This is] the beginning of the *good news* of Jesus Christ, the son of God" (Mark 1:1). Jesus's main message in the

Gospels is the *good news* of the kingdom of God that has come near in Jesus's life and ministry.

At this point you might be thinking, "If each of the Gospels tell the good news about Jesus's life and ministry, then why do we need four different Gospels? Wouldn't one be enough?" There are multiple reasons why the New Testament has four Gospels: the diversity of traditions about Jesus, the unique perspectives each writer provides, and the historical circumstances of the Gospels. First, the teachings of and about Jesus went through an oral period for about thirty years after Jesus's death and resurrection. During this time, different communities of Christians told and retold stories of Jesus, and traditions about him spread throughout the churches in the Roman Empire.

Finally, when the gospel writers (or evangelists, as we sometimes call them) began to weave the different oral and written pieces of the Jesus story together, they used numerous pieces of the traditions and patterned these into their Gospels. Each Gospel writer creates a distinct portrait of Jesus on their literary tapestry, emphasizing certain aspects of his character and highlighting what themes and motifs from his story served their purposes best. The evangelists did not write at the same time, from the same place, or to the same audiences. They each had a different *provenance*, or original background, and slightly different purposes, and so we have four complementary but diverse stories about Jesus's life, death, and resurrection.

The Gospels in Relationship

Although each Gospel has its own emphases, perspectives, and themes, they also have much in common with one another. Scholars who study the Gospels try to explain the connections between the Gospels by looking at their overlapping content and the sources they might have used. When comparing and contrasting the Gospels, it is clear that Matthew, Mark, and Luke share the most content. That is why scholars call these three Gospels—the Synoptic Gospels ("synoptic" means "seeing together"), and the study of their connections the Synoptic Problem or the Synoptic Puzzle.

The main problem or puzzle regarding Matthew, Mark, and Luke has to do with their sources and composition order. *Source criticism* seeks to discover and identify the written sources behind the Synoptic Gospels. The most widely accepted solution to the Synoptic Puzzle among source critics—those people seeking to answer these questions using this method—is the *Two-Document Theory*. This hypothesis proposes that: 1) Mark was written first; 2) the authors of Matthew and Luke used a copy or form of Mark's Gospel as a source for their narratives; 3) the books of Matthew and Luke both share yet another source, a collection of Jesus's sayings known to scholars as Q (*Quelle*, or "source" in German). An expanded form of this theory, called the *Four Document Hypothesis*, suggests that Matthew and Luke also had their own special material that they drew upon from another written source (called M for the Matthew material and L for the Luke material).

This likely scenario—in which Matthew and Luke set Mark as their template while adding their own perspectives and stories—shows us that we cannot think of the Gospels as modern history. That is not what they were written to be and not how we should read them. Instead, they are creatively crafted narrative biographies that sometimes take literary license in order to fulfill their ultimate goal: communicating the character and ministry of Jesus in a way that inspires people to follow him and his example.

The Gospel of John is an especially clear example of this artistic creativity because it breaks away from the Synoptic Gospels' storyline and narrates Jesus's life with vocabulary, themes, and theology that are quite different from the motifs in the other Gospels. Such artistry does not mean that we should take John less seriously than the Synoptic Gospels. It means we are fortunate to have different witnesses to the impact of Jesus in his world. What we need to do to appreciate those differing witnesses is to let them speak in the way that Gospels speak, with history and symbolism intertwined and with the portrait of Jesus centered—rather than the bare facts and dates that many contemporary readers prefer.

So let's take a closer look at those differing witnesses. In the following sections, we'll give some brief but densely packed summaries of each of the Gospels. You will notice that the section on Mark is longer than the Matthew and Luke ones. This is not because Mark is a longer book (Luke is actually the longest of the four Gospels), but because, as we discussed with the Synoptic Puzzle, his plotline is the original that Matthew and Luke build upon.

Note also that we will not be discussing Gospel authorship or provenance. The Gospels were all originally anonymous—no author signed their name to any—and their traditional identification with Matthew, Mark, Luke, and John probably didn't begin until the second century. This anonymity also makes it difficult to tell with any certainty when and in what specific context each of these Gospels was written. What we can and will do in these sections is home in on what it is possible for us to know: the plot of each Gospel, their literary themes, and each one's special emphases.

The Gospel of Mark

If there were a subtitle for Mark's Gospel, it might be something like "The Power of the Suffering Messiah" because Mark likes to highlight Jesus's miraculous power as a way to convince his readers that Jesus is the Messiah. However, Mark also makes it clear that Jesus was not the kind of messiah most Jewish people were expecting; instead of a messiah who would lead Israel to victory over their oppressors, Jesus proved to be one who suffered and died, despite his great power and importance.

Mark's story starts abruptly, without the birth story or childhood information we will see in Matthew and Luke. A man named John cries out in the wilderness, heralding the coming of one who is more powerful than him, one who will baptize not with water but with the Holy Spirit. Then Jesus arrives on the scene to be baptized by John. The heavens part (literally, "split open") and a voice cries from above, "You are my Son, the Beloved; with you I am well pleased" (1:11). This line is a powerful affirmation of Jesus's identity, and it sets the tone for the rest of the story: No matter how much misunderstanding and suffering Jesus encounters, we as readers should know that he is the beloved son of God and his mission pleases God. Then, immediately after this affirmation, the Spirit leads Jesus into the wilderness for forty days to be tempted by Satan (1:13). Following the temptation, Jesus begins his mission in earnest, traveling around Galilee and preaching about the kingdom of God.

Jesus's Traveling Ministry and Identity

Mark takes about half of his Gospel to describe Jesus's traveling ministry in Galilee, focusing much of the action on the fishing villages around the Sea of Galilee. This part of the story is fast-paced. Jesus gathers disciples, heals people with all sorts of ailments, and teaches in the synagogues. Men and women from all over Galilee follow Jesus, and Jesus chooses an inner circle of twelve, whom he calls "apostles."

Jesus's healing ministry is central to the early portion of Mark. It serves to illustrate the message that Jesus had first proclaimed in 1:15: "The time is fulfilled, and the kingdom of God has come near; repent, and believe in the good news." Part of the good news of the kingdom is that when God's reign appears on earth, people who were captive to all sorts of powers can experience freedom and healing. The miracles Jesus performs show that he has power over these forces, over the forces of sickness, nature, evil, and death.

In addition to showing divine authority through his powerful miracles, Jesus also exercises authority through his words. As he visits synagogues, Jesus teaches the people "as one having authority, and not as the scribes" (1:22). Jesus displays great skill in his teaching—he uses parables, hyperbole, figures of speech, and proverbs—and with each lesson, he gives his followers a fuller picture of what the kingdom of God looks like. The reign of God that Jesus was starting on earth was a present reality and a future hope.

A key theme of Mark's Gospel is that Jesus's mission as the Messiah required humble service, sacrifice, and suffering. Multiple times, the apostles seem confused about Jesus's identity and mission, even resistant to the truths he proclaims. When Jesus predicts his upcoming suffering and death, the disciples misunderstand and oppose his message.

They seem unable to fathom that the fate of the Messiah would not be glory and greatness but sacrifice and suffering. They are resistant to Jesus's insistence that discipleship also involves sacrifice and suffering. As Jesus says at a central moment in Mark's narrative: "If any wish to come after me, let them deny themselves and take up their cross and follow me. For those who want to save their life will lose it, and those who lose their life for my sake, and for the sake of the gospel, will save it" (8:34–35). Mark wants to make it clear to his audience that the same mission of sacrifice and suffering would fall to them as Jesus's followers.

A Race to the Cross

In Mark, as in the other Gospels, Jesus's healing and teaching both inspired a devoted following and instigated severe opposition. Jesus's opponents come in two forms in Mark—the demons who know who he is and shrink from his authority, and the Pharisees, scribes, and chief priests who deny who he is and reject his authority. When Jesus casts out demons (exorcisms are common in Mark), the demons succumb to his healing and liberating power. His battle is not so straightforward with the religious leaders. When Jesus teaches in the synagogues and the temple, the Pharisees, scribes, and chief priests contest his instruction and try to discredit him. Jesus debates with these foes throughout the Gospel, prevailing every time, but they are tenacious and refuse to let Jesus win in the end.

Mark's Gospel is sometimes described as a race to the cross, a story with a swiftly narrated beginning that surges forward until it reaches Jesus's last week—his passion week. (*Passio* is Latin for "suffering.") The first event of the week is Jesus's entry into Jerusalem, a symbolic and political act. Jesus rides through the gates of Jerusalem sitting on a donkey, an animal of peace rather than a war horse. Crowds lay their cloaks and palm branches on the road before him and cry, "Blessed is the one who comes in the name of the Lord! Blessed is the coming kingdom of our ancestor David! Hosanna in the highest heaven!"

Many Jewish expectations about the Messiah were that he would be a king in the same way his ancestor David was a king. He would come to wage war against their Roman oppressors and free Jewish people from their overlords. When Jesus rides into Jerusalem on a donkey, he is signaling to the people that he is not going to be that kind of messiah.

After the triumphal entry, Jesus visits the temple in Jerusalem and drives out the sellers and buyers there, overturning the tables of the money changers. He condemns the leaders of the temple, saying, "Is it not written, 'My house shall be called a house of prayer for all the nations'? But you have made it a den of robbers" (11:17). This accusation is the last straw for the chief priests and the scribes; they agree that Jesus must die.

Jesus teaches for several more days in Jerusalem, warning about the corruption in the temple and its future destruction while sparring with the religious leaders who dispute with him. Then, one of Jesus's own disciples—Judas Iscariot—seeks out the chief priests and scribes and agrees to hand Jesus over. When the night of the Passover feast arrives, Jesus comes together with his disciples, sharing a meal and fellowship with them. During the meal, Jesus predicts that one among them will betray him and another will deny him. After dinner, he retreats to the Garden of Gethsemane to pray.

In the garden scene, Jesus is troubled and asks God to remove the cup from him, to save him from the upcoming suffering. Despite this vulnerable, human request, Jesus concludes his prayer with resolve, saying, "yet, not what I want, but what you want" (14:36). After Jesus's moment of surrender, Judas arrives with a crowd armed with clubs and swords. They arrest Jesus and take him to the council of chief priests, elders, and scribes, who decide to take him before the Roman governor, Pontius Pilate. Pilate, unconvinced of his guilt, offers to release Jesus. The crowd refuses his conciliatory offer and demands that Pilate crucify Jesus. Pilate gives the crowd what they want.

When Mark describes Jesus's crucifixion, he emphasizes the cosmic significance of his tragic death. Darkness falls on the whole land from noon to three o'clock, and after Jesus exhales his last breath, the curtain of the temple tears in half. A centurion who witnesses the execution exclaims, "Truly this man was God's Son!" (15:39) The Gospel of Mark began with the declaration that Jesus was the Messiah, the Son of God, and now the author reminds his audience of that identity at Jesus's death. Jesus's obedient suffering on the cross confirms that the kingdom he represents and the road he has blazed for all those who follow him is one that is marked by humility and sacrifice.

Mystery and Misunderstanding

On Sunday after his death, some women disciples of Jesus come to the tomb to minister to his body, to prepare it in the way of Jewish custom. It is significant that the disciples are women. All of Jesus's male disciples had deserted him before his crucifixion, but the women disciples did not flee. They were at the cross, witnessing his death, and now came to the tomb in loving service. When the women arrive at the garden, they find the tomb empty and the stone that had sealed the grave rolled away. A man in white tells them that Jesus had risen from the dead and that they should go tell Peter and the disciples that Jesus would meet them in Galilee.

The end of Mark is strange, to say the least. After the man instructs the women to go, they flee from the tomb and say nothing to anyone. That is the very last verse of Mark's original Gospel. Any additional endings you might see in your Bible do not appear in the earliest copies, or manuscripts, of the Gospel of Mark. Most likely, Mark ended his Gospel in our chapter 16, verse 8, with no resolution to the women's silence and fearful fleeing. Why such an abrupt and unsatisfying ending?

Throughout Mark, there are themes of mystery and misunderstanding. Multiple times when Jesus heals people or when he reveals something about his identity, he instructs people to tell no one. Scholars have called this the "Messianic Secret." Also, recall that Mark consistently highlights the disciples' doubt and misunderstanding—sometimes even their fear and rejection of Jesus's suffering and death. Both of these themes find a climax in the scene at the tomb. The women disciples display doubt as they flee the tomb, and the abrupt ending leaves readers with questions and confusion. Perhaps that is by design, though. Mark concludes his Gospel the way he does to provoke questions in his audience, like "What would I have done at the tomb? What does Jesus's life, death, and resurrection mean? And who do I think this Jesus Christ is—the Messiah, the Son of God, or neither?"

The Gospel of Matthew

The Gospel of Matthew was probably written a decade or two after Mark, and although it follows Mark's basic storyline, it also creates a distinct portrait of Jesus. The author begins the story before Jesus is even born, starting with a genealogy of Jesus that ties him to Abraham's story, showing that Jesus will be a blessing to all the nations. The genealogy also hints at Jesus's royal lineage from David. These connections would have carried great significance for Matthew's readers because they would establish Jesus as the Davidic messiah.

Extraordinary Visits

After his genealogy, Matthew begins the more dramatic part of Jesus's origin story. In this account, which appears only in Matthew, an angel pays a visit to Joseph, the man whose lineage Matthew just outlined. Joseph is at this point in the story engaged to Mary, who is pregnant with a child that is not Joseph's. This would have been a shameful and dangerous situation in their first-century culture. The angel has come to assure Joseph that he does not need to condemn Mary or send her away—and that this baby conceived by the Holy Spirit will save Joseph's people from their sins.

Matthew also is the only Gospel that relates the story about the magi from the East and Herod's slaughter of baby boys. The magi, wise men from far away, had followed a star to find the baby who would be born king of the Jews. They sought directions in Jerusalem from Herod the Great, the current king of the Jews, but the power-hungry king did not take the news of a new king well. As a result, Herod has all the boys in the area under age two killed to make sure he eliminates the threat to his throne. Fortunately, an angel warns Joseph in a dream to flee to Egypt with Mary and Jesus as refugees. With this miraculous intervention, the attempt on Jesus's life is foiled, and the family stays in Egypt until Herod the Great dies.

The Five Discourses

Matthew's innovations to Mark's account extend beyond Jesus's birth story. In Matthew, Jesus does everything he does in Mark—preach, gather disciples, heal, and debate with religious leaders—but his teaching material, rather than Mark's fast-moving action, is the anchor of the story. Matthew adds five key discourses or teaching sections to Mark's structure, paralleling the five books of the Pentateuch.

These five discourses group Jesus's teachings around specific topics related to life in the kingdom or the church. The most famous of these teaching sections is the Sermon on the Mount, which outlines characteristics of the kingdom and kingdom people. Kingdom language in the Synoptic Gospels refers to the reality that Jesus is announcing and beginning in his ministry, a new era in which people who accept the kingdom will start to live out God's priorities on earth. The sermon kicks off with the Beatitudes (5:3–11), which establish the upside-down nature of God's priorities.

> *Blessed are the poor in spirit, for theirs is the kingdom of heaven.*
> *Blessed are those who mourn, for they will be comforted.*
> *Blessed are the meek, for they will inherit the earth.*
> *Blessed are those who hunger and thirst for righteousness, for they will be filled.*

> *Blessed are the merciful, for they will receive mercy.*
> *Blessed are the pure in heart, for they will see God.*
> *Blessed are the peacemakers, for they will be called children of God.*
> *Blessed are those who are persecuted for righteousness' sake, for theirs is the kingdom of heaven.*

In this section, Matthew is communicating that the people the world considers lowly or unfortunate will experience contentment when God's kingdom comes fully. It also suggests that the meek and the persecuted are those who are most likely to grasp kingdom values and thrive in God's reign.

In the Sermon on the Mount and throughout Jesus's other discourses, Matthew helps his audience begin to understand and live out the ethics of God's kingdom in their lives. Kingdom people should examine the attitudes of their hearts, those inner motivations that lead to destructive actions. Jesus tells his disciples that they should avoid the anger that leads to murder, reject the lust that leads to adultery, and remove the hatred and vengeance that creates enemies; instead, they should love their enemies and pray for those who persecute them (5:21–48). It is not enough to change the outside and put on the appearance of a religious, law-abiding follower of God; in the kingdom, transformation is radically countercultural and happens from the inside out.

A Satisfying Ending

When Matthew narrates Jesus's last week in Jerusalem, he follows Mark's timeline closely. The main point of departure comes when the story reaches Jesus's resurrection. While Mark ends with the women disciples afraid and fleeing from the tomb, Matthew's disciples leave with fear but also joy, ready to tell the disciples the news.

Matthew has a much more satisfying ending than Mark, with Jesus giving final instructions to his disciples on a mountain and challenging them with the Great Commission: "Go therefore and make disciples of all nations, baptizing them in the name of the Father and of the Son and of the Holy Spirit, and teaching them to obey everything that I have commanded you. And remember, I am with you always, to the end of the age" (28:19–20). Matthew leaves his readers anticipating the future disciples from all nations that, by the time the Gospel is written, had already begun to join the Jesus movement across the Mediterranean world.

The Gospel of Luke

Luke, like Matthew, follows the basic storyline and the main teachings laid out in Mark. Luke includes an infancy narrative and a genealogy as Matthew does, but his story begins in the temple in Jerusalem, where the angel Gabriel appears to a priest named Zechariah.

The angel announces that Zechariah's wife, Elizabeth, is pregnant despite being too old to conceive. The baby Elizabeth carries will be John the Baptist, the prophet who will turn his people back to God and prepare the way for the Lord. In a parallel scene, Gabriel visits Mary, Elizabeth's relative, and he delivers a message about another miraculous birth. Mary learns from the angel that she will give birth to the Son of God through the Holy Spirit. Mary accepts her awesome responsibility with words that echo those of the prophet Isaiah: "Here am I, the servant of the Lord; let it be with me according to your word" (1:38). These two women, Elizabeth and Mary, become key figures in Luke's salvation history, the two of them not only giving birth to a prophet and a king but also fulfilling the role of prophets themselves. (See Elizabeth's prediction of Mary's importance in 1:41–45, then Mary's words in 1:46–55 that prophecy the nature of Jesus's ministry.)

Mary eventually travels to Bethlehem with Joseph because the taking of a census requires it, and she gives birth there, wrapping the baby in swaddling clothes and resting him in a manger (an animal's feeding trough) instead of a bed. Meanwhile, shepherds who are watching their flocks hear an angel announcing good news of great joy and peace on earth. These familiar details from the Christmas story are all found uniquely in Luke. All the supernatural elements from this story—the angels and the spirit pregnancy—draw the audience's attention to the divine attributes of Jesus. The mundane details—a census, the shepherds in the field, the cloths and feeding troughs—demonstrate that the divine has come to be a part of the lowly and common.

Jesus's Liberating Message

After the nativity scene, Luke mostly follows Mark's timeline, with a few significant departures. The first difference comes at the beginning of

Jesus's ministry, when instead of narrating Mark's story of Jesus healing a demon-possessed man, Luke writes about Jesus visiting his hometown synagogue. One of the book's major purposes is to depict the liberating nature of God's reign, and here is where that theme bursts onto the pages. In the synagogue, Jesus stands up and reads the following from the scroll of Isaiah:

> *The Spirit of the Lord is upon me,*
> *because he has anointed me*
> *to bring good news to the poor.*
> *He has sent me to proclaim release to the captives*
> *and recovery of sight to the blind,*
> *to let the oppressed go free,*
> *to proclaim the year of the Lord's favor.*
> (Luke 4:18–19)

When Jesus reads this passage, he announces to everyone present, "Today this Scripture has been fulfilled in your hearing." With these words, Jesus aligns his work and mission with the salvific agenda that God described in Isaiah 61. There is layered significance to this passage in Isaiah: It speaks of God's justice and mercy while referring to Jubilee, a practice that was supposed to occur every fifty years and involved freeing prisoners, returning land, and forgiving debts. When Jesus claims the fulfillment of this passage, he connects the kingdom with Jubilee (known as "the year of the Lord's favor"), which was a political and economic rearrangement. The reign of God announced in Jesus's ministry was a reality that would bring freedom and healing to the poor and captive.

Marginalized Groups

A second significant departure from Mark is the depiction of Jesus's attention to marginalized groups. Throughout the rest of the Gospel, the author highlights Jesus's ministry among marginalized groups in first-century Judea, including women, outcasts, and the poor.

Women living in Jesus's time were largely marginalized and oppressed, as they had little personal agency, few opportunities to independently support themselves, and bore the physical and emotional burden of poverty in their culture. Starting with Mary and Elizabeth, the book of Luke shows that women play a central role in the ministry of Jesus, and the author focuses on the numerous instances that Jesus interacts with women and lifts their social and religious position.

Jesus also ministered to outcasts. Various groups were treated as outcasts in Jesus's environment, pushed to the edges of society because of their differences. The sick and disabled faced economic challenges, social ostracism, and judgment in their culture because infirmity was often thought to be divine punishment. People like tax collectors and prostitutes were also shoved to the margins and judged harshly as "sinners," unworthy of mercy. These outcast groups, denied their full humanity by some of the religious leaders, were those to whom we see Jesus offer the most attention and grace.

The final marginalized group that Luke highlights in his Gospel are the poor, those who were oppressed and held captive by the Roman economic system, which made it difficult for them to survive. Jesus's teaching and healing ministry takes place among the most destitute of people, and Luke is careful to include passages that warn against the dangers of wealth.

Luke is also the only Gospel to give us the story of the wealthy tax collector, Zacchaeus, whose salvation Jesus affirms after he gives up half his wealth. The Zacchaeus story illustrates what the year of Jubilee might look like, when those who are rich begin to live under God's reign by relinquishing their wealth and righting the economic wrongs of their society. This is salvation for Luke: Jesus offering freedom to people weighed down by greed and hypocrisy, while giving release to those victims of greed and hypocrisy as well. When Jesus brings the good news in Luke, it is good news for everyone, especially those who are captive and oppressed.

The Good Samaritan

A third significant departure from Mark found in Luke is the book's clarification of what it looks like to love God and love our neighbor. All the Synoptic Gospels agree that Jesus's teaching revolves around the Old Testament emphasis on loving God and our neighbor (see Leviticus 19:18 and Deuteronomy 6:5), but Luke alone tells the parable of the good Samaritan (Luke 10), which illustrates who our neighbors are. (Surprise! They are our enemies.)

The story's setup makes it clear that this parable from Jesus teaches that love of God and love of neighbor are not two separate actions but one and the same; we cannot love God and refuse to show mercy or compassion to our neighbors. The lost parables in Luke 15—the lost sheep, the lost coin, and the lost (or prodigal) son—also teach readers about love. When Jesus tells the story of a father who welcomes his rebellious son back with open arms and celebration, he gives us a picture of God's love for even the most rebellious people. It is this kind of love—the unconditional and unwavering love of God—that inspires humanity to practice the love of God and love of neighbor that Jesus preaches.

Dining with Jesus

The final departure Luke makes from Mark's Gospel involves Jesus's dining practices—an image especially noteworthy in a book that draws on the metaphor of cooking. Meals are an important motif in Luke. In multiple scenes throughout the Gospel, Jesus sits down to eat, often teaching people as he dines.

He eats with Pharisees and lawyers, with tax collectors and "sinners," with the apostles at the Last Supper and with other disciples like Mary and Martha. These meal scenes, then, reveal important truths about community and the kingdom—the importance of forgiveness, the universality of the Gospel, and the significance of Jesus's death—all themes that Luke takes great care to highlight throughout his Gospel narrative.

Luke's Gospel even ends with meals; two resurrection appearance stories take place around a table. In one of these meal scenes, Luke relates the tale of two disciples who are walking on the road from Jerusalem to Emmaus. As they talk about everything that had happened, the resurrected Jesus appears next to them, but they do not recognize him. They express to him their grief surrounding the death of their prophet and would-have-been Messiah, and then they tell him about the empty tomb. In response, the incognito Jesus explains how the Scriptures had pointed to the Messiah's suffering and glory.

Then, the disciples invite Jesus to dine at their table and share a meal with them. It is when Jesus blesses the bread and breaks it that they finally recognize him, as if the act of sharing a meal with Jesus were so familiar that they could not help but finally see him.

The Gospel of John

As we noted earlier in this chapter, John's Gospel is not one of the Synoptic Gospels—meaning, it does not follow Mark's storyline closely like Matthew and Luke. However, it does seem as though John knew of Mark's Gospel or was at least aware of the Jesus traditions upon which the other Gospels build. From the first words of John's Gospel, a reader may sense that the author wants to take the Jesus story to another level—to set the life and ministry of the Messiah on the cosmic stage.

Jesus, According to John

The Gospel opens with an image of Jesus as the divine Word that played a role in the creation of the world. John 1:1 reads: "In the beginning was the word." This echoes Genesis 1:1: "In the beginning, God created. . ." In this way, John's prologue—the term used for his introductory section—traces Jesus's origin not back to Abraham, like Matthew's genealogy, but all the way back before the dawn of creation.

Like he does in the other Gospels, John the Baptist plays an important role in John's story, testifying to and preparing the way for Jesus the Messiah. John's Gospel also recounts how Jesus gathered disciples and traveled around healing and teaching, just as Mark's does. The miraculous works of Jesus and the content of his preaching, however, are quite different in John than they are in the Synoptic Gospels.

John arranges the first half of his Gospel around seven "signs" that Jesus does in the presence of his disciples and others. John uses the word "sign" instead of "miracle" because each of the miraculous deeds that Jesus performs are carefully chosen and are narrated so that they point, like signs, to Jesus's identity and purpose. All the signs in John reveal different aspects of Jesus's authority and identity, and they also connect his ministry to traditions and stories from the Hebrew Bible.

Unlike Mark, who concentrates on the suffering in Jesus's sacrificial death, John portrays Jesus's death and resurrection as his glorification. The glory of God revealed in Jesus is a theme throughout this Gospel—we see it in the prologue, in the signs, and especially in conjunction with Jesus's death on the cross. John counteracts the shame that is associated with crucifixion by depicting Jesus's arrest, trial, and death as voluntary and heroic. This is why in John, Jesus does not pray in the garden for the cup to be removed from him; instead, Jesus insists, "And what should I say—'Father, save me from this hour'? No, it is for this reason that I have come to this hour. Father, glorify your name" (12:27–28).

Divergent Timelines and Theology

John's portrayal of Jesus's death is not his only divergence from the Synoptic Gospels. The timeline deviates as well. Jesus's ministry in John relies on a three-year period (three trips to Jerusalem for Passover); the vague Synoptic timeline seems to last about a year. Also in John, Jesus clears the temple at the beginning of the Gospel (chapter 2), while the Synoptics place this event in Jesus's last week. John 13 describes Jesus washing his disciples' feet on the night before he dies; the other Gospels report the Passover meal and the institution of the Lord's Supper.

Theological differences between John and the Synoptics also occur. These differences can be found in Jesus's teachings about his identity and connection to the Father. In the book of Mark, the narrator calls Jesus the "Son of God," but Jesus uses the term "Son of Man" to refer to himself and prefers to keep his messiahship a secret. In John, however, Jesus emphasizes his connection to God. "The Father and I are one," Jesus says in 10:30, and in 16:15, "All that the Father has is mine." Jesus also utters a series of "I am" statements that echo God's name (YHWH, "I am") given to Moses in Exodus.

A New Community

In narrating Jesus's passion week, John eliminates the appearance of weakness or shame—for example, Jesus does not cry out on the cross as one forsaken; instead, he cries out in victory, "It is finished!"

Other than small variations like this, John follows the basic storyline from Mark's crucifixion account. One scene stands out as distinct and meaningful, however. In John 19:25–27, Jesus's mother stands near the cross, and with some of his last breaths, Jesus commits her into the care of "the disciple whom he loved."

This mysterious "beloved disciple" appears throughout the latter part of the Gospel, and while the text itself does not give the disciple a name, tradition identifies him as the apostle John, the possible author of the Gospel. When Jesus tells his mother and his beloved disciple to take care of each other, it feels like a new family begins, a community of believers who are like mothers and brothers and sisters to one another because they love each other and follow Jesus's commands.

That You May Believe

Near the end of John, in 20:30–31, the author summarizes the purpose of the Gospel: "Jesus performed many other signs in the presence of his disciples, which are not recorded in this book. But these are written that you may believe (or continue to believe) that Jesus is the Messiah, the Son of God, and that by believing you may have life in his name." (my translation)

Each story told in John's Gospel serves to convince readers to believe or persist in their belief that Jesus is the Messiah, the Son of God. Even the final scenes of John, the resurrection appearances, demonstrate various types of belief in Jesus.

Mary Magdalene mistakes the resurrected Jesus for the gardener but eventually recognizes him and believes. When she tells some other disciples, they don't believe her, but then Jesus appears to them, and they finally trust it is him. Next, a disciple named Thomas insists on touching Jesus's crucifixion wounds before he will believe, but in the end, he has faith without needing to touch Jesus. In the final scene, Jesus charges Peter with putting his love and belief into action by feeding his sheep. All these responses to Jesus's resurrection follow the pattern laid out across the whole Gospel—the signs of Jesus, whether they involve healing or feeding or raising people from the dead, should move people toward faith and the abundant life that Jesus offers.

Tips for Interpreting the Gospels

The Gospels are key texts for people who follow God and want to interpret the Bible. But as universal as the stories are, it is still difficult for twenty-first century people to understand first-century narratives. So, we want to offer some tips for reading the Gospels well.

1. Keep Narrative Plot and Characterization in Mind

As we noted earlier, the Gospels share much in common with ancient biographies, and that means that at their core, the Gospels fall under the genre of narrative. Storytelling varies from culture to culture and era to era, but there are some elements of stories that remain consistent. All stories have some kind of narrative structure or plot, and they all have characters.

When reading passages from the Gospel, it is imperative that interpreters understand where that passage fits in the overall plot of the narrative. Ideally, one should read a whole Gospel to understand its parts more holistically.

Smaller stories within the overarching story also have their own plot features. Generally speaking, plot can be thought of as a combination of characters, cause, conflict, and resolution. Stories start with exposition that introduces characters and an initial cause of conflict. This is followed by stages of the story known as the rising action, climax, and falling action. All of this ends in a resolution or *denouement*. Noticing plot can help us understand the key ideas and movement in a passage.

Let's try an example. Read the following pericope (a term for a small narrative unit) from Matthew, and pay particular attention to the plotline.

> Jesus left that place and went away to the district of Tyre and Sidon. Just then a Canaanite woman from that region came out and started shouting, "Have mercy on me, Lord, Son of David; my daughter is tormented by a demon." But he did not answer her at all. And his disciples came and urged him, saying, "Send her away, for she keeps shouting after us." He answered, "I was sent only to the lost sheep of the house of Israel." But she came and knelt before him, saying, "Lord, help me." He answered, "It is not fair to take the children's food and throw it to the dogs." She said, "Yes, Lord, yet even the dogs eat the crumbs that fall from their masters' table." Then Jesus answered her, "Woman, great is your faith! Let it be done for you as you wish." And her daughter was healed from that moment.
>
> Matthew 15:21–28

By tracing the conflicts, climax, and resolution here, an interpreter can see that the daughter's ailment is not the focal problem of this story. Rather, the climactic statement, spoken here by a woman, is the main idea of this healing story: People other than the children of Israel can and will benefit from Jesus's ministry.

This story fits into the larger narrative of Matthew perfectly. From the beginning of the story, when the Eastern magi come to Jesus and the holy family flee to Egypt, to the end when Jesus tells his followers to make disciples of all nations, Matthew is emphasizing the universal ministry of Jesus. The Canaanite woman in this story furthers the plot by pushing Jesus out of his Israelite comfort zone.

Her statement illustrates two important truths: Jesus's ministry will have a future impact on other nations and faith in Jesus among foreigners (non-Israelites) will be important in the early Christian movement. A narrative analysis of this passage demonstrates how attending to plotline and character can help us see key messages in a story.

2. Pay Attention to Dialogue

In addition to analyzing plot, it is a good idea to pay attention to dialogue in the Gospels. Often, authors embed vital information and emphatic points in conversation or direct speech. That is true in the story of the Canaanite woman above. As we just saw, the main ideas in that story were introduced in direct speech.

John's Gospel introduces central ideas and motifs in the long conversations that Jesus has with people like Nicodemus and the Samaritan woman. Ancient histories and biographies often employed carefully crafted speeches or dialogue in this way.

We must point out, however, that ancient readers did not assume that these speeches were word-for-word quotations from historical figures. Instead, they knew that authors used creative license to capture the essence of a character or an idea.

3. Be Aware That the Gospels Are Two-Level Dramas

The Gospels were written fifty to seventy-five years after the time of the events they narrate. Because of this, interpreters of the Gospels must be aware that when the authors are telling their story of Jesus, they are also addressing problems that their own Jesus communities were facing in the late first century.

Scholars believe that the story of the Canaanite woman not only reveals truths about Jesus's time but also speaks into the life situations of Matthew's first readers. They were grappling with the multinational character of the new Jesus movement and would find the importance of a foreign woman in Jesus's ministry helpful and encouraging in their mixed cultural context. To read the Gospels well, interpreters must be attentive to the two contexts in the books: the story's setting and the times during which the authors were writing.

The Book of Acts

In the four Gospels, we have four distinct witnesses to the life and ministry of Jesus, but when it comes to the inception and spread of the early Church, we only have one narrative account from the first century: the book of Acts. Fortunately, that account comes from the same person the Gospel of Luke is attributed to. (We tend to just call him Luke, even though he is not named explicitly). In this way, Acts then serves as a continuation of Luke's story of Jesus, giving the audience a glimpse of how the followers of Jesus carried Jesus's legacy and teachings beyond his life and ministry.

The genre of Acts has sometimes been described as theological history. That implies that Acts does not attempt to tell the complete history of the apostles and the earliest churches. Rather, it is a selective history with a narrow focus. It also has guiding theological purposes that make it read more like a Christian defense of the Jesus movement than like a disinterested, historical report.

In Acts, we don't learn about all the various paths that the Jesus movement spread. The book doesn't tell us how the good news spread to Egypt or India or Nubia or Cyrene. Instead, Luke curates a specific path in the expansion of the church.

Jesus first tells his disciples, "But you will receive power when the Holy Spirit has come upon you; and you will be my witnesses in Jerusalem, in all Judea and Samaria, and to the ends of the earth" (Acts 1:7–8). With this deceptively simple prediction from Jesus, Luke lays out the geographical structure of the book of Acts. Jesus's Gospel will move from Jerusalem (chapters 1–7), into the surrounding areas of Judea and

Samaria (chapters 8–12), and finally to Rome, the "ends of the earth" for the purposes of this story (chapters 13–28).

Beginning in Jerusalem

The first seven chapters, focused on Jerusalem and Peter's ministry, have several key scenes. In Acts 2, during the celebration of Pentecost following Jesus's ascension, God's presence in the Spirit makes an appearance among the people in a new and dynamic way. A group of Jesus's disciples, including his mother Mary, are gathered together in a house in Jerusalem. Suddenly, a violent wind blows in, and something like tongues of fire come to rest on them. The disciples are filled with the Holy Spirit and begin to speak in tongues, or languages they did not know previously. Many Jews from around the world were visiting Jerusalem for Pentecost, so with this gift of tongues, the Galilean disciples are able to speak to them in their own languages. Then, the apostle Peter stands up and preaches to the Pentecost crowd about God's work through Jesus and the Holy Spirit.

In the sermon, Peter references a prophecy from the Old Testament book of Joel: "In the last days, God says, I will pour out my Spirit on all people. Your sons and daughters will prophesy, your young men will see visions, your old men will dream dreams. Even on my servants, both men and women, I will pour out my Spirit in those days, and they will prophecy" (Acts 2:17–18; Joel 2:28–29). Peter is relating God's vision for the restoration of the divine kingdom with what was happening among them on Pentecost; the Spirit was being poured out on all people, encouraging participation for men and women, young and old, slave and free. The climax of Peter's sermon is his message about Jesus, a message that would become the core of apostles' preaching in the early Church. After his sermon, thousands of people are baptized in the name of Jesus Christ.

A second key event in Jerusalem is the martyrdom of Stephen. Luke's depiction of the early Jesus followers in Acts parallels his description of Jesus's ministry in the Gospel. The apostles teach and preach in the synagogue like Jesus did, perform miraculous healings, share meals, pray together, and take care of the needy among them. These early believers also meet resistance from the religious leaders as Jesus had, some of them being arrested and even killed for their faith. The first follower of Jesus to become a martyr and die for the faith was a man named Stephen. In Acts 7, Luke describes the stoning of Stephen by the Jewish authorities in a way that echoes Jesus's own death. As the crowd throws stones at him, Stephen asks that Jesus receive his spirit, and then he prays forgiveness over his murderers.

After Stephen's death, a wave of persecution breaks out against the church in Jerusalem, and most Jesus followers flee from the city. As they spread to cities throughout the Mediterranean world, they take the Gospel message with them. The good news about the life, death, and resurrection of the Messiah starts to breaks through barriers—social, national, and ethnic boundaries that had kept people apart—and the church of Jesus Christ begins to take on a multinational, multicultural character.

In Judea and Samaria

The second section in Acts shows this boundary-breaking message moving throughout Judea and Samaria. First, in Acts 8, a believer named Philip preaches the Messiah to people in Samaria, many of whom become Jesus followers. Philip also baptizes an Ethiopian official on his way back to Africa. Both of these evangelistic acts show how the Gospel reaches across national, ethnic, and social boundaries.

Next, Acts reports the supernatural calling story of Saul/Paul, who transformed from a zealous persecutor of early Jesus followers into a dedicated apostle of Jesus who spreads the Gospel to the Gentile (non-Jewish) world. This story pairs with the account of Peter the Jewish apostle and Cornelius the Gentile centurion. After Peter gets a vision about eating unclean animals, he starts to realize that God is opening up the door to Gentiles becoming Jesus followers without becoming Jewish converts.

At the climax of this story, Peter visits the Gentile centurion, and the people in Cornelius's household accept the message about Jesus that Peter speaks. The Holy Spirit comes upon them just like it did on the Jewish believers at Pentecost. This demonstrates that people do not need to be Jewish to receive the Holy Spirit and become part of God's family. Although the acceptance and implementation of this truth will take time, it is truly a turning point in the Jesus movement. The power of the Gospel and the movement of the Spirit had broken through yet another human boundary—the long-standing barrier between the Jew and the Gentile.

To the Ends of the Earth

All of this brings us to the last section of Acts, what we like to call the "to the ends of the earth" portion of the book. These chapters, Acts 13–28, read like a travel journal mixed in with some legal trial reports. Paul participates in three missionary journeys, preaching about Jesus in the cities he visits. The first journey runs through Asia Minor, and Paul and his partner Barnabas end up starting quite a few house churches among Jewish people and more Gentile populations. Paul picks up new travel buddies on the second journey: Silas, Timothy, and even Luke for a while. They plant more churches in the areas surrounding Greece. The third journey takes Paul to cities he has already visited, and on this excursion, he also writes many letters to churches he is advising and encouraging in a long-distance way.

In the latter part of his journeys, Paul finds his way to Jerusalem and encounters trouble from the Jewish leaders and the Roman authorities there. He is imprisoned in a couple of different cities, continuing to write letters to the churches he had started. Eventually, Paul participates in a series of trials before various Roman governors and, after a harrowing voyage across the Mediterranean Sea, arrives at Rome to await an audience with the emperor.

Finally, Acts ends quite abruptly, without giving information about Paul's meeting with Roman authorities or his final fate. Still, by that point the Gospel has reached Rome, the center of the empire and the place designated "the ends of the earth" in Jesus's speech to the disciples at the beginning of Acts.

Tips for Interpreting Acts

Luke's narrative of the early church in Acts does not check all the boxes for everything we might want in a modern account of the history of nascent Christianity. But it does what it sets out to do: It hints at the scope and diversity of the early Jesus movement, and it gives later readers a glimpse of how the Holy Spirit moved the apostles and other followers of Jesus to spread the Gospel across the Roman Empire despite the opposition they faced.

Consider the following pointers to help you as you're interpreting the book of Acts.

1. Keep the Authors' Purposes in Mind

It is good interpretive practice to keep the purposes for which a book's author might have written at the forefront of your mind as you read their accounts. This is especially true of Luke and Acts, because this author seems to have had strong guiding purposes when writing about Jesus and the early church. Many scholars in fact recognize an apologetic rationale—that is, an argument made to justify something—in the book of Acts. Luke's story seems to defend Christians against some of the accusations that the Roman Empire was at the time making against them.

Roman historian Tacitus recounts that Romans thought of early Christians as a dangerously superstitious sect with antisocial tendencies that participated in shameful practices like cannibalism (a misunderstanding of Communion). Christians were also suspected of treason against the empire.

In Acts, Luke is careful to portray the early Jesus movement as a benign sect that is centered around service and love, showing that political machinations or sedition played no part in the inception of Christianity. For example, Luke's narration of Paul's legal trials makes it clear that Rome's government officials did not see him as guilty of treason or any other political treachery. The message to the reader is a decisive one: If Paul, one of Christianity's most active missionaries, posed no threat to the Roman Empire, then surely the Jewish sect was harmless.

When interpreting Acts, we must keep in mind that the stories Luke chooses to tell and the details that he includes are not incidental. Luke is shaping his history in a way that paints Christianity in a particular light. So, when we read Acts, the question that should dominate our thinking is not "Is this the way it happened?" but instead "What is Luke trying to communicate by including this story and these details?"

2. Remember: The Gospel Speeches in Acts Are Specifically Crafted, Not Comprehensive

At various key moments in Acts, a leader in the early Jesus movement gives a speech in front of a crowd. The first one of these, Peter's Pentecost sermon in Acts 2:14–36, is perhaps the most famous, but there are several more. These sermon-like speeches reach a wide range of audiences, from a multiethnic Jewish festival crowd (Acts 2) to Greek philosophers on Athen's Areopagus (Acts 17).

Despite the contradictory contexts and diversity of listeners, the speeches seem to echo one another. Scholars argue that the unifying message and themes exist because Luke carefully composes these speeches as a cohesive "gospel" for his narrative. This means that when we read Acts, we should not expect these sermons to give us a full picture of the preaching from the early church and we should not base our ideas about the Gospel on just these speeches. What we should do is read them alongside one another and ask: "Why is Luke laying out the Gospel in this particular way, and what might be missing from his articulation?"

Conclusion

The Gospels and Acts present the narrative groundwork for the whole of the New Testament. We learn about Jesus's teachings, ministry, death, and resurrection, the core basis for the Christian movement. Then we glimpse pieces of the church's earliest history in Acts, an account that provides a backdrop for the letters of the New Testament. Becoming familiar with the Gospels and Acts, and practicing responsible interpretation of them, is as important as a chef learning the basics of cooking. If one can master these foundational skills, they are on their way to prepare a multitude of dishes, whether they are of the culinary or biblical variety.

CHAPTER 9

New Testament Epistles and Revelation

I (JENNIFER) RECENTLY saw a cookbook entitled *Mastering My Mistakes in the Kitchen* by Dana Cown. The book lays out the misadventures the author experienced in her cooking journey, detailing her early ineptitude in the kitchen and how she improved alongside other, more experienced chefs. The cookbook is popular because untried or unconfident cooks can not only learn from someone else's mistakes but also advance their own skills through the examples she provides.

It is similarly helpful to look at the letters and apocalyptic literature of the New Testament as a record of the missteps and challenges of early Christians, problems that we can relate to and maybe even avoid if we learn from their mistakes. Readers can also benefit from the encouraging advice and spiritual metaphors woven throughout the epistles and Revelation, especially if they interpret these solidly within the limitations of their genres and historical contexts.

With such limitations in mind, this chapter will give an introduction to the genre and authorship matters of ancient letters, discuss the general content of the New Testament Epistles, and provide tips for interpreting these letters well. Then, we will tackle the genre of apocalyptic literature and give some advice on reading Revelation with restraint and competence.

The Epistles

"Epistle" is another word for letter, and this genre of literature was a very important form of communication in the ancient world. Epistles served as formal substitutes for personal presence when military, religious, and family leaders were unable to travel to send messages. They are also examples of something called "situational literature" or "occasional literature"—that is, pieces of writing whose purpose is to address situations or occasions particular to a certain time period and group of people. Epistles were written with a very specific audience in mind—either an individual or a small group.

New Testament epistles can be broken into two categories: Paul's letters and general letters (also known as "catholic letters," with a small *c*, meaning letters that were written to a general audience and not to a specific person or church).

Paul's Letters

Paul was a multicultural individual. In his case, he was Jewish by birth and heritage, but he was raised and educated in the Greek city of Tarsus, and he was a Roman citizen who traveled widely across the empire during his life. It should not surprise anyone, then, that when he wrote to the churches he had started (and to some he hadn't) across the Mediterranean world, he used the writing genre that was then common in Greco-Roman society—the epistle. Paul wrote epistles to churches as a way of replicating his authoritative presence so he could guide and inspire struggling churches when he couldn't visit them in person.

Thirteen letters in the New Testament are attributed to Paul, but most contemporary scholars agree that Paul did not write all thirteen of these. We cannot be certain about which ones he did or didn't write, nor can we know who the alternative authors are. Determining authorship of letters from the ancient world is a tricky business. There are a number of reasons for this.

First, senders of letters during the first century almost never wrote their letters with their own hands. That's what a scribe, or an amanuensis, was for. We know for sure that some of Paul's letters were penned by an amanuensis. That's because in several cases they introduce themselves in the letters (see Romans 16:22: "I Tertius, the writer of this letter, greet you in the Lord"). Still, it is likely that in each of these cases, Paul dictated the letter in question.

There are two other ancient practices that complicate the question of authorship: delegated authorship and pseudepigraphy. In cases of delegated authorship, a sender would assign a trusted companion or coworker the job of writing a letter in their name.

For example, Paul might have asked one of his missionary buddies, like Silas or Timothy, to write a letter to a church in his name. The content of the letter might be very close to what Paul would have written himself, but the exact words could have been formed by an associate. In other words, the letter would have Paul's name on it, and the recipients might consider it to be from Paul, but the vocabulary and sentence structure could sound different from letters Paul dictated. We also know that many of Paul's letters were cowritten with his companions, and any of those may have a different feel because other authors contributed to the content.

Pseudepigraphy is another common practice in ancient letter writing. A book or letter is considered pseudepigraphal when one person writes it but another person is named as the author, usually without that person's permission or knowledge. A majority of contemporary New Testament scholars consider the letters of 1 and 2 Timothy and Titus to be pseudepigraphal epistles, written to Timothy and Titus after Paul's death but purporting to be from Paul. The fact that Paul didn't actually pen a letter, however, doesn't mean it is useless or should be thrown out of the Bible. We just have to be careful about including such letters in our *Well, Paul said this. . .* arguments, and we should also acknowledge that the letters may be from a later time period or reflect theology that does not fit well with Paul's ideals and practices.

Paul's letters share some common themes, but more often than not, the content of his correspondences with churches focused on different issues depending on the recipients and their circumstances. The following list shows the New Testament letters that are attributed to Paul with some brief descriptions. The letters with asterisks are those considered to have genuine Pauline authorship, and the ones with the hashtags are disputed letters, considered by many scholars to be pseudepigraphal. Note that the list is in canonical order (how the letters appear in the New Testament) rather than chronological order (which we cannot know with certainty).

- Romans*: Paul introduces himself to the church in Rome, which he has never visited, and he explains key pieces of the gospel to them in a way that addresses divisions and misconceptions that plague them.
- 1 Corinthians*: Paul addresses specific problems Corinthian Christians are dealing with, like division and the lure of their former pagan practices and philosophies.
- 2 Corinthians*: Paul writes again after an estrangement with the Corinthians, defending his ministry and offering reconciliation.

- Galatians*: Paul is angry at the Galatians for believing a different gospel than the one he preached to them.
- Ephesians#: Paul encourages believers to be united and live Spirit-centered lives as they navigate their Roman culture.
- Philippians*: Paul reassures the church that he is doing fine in prison and urges them to be humble (like Jesus) in the midst of church conflict.
- Colossians#: Paul writes that Jesus is greater than any religious or spiritual tradition they might want to adopt.
- 1 Thessalonians*: Paul motivates his audience in the midst of the persecution they are facing.
- 2 Thessalonians#: This one is similar to but more insistent than 1 Thessalonians.
- 1 Timothy#: Paul writes to Timothy about the problems he is facing leading a church.
- 2 Timothy#: Paul looks back over his ministry at the end of his life.
- Titus#: Paul helps Titus deal with the Cretans to whom he is ministering
- Philemon*: Paul persuades a slaveowner to accept his runaway slave back and treat him like a family member.

Looking at this list, we can see how complicated the issue of Pauline authorship is, and we can also recognize how the authors tailored their letter content to specific recipients. The letters attributed to Paul act as a window into one strand of early Christianity, and they help contemporary readers get a glimpse of the difficulties that early followers of Jesus faced in the Roman Empire. We should not, however, use them as a source for systematic theology or a definitive guide to how early Christianity operated. Let us explain why.

Yes, it is true that Pauline letters provide some helpful advice for Christian living that can sometimes cross over well into our context. They also offer us beautiful metaphors about community, the cross, love, and unity. However, the authors were primarily concerned with addressing the particular and contextual needs of specific people and congregations, and they had no idea we would be reading their words almost two thousand years later and quoting their letters on our youth camp T-shirts (*I can do all things through Christ who strengthens me!*).

The General (or Catholic) Letters

The letters in the New Testament that aren't attributed to Paul are even more difficult to pin down authorship for than the Pauline epistles. These letters are often called the "general" or "catholic letters" because (with the exception of 2 and 3 John) they tend to be addressed to audiences that are wider than just one congregation. The general epistles include Hebrews (which is not really a letter at all), James, 1 and 2 Peter, 1–3 John (also known as the Johannine epistles), and Jude. Each of these is attributed to an apostle except Hebrews, but scholars tell us that it is unlikely that any of them were actually written by the apostle with whom they are associated.

Despite their dubious authorship, these letters are still excellent sources of information that can teach us about the community life and struggles of the earliest Christians. For example, the Johannine letters, 2 Peter, and Jude give us a particular glimpse into the main challenges of the early church; namely, the diverse and false teachings about Jesus that were widespread in the first century, and the persecution that some Christians faced under Roman rule.

Scholars agree that 1 Peter is addressed to churches that were experiencing trials and persecution for their faith. Hebrews shows us that some Christians were becoming complacent in living out their lives of faith, failing to persevere during times of testing or doubt. James paints a picture of Christ followers who had devolved into expressing their faith merely as a feeling or mental assent instead of enacting their faith through kind and generous actions in their community.

As you can see, the specifics varied from epistle to epistle. But all of these letters contain strong encouragement for believers around the Mediterranean world as they strived to live as a minority religious group in a society that could be antagonistic and even hostile toward them.

Tips for Interpreting Epistles

Here are some tips for studying epistles in their context:

1. Remember We Aren't the First Audience

Ancient letters are what's known as situational or occasional literature, written with a specific audience and specific problems in mind. This means that when twenty-first century people try to read and interpret epistles written to first-century Jews, Greeks, and Romans, we face quite an interpretive gap. We don't know all the circumstances of the people who received a letter like 1 Corinthians, their ethnic and cultural makeup or their social problems and situations. We can do our best to piece information together from the letters themselves and from some historical information, but we are never going to understand it all. We are essentially listening in on one side of a two-sided conversation, like someone trying to guess what another person is saying on the other side of a cell phone call by just hearing the person in front of them. When we interpret letters, then, we must refrain from filling in gaps with our own cultural experience, and we must be careful not to apply the advice given to the original audience directly to our context.

For example, in 1 Corinthians 14:34, Paul writes, "Women should be silent in the churches. For they are not permitted to speak but should be subordinate." It would be irresponsible for us to apply this directly to our churches today because there is a specific problem that Paul is addressing here. Earlier in the letter, he talked about women praying and prophesying in church, and this verse is a continuation of that circumstance. Thus, his admonition in chapter 14 cannot be a rule to be enforced at all churches in all times. It is meant to be a response to a particular problem. We cannot be certain today what exact problem he refers to; he is not clear about that. However, we should take care when we interpret this passage for our context because it was not written for us in our time. This care should also be taken with other passages throughout the letters because many of the issues the biblical authors address are specific to their time and circumstances.

2. Be Aware of the Patriarchal Nature of Household Codes

There is one specific subgenre in the New Testament letters that has caused much pain and harm to people in our contemporary context, and that is a category of biblical texts known as "household codes." In several places in the epistles (Ephesians 5, Colossians 3, 1 Peter 2, and in the background of 1 Timothy and Titus), the authors make use of Greco-Roman household codes when giving advice to Christians. Such household codes were often written by philosophers like Aristotle and detailed how various members of a family should relate to their *paterfamilias*, or the head of the household.

What's important to remember about this is that the family structure in the Roman Empire was rigidly patriarchal and the oldest male had complete power over the wives, concubines, children, slaves, and other relatives that belonged to their household. These groups had to obey their master in everything and were often subject to abuse at the hands of the *paterfamilias*. This was a key feature of the culture of the time.

When New Testament writers replicate these codes in the epistles, they make small changes to tailor them to the Christian family and household. They do not, however, completely alter the structure that was so central to family life in the empire. It is worth noting that many of the New Testament writers assumed that Jesus was going to return within their lifetimes. Therefore, fighting against their culture by completely altering the structure of the family would not have been a pressing concern. Such countercultural measures would not likely have been immediately successful even if they had been pursued.

When interpreting the passages that include household codes, it is vital to remember that these passages tell us much more about how people in the Roman Empire structured their family than they do about how God wanted Christians to structure their families for all of human history.

The Book of Revelation

There is no book quite like Revelation in the New Testament. Curiously, though it is one book, it is in fact a combination of several different genres of literature. The first three chapters are structured like a set of letters, sent to the seven churches in Asia Minor. But the book also claims to be a prophecy (Revelation 1:3) (a common genre from the Hebrew Bible) and a genre known as a literary apocalypse (*apokalupsis* in Greek, which means to uncover or reveal, hence the name Revelation). It is this last type of literature that gives the book its dramatic and otherworldly flair. Apocalyptic literature is a genre that can be found in the Hebrew Bible and in other Jewish literature that was written in the Second Temple period (roughly 516 BCE–70 CE).

Apocalyptic literature first became popular during times of oppression and persecution for the Jewish people. The book of Daniel, for example, was written after Israel had been under the rule of several different empires, and its visions of beasts and angels amplify the situation the people are facing by merging the earthly troubles of human empires with drama in the heavenly realm between good and evil creatures. Revelation does the same thing, using images from Daniel, Ezekiel, and Zechariah to speak to the situation of Christians living in the Roman Empire at the end of the first century.

Although various interpreters throughout church history have tried to make Revelation into a book whose vivid imagery literally scares the hell out of people, the book is in fact meant to be a beacon of hope for people whose faith may be wavering as they suffer under the greed and violence of empire. The message that John, the named author of Revelation, receives and passes on to the seven churches is one that wakes them up to the real possibility that they will lose their faith and—yes—experience suffering. But Revelation also encourages them with the message that no matter how bad things may seem, no matter how long evil seems to have had the upper hand, Jesus will return to set things right. Good will triumph in the end, Revelation exhorts its audience, telling them that whatever is happening, just hold on a little longer.

Tips for Interpreting Apocalyptic Literature

It is very common for Christians to misinterpret apocalyptic literature or to have picked up fantastical and erroneous readings from pastors and pop culture. For this reason, we have some suggestions for how to interpret Revelation with historical and literary prowess.

1. Keep Historical Context in Mind

Revelation has fascinated biblical readers for generations, so there is naturally a rich and convoluted history of interpretation for the book. There are people who have favored a futurist view of the symbols and references in it, claiming that the author was laying out a map to the end times, complete with accurate descriptions of what will happen to people when Jesus comes back.

There are others who have held a historicist view, ascribing the various visions in Revelation to particular time periods in human history. To these interpreters, Revelation is a map of major events from history, including wars and other disasters, even those in the modern era. Neither of these approaches, however, takes seriously the genre or context of Revelation.

The two most responsible ways to read the apocalyptic portions of Revelation are by taking what are called the "preterist" and "idealist" views. Preterists rightly read Revelation as speaking to its own historical context—that is, the time period in which it was written, the Roman Empire in the first century. In this view, the symbols refer to figures from the early church, and the events shown in the visions all find fulfillment in the first century or soon after. Those with an idealist approach, for their part, interpret Revelation as a general account of good versus evil, a tale with a goal similar to Tolkien's *Lord of the Rings*.

These are two different approaches, but they can also be combined. An interpreter doesn't have to choose between them. For example, one could read most of the symbols as referring to real situations in the first century but also interpret some of the visions as sketching a *general* picture of how good will defeat evil in the end.

The recipe for responsible interpretation of Revelation, then, might look like this: Apply a hefty portion of historical and contextual investigation with a dash of faith concerning God's ability to set things right in the future.

2. Know Your Hebrew Bible

A large number of the symbols in Revelation refer back to other Jewish apocalyptic literature. For example, the four horsemen and creatures from Revelation 4–8 allude to the horses and riders mentioned in Zechariah 6 and the four creatures from Ezekiel 1 and 14. Some of the references are subtle, but dozens of the allusions and motifs that the author of Revelation uses can be traced back to the literature of the Hebrew Bible.

If you want to even begin to understand what the symbols in Revelation mean, you have to go back to their Old Testaments roots (and even then, you won't be able to catch all the references). So, do your Hebrew Bible cross-reference homework when it comes to Revelation—large language models (ChatGPT and the like) may not do a great job of theological interpretation, but they can help you identify what images and motifs appear in other literary works. Just make sure to use discernment when using AI, because it can suggest false or biased connections as it pulls from nonacademic sources across the internet.

3. Keep Hyperbolic Warnings and Violent Rhetoric in Their Place

There are violent images and disturbing warnings throughout Revelation, each designed to elicit emotional response in its audience. Some of them are hyperbolic or exaggerative warnings that serve to jolt empire-compromised readers into repentance, and others paint disturbing depictions of the war, pestilence, and death that will be rained down on the enemies who have oppressed God's people.

It is important to keep in mind that such extreme descriptions are an inherent part of apocalyptic literature; the ancient genre operates from an understanding that fear is a strong catalyst for change and that oppressed people feel a sense of rightness or even comfort when they know their persecutors will face justice one day. First-century Jesus followers (and other people harmed by empire throughout history) needed great change in their situation to imagine survival and salvation. The rhetoric of Revelation prompts such change in its readers and promises (in disconcerting detail) that the tables *will* turn for the powerful and the powerless; it may just be painful for Christians until that revolution occurs.

Conclusion

The Epistles and the book of Revelation provide contemporary readers with a greater understanding about the challenges and growing pains the first-century church experienced as a new religious movement in the Roman Empire. We can learn much from the trials early Christians faced and the missteps they took as they acclimated to their new beliefs and practices.

In fact, the entire history of the church can serve as a handbook of "lessons learned" for contemporary Christians. The next chapter provides a sliver of that history as we discuss the ways that people have interpreted the Bible throughout the centuries. The history of biblical interpretation often ends up feeling like a chronicle of what not to do when it comes to reading Scripture, but there is much for us to learn from both the positive and negative examples of our ancestors in the faith.

CHAPTER 10

The History of Biblical Interpretation

It would be very difficult to ask someone to make food if they had never seen food made before. And yet we often interpret the Bible without having any sense of how the Bible has been interpreted by communities before us in history. As with most things in life, it's easy to assume that the way we do things is the way things have always been done. But also as with most things in life, this is rarely true. The way we interpret the Bible today is often quite different from the way religious and non-religious people have interpreted the Bible in the past.

Knowing that gives us freedom, because if the way the Bible has been interpreted has changed over time, then it can and will change again. If you feel trapped by the interpretations of people around you, you can rest assured that those interpretations will pass. And if you feel inspired by the interpretations of people around you, you can feel grateful that you're living in a time and a place where those interpretations exist and then take an active role in preserving them for as long as possible.

With all that in mind, let's take a moment to explore the way the Bible has been interpreted. Just as you might get ideas for cooking from watching a documentary on famous foods made in the past, you might find some new ideas about ways to interpret Scripture.

Interpretation Within the Hebrew Bible

When thinking about biblical interpretation, people sometimes find themselves wondering about the origins of the process. Given all we've discussed thus far, it's reasonable to ask the questions "Who was the first person to interpret the Hebrew Bible, and how did they do it?" The answers might surprise you. The interpretation of the Hebrew Bible began even before the Hebrew Bible in its current form existed. Interpretation of the Hebrew Bible, in fact, begins in the Hebrew Bible itself.

Here's what we mean by that: Since the texts that make up the Hebrew Bible were written over the course of centuries, some of the ones written latest were composed by people who knew about and had access to some of those that were written earliest. This knowledge and access made it possible for them to interpret these earlier texts, which they did, sometimes in very surprising ways.

In chapter 5 of this book, which introduces the Pentateuch, we mentioned that some later laws are reinterpretations and reworkings of earlier laws. And in chapter 7, which introduces the Writings, we mentioned that 1 and 2 Chronicles retell the history of ancient Israel and rewrite many of its major characters. Let's look at a couple more examples of later texts that interpret earlier ones.

Micah Is Saved by Jeremiah

Deuteronomy 18:14–22 describes what a prophet is supposed to be able to do: The criteria for distinguishing between a false prophet and an authentic one is the prophet's ability to accurately predict the future. In other words, if what a prophet says will happen comes true, then they're legit.

There are some practical problems with this criteria. The main one is that if a prophet foretells doom, then having to wait until after the doom arrives (or doesn't) to know whether or not they're legitimate is a bit of a bummer. In practical terms, a prophet's legitimacy becomes something that future generations, not the prophet's contemporaries, get to decide. The book of Micah offers an important biblical example of this.

Writing in the latter part of the eighth century BCE, when the Neo-Assyrian Empire is coming to destroy Jerusalem, Micah prophesies that the city will be destroyed, saying, "Zion will be plowed like a field. Jerusalem will become a heap of rubble, the temple hill a mound overgrown with thickets" (3:12). He is foretelling that Jerusalem will be destroyed, just like the capital of northern Israel, Samaria, was destroyed a short time before.

It turns out, though, that Jerusalem is not destroyed in Micah's lifetime or at any time in the next century. Anyone living in Micah's time would have believed him to be a false prophet according to the criteria set down in Deuteronomy 18.

But the story has an interesting twist. More than a hundred years later, at the beginning of the sixth century BCE, the prophet Jeremiah found himself about to be executed for prophesying the destruction of

Jerusalem at the hands of the Babylonians—a message that was considered by King Zedekiah's officials to be treasonous. However, Jeremiah 26:16–18 says that the prophet's execution is halted when some gathered elders recall that Micah prophesied the same thing.

In this way, a later generation retroactively legitimized Micah's prophetic career by finding a new way to interpret his words. Micah had been speaking about the crisis of the Neo-Assyrian empire, but Jeremiah's audience found it more helpful to apply his words to the Babylonian crisis of a different period. And lo and behold, the Babylonians do in fact destroy Jerusalem in Jeremiah's lifetime.

As you'll see, when we discuss the New Testament's use of the Hebrew Bible, later communities finding new meaning in older texts is quite common.

Wrestling with Multivocality in 2 Chronicles

The books of 1 and 2 Chronicles do interesting interpretive work in the way that they handle tensions and contradictions in earlier texts. As we've noted, the Bible is a multivocal text. Even the Bible itself acknowledges this when it goes out of its way to try to "fix" things that came before.

For example, Exodus 12:9 gives specific instructions on how the Passover meal is to be prepared. The verse is clear that the meat *should not* be boiled (the Hebrew word is *bashel*) but roasted over a fire instead. Yet Deuteronomy 16:7 explicitly instructs that the meat is to be boiled (again, *bashel*). Such contradictory directions can't be followed in real-life practice. Either you follow one instruction or the other.

So what is the author of 2 Chronicles 35:13 supposed to say when describing the way the king, Josiah, perfectly celebrates the Passover? The answer is one of interpretation: The author puts the commands together, saying Josiah had the meat "boiled in fire." Since boiling requires a liquid and fire doesn't do so well in liquid, this statement is, strictly speaking, silly. It's also a valuable illustration of one ancient way that interpreters attempted to deal with the multivocality of Scripture.

Contradictions Concerning David

Another interesting interpretation of Hebrew Scripture within Hebrew Scripture concerns the slaying of Goliath. In one of the most famous stories in the Bible, found in 1 Samuel 17, David kills Goliath. But in 2 Samuel 21:19, one of David's elite warriors, a man named Elhanan, kills Goliath instead. So who actually killed Goliath?

One Chronicles 20:5 gets around this contradiction by repeating the story found in 2 Samuel 21, but changing it to say that Elhanan didn't kill Goliath but rather Goliath's brother. This change is entirely fictitious. The author took the word for Elhanan's place of origin, "Bethlemite," and chopped it up to invent the name "Lachmi" that is used for Goliath's brother. The word *lachmi* would mean "my bread" and isn't a real name.

The two books of Chronicles not only attempt to correct contradictions but they also introduce new contradictions of their own. One good example of this concerns the census David takes near the very end of his life. In 2 Samuel 24:1, God incites David to take a census of his people, and then later punishes David for taking the census. This portrait of God is quite fickle, malicious even. But the author of 1 Chronicles 21:1 clearly didn't think this was an accurate way to tell the story, because in their retelling of the story, that verse is changed to say that *Satan* incites David to take the census instead.

Well, who incited David, then, God or Satan? There's a big difference between the two, with the answer holding potentially profound theological implications. So how does one decide?

While we can't read the minds of ancient authors, it's not difficult to see why someone would be more comfortable with the prospect of Satan doing a bad thing than God doing a bad thing. Thinking back on all the changes 1 and 2 Chronicles makes, we feel prompted to ask: Is someone's comfort what ultimately decides the content of biblical stories? And in a very real way, the answer is *yes*.

Writing for Comfort

As we've established, biblical authors were writing for communities with certain desires, concerns, and beliefs. Meeting those desires, addressing those concerns, and respecting those beliefs made a text feel comfortable for those communities. Yet the criteria for comfort is not static. In the centuries between the earliest texts in the Hebrew Bible and the latest ones, people's desires, concerns, and beliefs changed, and so newer biblical authors responded by reinterpreting old stories so the stories could make them comfortable again.

We may find ourselves surprised by how thoroughly and how radically later parts of the Hebrew Bible interpret earlier parts. This is especially true for those of us who used to believe, or continue to believe, that the Bible is the inerrant word of God—always correct, unchangeable, and sacrosanct—and that altering it is tantamount to heresy. The authors of the Hebrew Bible, however, didn't share this view. They wanted to create a text that served their needs, and they made bold interpretive moves to get it.

The New Testament Use of the Hebrew Bible

One fascinating aspect of human life is that people are master imitators. We learn language and culture and habits and manners by imitating the people around us. We learn to cook and to master recipes by imitating others, whether it be a parent or a famous chef.

We also learn to interpret the Bible by imitating the way others interpret. Many of us unconsciously (or consciously) learn ways to read Scripture from our pastors or our parents or even religious social media creators. We may even pick up ways to interpret the Bible from the biblical writers themselves.

Think about it. The New Testament authors use quotes and stories from their sacred Scriptures throughout their writings; in fact, about 10 percent of the New Testament contains references to the Hebrew Bible! Every time these authors quote or allude to these Scriptures, they are illustrating different ways to interpret.

The question for us is: Do the New Testament authors model helpful interpretive methods or do they utilize Scripture in ways that we should avoid? Let's take a look at some of the characteristics of the New Testament authors' use of the Old Testament to see which ones are model-worthy and which ones aren't.

Appreciate, Don't Emulate

Foundationally, it is important to recognize that the writers of the New Testament frequently did not reference the Hebrew Scripture in the ways we would expect them to. Instead of quoting it word for word, they often paraphrased its content, communicated the gist of its stories, alluded to its ideas, and loosely used its motifs, themes, and images.

That may bother some of us contemporary readers of Scripture—we like to be precise in our quotation of Scripture—but this practice was common for first-century Jews. Not many people in Roman-occupied Judea and Galilee were literate, so it makes sense that general references to Scripture leaned more toward summary or gist than exact citation. Very few people had access to the scrolls that contained the texts. Oral traditions concerning the content of the Bible also influenced people's recollections and interpretations of passages.

A quick example from the Gospel of John can illustrate the kind of allusion that New Testament authors often used. In a conversation with Nicodemus narrated in John 3, Jesus says, "And just as Moses lifted up the serpent in the wilderness, so must the Son of Man be lifted up, that whoever believes in him may have eternal life." This line is a nebulous reference to a story from Numbers 21, in which Moses fashions a bronze serpent to heal people who were bitten by poisonous snakes.

The book of John does not quote any part of the Numbers story or even explain the content of the strange incident in the wilderness; instead, the author simply makes a brief reference, assuming that his audience will know what he is alluding to. Such use of the Hebrew Bible is common in the New Testament, but it may be dangerous for us to emulate this kind of approximation today.

Why? Because if we try to communicate biblical ideas with vague allusions to stories and figures from the Hebrew Bible, we will likely fail. People today just don't have the same level of familiarity with the Jewish Scriptures that early Christians would have had. If we want to responsibly interpret Scripture for ourselves and our communities, we need to understand that sometimes the New Testament writers use references to the Hebrew Bible that are obscure and elusive to modern readers. This was their ancient style. But just because they approximate their interpretations when they communicate does not mean we should do the same in our quotations and interpretations of Scripture today.

Out-of-Context Interpretation

Like authors of later books in the Old Testament, the New Testament writers also used some passages from the Hebrew Bible in ways that did not match their original literary contexts. In fact, these writers sometimes interpreted verses to mean something quite different from what they originally meant. The key to understanding such use is to recognize that this kind of citation usually happened in service of the author's own persuasive arguments or purposes.

One popular example of an out-of-context Hebrew Bible reference is found in Matthew 2, when the author narrates Jesus, Mary, and Joseph returning from Egypt after their time as refugees. The author of Matthew boldly quotes from Hosea 11 with the line, "Out of Egypt I have called my son." In its original context, the verse refers to God liberating Israel from Egyptian slavery. When Matthew cites it to refer to Jesus leaving Egypt to go back to Nazareth, it may seem to the reader like a stretch.

However, this reference does fit within a creative theme found in the book Matthew—the portrait of Jesus as a new Moses. Matthew weaves several details into the narrative that forge literary links between Moses and Jesus, including Herod killing baby boys, just like Pharaoh did, and Jesus fasting in the wilderness for forty days, just like the forty-year wandering of Moses and the Israelites. Exercising creative license, Matthew's author applies the Hosea passage to his message because it adds to this motif about Jesus being a new Moses.

So, is Matthew's use of the Hosea passage consistent with its original context? No, but original context isn't the concern here. Connecting Jesus to the figure and work of Moses is the much more important goal.

What does this mean to interpreters of Scripture today? You may wonder: Should contemporary interpreters use the Hebrew Bible in the way that Matthew does?

Our view is that in most cases this is best avoided. Instead, we urge people to familiarize themselves with the original contexts of Old Testament passages and use them in ways that honors those contexts rather than deviate from them. Doing this will ensure that we don't misuse or diminish the importance of the Hebrew Bible by ignoring its backgrounds and messages.

Typology and Other Jesus-Centered Readings

Our example of out-of-context interpretation leads us to another kind of interpretation that the New Testament writers use—typology. *Typology* is a kind of interpretation in which symbols, people, or events in the

Hebrew Bible are interpreted as "types" that foreshadow the work of Jesus.

In one on-the-nose example, Paul describes Adam as a "pattern" or "type" of Jesus, or "the one who is to come" (Romans 5:14). By using the Adam figure from Genesis to point to Jesus, Paul is trying to make a point about sin and grace. It is unlikely that Paul means that Adam's story was written with Jesus's story in mind. Rather, he is using it to argue rhetorically for the necessity of grace.

Despite this, many well-meaning Christians today follow the examples of typology provided by New Testament authors like Paul and try to find Jesus all over the Hebrew Bible. "Remember the mysterious figure spotted in the fiery furnace with Shadrach, Meshach, and Abednego?" an enthusiastic typological interpreter might say. "That must have been Jesus, and this story foreshadows Jesus's power over death." We must be careful not to "find" Jesus under every rock in the Old Testament. When we do that, we fail to let the Hebrew Scriptures speak in their own context, on their own terms. This can lead to us disrespecting the Jewish Scriptures—and misinterpreting them as well.

Modern-day interpreters are not in the same situation that New Testament ones were. The New Testament writers were interpreting the Hebrew Bible in light of the Jesus event—his ministry and teachings and death and resurrection. Their audiences were familiar with Old Testament characters and stories, so they used them for a specific purpose: to communicate their theological points and forge a connection between the fledgling Christians and their Jewish Scriptures and background.

Interpreters of the Hebrew Bible today should not imitate this interpretive strategy. There are much better ways to read the Hebrew Bible, ways that will honor the original authors and contexts of the Scriptures and communicate to our contemporary context more effectively. We will address those better ways in the next several chapters.

Early Jewish Interpretation

Many lessons can be learned from the ways ancient and medieval Jewish people interpreted the Hebrew Bible. Of particular note is a prominent style of Jewish interpretation used during these time periods called midrash, from the Hebrew word for "to seek." The practice of midrash often involves the creative invention of stories that exist parallel to biblical passages. Midrash was often employed when Jewish interpreters encountered tensions and contradictions in the biblical text. Rather than see these factors as obstacles, the interpreters saw them as opportunities, perhaps even invitations, to add to the text's divine revelation.

Midrash in Practice

Consider, for example, some of the prominent contradictions in the flood stories of Genesis 6–9, which we discussed in chapter 5. Did Noah bring one pair of animals onto the ark (Genesis 6:19–20) or seven pairs of clean and one pair of unclean animals (Genesis 7:2–3)? The thirteenth-century Jewish sage Nachmanides addresses this inconsistency with a story, saying that one pair of animals came to the ark by themselves, but then Noah had to go out and capture the additional seven pairs of clean animals himself.

Here's another example: Did the flood come from heaven and earth bursting open (Genesis 7:11), or from more conventional rain (Genesis 7:12)? The Zohar Chadash, a collection of mystical commentaries from the late medieval period, claims that it's both, saying that the flood came first as a merciful rain, which gave humanity an opportunity to repent. Only after that did the waters come as a more devastating flood.

And what about the bird Noah sends out after the completion of the flood? Is it a raven (as stated in Genesis 8:7) or a dove (Genesis 8:8–12)? Rashi, a twelfth-century Jewish sage, explains that the raven didn't do what Noah wanted because it was destined to serve Elijah generations later in 1 Kings 17:6. As a result, Noah switched and sent out the dove.

Now, does the biblical text itself say any of these things? No. Nevertheless, centuries of Jewish interpreters felt free to compose bite-sized parallel stories that, when read in combination with the biblical stories, turn tension into fruitful reflection. These parallel stories don't change the biblical text, and they don't *have* to be read alongside the biblical text. As a result, they respect the multivocality of the Bible by letting the Bible be what it is.

Letting Anachronisms Be Anachronisms

Midrash was not, however, used by all ancient and medieval Jewish thinkers to interpret tensions in the biblical text. Some in fact approached these tensions in ways that anticipated the concerns of biblical scholars from the later modern period—roughly the late eighteenth to the early nineteenth centuries. One such thinker was Abraham Ibn Ezra, also known as Abenezra, a twelfth-century poet, Jewish philosopher, and biblical scholar born in modern-day Spain.

In Abenezra's commentary on the Pentateuch, instead of employing the practice of midrash, he points out several anachronisms in the text that require an author other than Moses. For example, Deuteronomy 1:1 says, "These are the words Moses spoke to all Israel *on the other side* of the Jordan River." Such a statement could only be made from the perspective of someone who is already in the land of Israel, west of the Jordan, while Moses is standing on the eastern shore and forbidden from crossing over. Other anachronisms include the description of Moses's death in Deuteronomy 34 (which Moses couldn't have written himself) and the statement in Genesis 12:6 that the Canaanites were in the land *then* rather than now.

Midrash generally assumes that biblical texts are special, and that the tensions and contradictions in those texts exist for the spiritual benefit of its readers. Viewed through this lens, the tensions and contradictions aren't accidents but rather indications of deeper divine revelation waiting to be gleaned by those who are sufficiently attentive and imaginative. There's nothing wrong with treating the Bible as though it's special in this way; religious people do this with their sacred books all the time, but that's obviously not the kind of assumption we make with normal, everyday texts.

Yet when Abenezra treats anachronisms as anachronisms and contradictions as contradictions, he's treating biblical texts in the same way we treat normal, everyday texts. And when the text is treated in this way, a whole new set of questions come up.

Once we no longer assume that something special is happening in the text, anachronisms and contradictions raise important questions about the text's composition, including from whom, when, why, and how did the text come together such that it has these features? Because earlier generations of Bible readers tended to make assumptions about the text's special nature, these questions of composition tended not to come up. But once those assumptions began to fade, these questions come to dominate many scholars' study of the Bible.

Early and Medieval Christian Interpretation

The method of biblical interpretation used in the early centuries of the church and throughout the Middle Ages is called *premodern interpretation*. It is characterized by diverse methods of interpretation that often lean toward spiritual or practical concerns. This means that early and medieval interpreters often focused their study of Scripture on what they called the *sensus plenior*—that is, the fuller sense or meaning of the text that they believed was intended by God. They also used interpretations of Scripture to defend the legitimacy of their Christian faith.

Why did it need defending? Because in its first three centuries, Christianity was essentially a fledgling sect that had to negotiate its place in the religious landscape of the Roman Empire. Christians were so new on the scene that they were considered untrustworthy; because of this, they became scapegoats, were accused of engaging in moral taboos, and faced some persecution.

Understandably, Christian thinkers tried to establish Christianity as a stable religious sect that posed no threat to the empire. One way that they went about this was through *apologetic interpretation*: using reasoned arguments to defend or justify beliefs. Justin Martyr, one early apologist for the faith, wrote his First Apology around 150 CE. In it, he defended the morality of Christians and the philosophical legitimacy of the Christian faith.

Justin claimed in the First Apology that the Hebrew Bible was full of predictive oracles—from Moses, David, Isaiah, and others—who divinely prophesied details of Jesus's life, ministry, and death. He also expanded the typological interpretation of the Hebrew Bible by the New Testament authors, providing in his apology even more scriptural evidence for the events recorded in the Gospels. As we discussed above, typology is a kind of allegorical interpretation that seeks a deeper meaning in texts: specifically, meaning that looks forward to what kind of person Jesus is and what things he will do.

Here's one example of apologetic and typological interpretation by Justin Martyr: He claimed that Psalm 22, including the line "they divide my clothes among themselves" (v. 18), prophesies the details of Jesus's crucifixion. This interpretation lends credence to Christianity because it suggests that the death of their Lord and leader was part of the message of an ancient, religious source (the Hebrew Bible). It is true that the Gospel writers use lines from Psalm 22 in their accounts of Jesus's crucifixion, and Mark may even have constructed his passion account around the psalm. But that does not mean the psalmist wrote it to prophesy Jesus's suffering, as apologetic and typological interpretation implies.

In a similar vein, an important church father from the third century, Origen, used *analogy* or *allegorical interpretation* in his treatment of Scripture. Origen insisted that divine wisdom in Scripture was best accessed through allegorical interpretation, especially when the literal reading produced a picture of God that did not measure up to the divine character. Origen further believed that there were three senses to Scripture—the literal, the moral, and the spiritual.

Augustine of Hippo, perhaps the most influential Christian leader from early Church history, built upon Origen's three senses and argued for the fourfold sense of Scripture. These are:

- The literal sense: The text's surface meaning, which refers to real people, places, events from the past
- The allegorical sense: The text's symbolic or metaphorical meanings
- The moral sense: The text's teachings applied to our own lives
- The anagogical sense: The text's spiritual and heavenly significance

Augustine believed that Christian interpreters should read the Bible for the purpose of pursuing holy living, focusing on the three virtues of faith in God, hope in God, and love of God. For Augustine, if the literal meaning of a passage did not lead a reader to the love of God or love of neighbor, then the interpreter should find meaning in one of the other senses.

Interpretation in the Middle Ages generally falls in line with earlier Christian interpretations. Church theologians like Thomas Aquinas defended the idea that there were multiple meanings in a text, although he prioritized the literal sense. Aquinas also grouped the allegorical, moral, and anagogical sense under the heading of the "spiritual sense" of Scripture. For Aquinas, then, two main senses of Scripture exist: the literal and the spiritual.

Another type of interpretation that comes out of the Middle Ages—*mystical* or *experiential interpretation*—can be observed in the writings of mystics like Julian of Norwich. Julian was an anchorite who lived in fourteenth century England. An anchorite is someone who withdraws from society in order to experience God more profoundly but lives connected to a town church rather than moving away. Julian describes her visionary experiences of God and the passion of Christ in her book *Revelations of Divine Love*. The book is aptly titled because in it she demonstrates how she interprets Scripture through the lens of her experience of God's loving character. Julian believed that passages in the Bible that contradict the character of God we experience in Christ could not be true depictions of God.

Early and medieval models for interpreting Scripture should feel familiar to most contemporary Christians because searching for deeper, spiritual meaning in Bible passages is a common practice in churches today. Preaching also often involves communicating various senses of a text to a congregation, such as the moral or spiritual senses. Let the Bible interpreter be warned, however, because it is easy to let our imaginations and biases lead us far away from the text's original context and message.

The Rise of Critical Biblical Studies

In 1656, a Jewish Portuguese philosopher named Baruch Spinoza was forced out of his Jewish community for, among other things, denying that Moses wrote the Pentateuch. Mosaic authorship of the Pentateuch had been tradition since at least the Talmud from the second to the fifth century and had been made an essential article of the Jewish faith by Maimonides, a twelfth-century Jewish philosopher and theologian.

Spinoza cited Abenezra's commentary and the anachronisms he recorded as his reasons for denying Mosaic authorship. However, this wasn't a sufficient defense to spare him excommunication. Spinoza went on to have a robust career in philosophy, and his works on theology, politics, and ethics are often credited with helping provide the foundations of modern liberal democratic societies and the separation of church and state.

Key to Spinoza's approach to the Bible was the idea that it was a normal, everyday text, a product of its time, and prone to institutional abuse. Viewing it through this lens, Spinoza described the Bible as contradictory, fragmentary, and historically unreliable—evaluations that most biblical scholars share today.

Spinoza believed that the biblical text had come together through a very long and human process, and he thought that Ezra (the scribe from the book of Ezra) was a likely candidate for having composed the Pentateuch, while the rest of the canon was ultimately chosen from a range of available texts written by Pharisees in the second century BCE who studied and preserved those texts. He was convinced that it was human ideologies and powerful institutions that had enshrined these ideologies regarding who composed the various texts, as well when, why, and how the texts were written.

Critical Bible Scholarship

Another philosopher living at around this time shared Spinoza's approach to the Bible. Thomas Hobbes is best known in the field of intellectual history for his work on social contract theory and for his description of the natural state of life as "nasty, brutish, and short."

In the thirty-third chapter of Hobbes's most famous work, *Leviathan*, he undertakes the task of determining when all the canonical biblical books were composed. He dispenses with the possibility that Moses wrote the Pentateuch by appealing to many of the same anachronisms Abenezra noted and Spinoza repeated. He then continues in this vein, finding instances all throughout the historical books where the narrator says words to the effect of "and it is still that way to this day" and using them to argue that most biblical books were composed long after the time their stories are set. He concludes that Ezra brought most of the Hebrew Bible together, and that Christian councils decided the content of the New Testament.

He rehearses this history of composition in order to make the points that it's human authority that's ultimately responsible for the Bible we have today, and it's only through human authority that we have any knowledge of the divine revelation people supposedly received throughout history. Once again, the who, when, and why of the text's composition is attributed to human action—human action that can be understood with the same tools we'd use for any normal, everyday text.

Treating the Bible this way and subjecting it to the same kinds of questions we'd ask of any other text is called *critical biblical scholarship.*

Spinoza and Hobbes laid the foundations of critical biblical scholarship, which continued to flourish in the centuries after them.

Stitching the Bible Together

Later, in the eighteenth century, the French scholar Jean Astruc wanted to find a more systematic way to understand the repetitious and contradictory stories in the Pentateuch, such as the two creation stories, the two flood stories, and the two stories of Abraham's covenant. He examined the book of Genesis and noticed that whenever we see these repetitions, in one version of the story God is referred to by the generic title "Elohim," which just means "god" or "gods." But in the other version of the story, God is referred to by God's personal name, Yahweh.

Astruc came to believe that prior to the composition of Genesis, there were originally two ancient documents: one with a set of stories about God as Elohim and one with a set of stories about God as Yahweh. He concluded that a third party had later edited the two documents together to become the book of Genesis we have today. Although Astruc didn't have these original documents (nor have such documents been found since), the theory of their existence explained many things about the biblical text. Whereas early Christian allegories and Jewish Midrash had to invent new stories to explain each tension, contradiction, repetition, et cetera, Astruc's hypothesis explained many of these features all at once.

The nineteenth century saw Astruc's line of reasoning expanded. Eventually biblical scholars came to believe that there were a total of four originally independent documents behind the Pentateuch, each written in different times and different places, by different authors with very different theologies, which were then edited together to create the first five books of the Bible. This was called the "documentary hypothesis," and the hypothesis remained a dominant paradigm for thinking about the Pentateuch's composition up through the middle of the twentieth century, when it took on more nuanced forms. The nineteenth century also saw the identification of three authors for the book of Isaiah, who wrote their respective sections (First Isaiah, chapters 1–39; Second Isaiah, chapters 40–55; and Third Isaiah, chapters 56–66) over a period of two centuries.

Critical Bible scholarship continued into the twentieth century, when biblical scholars reasoned that Joshua, Judges, 1 and 2 Samuel, and

1 and 2 Kings were partially composed and then edited together during the Babylonian exile (597–539 BCE) by a historian who used the theology of the book of Deuteronomy to help explain why Jerusalem was destroyed and its line of Davidic kings ended. Studies of the social contexts in which psalms might be used implied that they hadn't been written by David, as widely believed, but rather by many different people over the centuries for a variety of religious purposes. Some of them, like Psalm 82, even preserved very old polytheistic theology. Similarly, linguistic and ideological studies on Proverbs and Ecclesiastes demonstrated that they weren't written by Solomon but rather were better explained as products of fifth century BCE or later, when languages like Persian became available to biblical authors and interethnic marriage became a hot button issue.

The twentieth century also enshrined important scholarly consensuses related to the New Testament, including the idea that only seven epistles—1 Thessalonians, Galatians, 1 and 2 Corinthians, Romans, Philemon, and Philippians—were authentically written by Paul, with the rest written by someone else in his name (these disputed letters are known as the deuteropauline letters). Also, the idea that the Gospels weren't composed until 70 CE or later—with Mark being written first, Matthew and Luke second, and John last—became solidified in biblical scholarship. Many of these consensus positions remain significant even today.

It's worth reiterating that these discoveries were only possible once Bible readers began to investigate the human dimensions of the biblical text using the same tools and theories they would use for any other piece of literature. In acknowledging this, we are *not* saying that the Bible isn't a special text or *cannot* be divinely inspired. We are simply noting that certain valuable insights about its history and composition are available to us only when it's read in a particular light.

The Fundamentalist Response

The last phase of biblical interpretation we'll discuss is best described as being a part of the *fundamentalist movement*, which was a reaction against modernist ideas and critical biblical scholarship. But the fundamentalist movement was more than just a response to what was happening in the academic world of biblical interpretation; it also served as a backlash countermovement to what was happening in society and in the sciences.

The fundamentalist movement got its start in the late nineteenth and early twentieth centuries as a reaction to yet another movement within American Protestant churches. Called the *social gospel* (or *social justice*) *movement*, this branch of Christians focused their energy on activism in urban areas and general social reform rather than on doctrine and religious traditions. The combination of the social changes caused by the Industrial Revolution, such as immigration and increased urbanization, and the pragmatic activism of Social Gospel proponents, frightened the more conservative sectors of American Christians. They feared that Christianity was losing its traditional values and moving away from the doctrine of *sola Scriptura* ("Scripture alone is important"), the idea that Scripture and not tradition, reason, or anything else is the ultimate authority for Christians, an idea which had dominated Protestantism since Martin Luther and the Reformation.

And social and theological shifts weren't the only threats that some Christians perceived. At the same time that the social gospel movement was spreading, the theory of natural selection launched by Charles Darwin and his contemporaries was changing the scientific world. The ripple effects of his theory of evolution created further panic among conservative Christians.

The new theory of evolution (and the archaeological evidence suggesting that the world was millions of years old) contradicted a literal interpretation of the first creation story in Genesis. In response, theologians and Bible scholars tried to reconcile traditional readings of Scripture with these new scientific principles. As part of this pursuit, some European and American scholars leaned further into modernism, adopting *theological liberalism*, meaning they used modern critical methods on the Bible and emphasized the ethical teachings over traditional doctrines. Other Protestant scholars and pastors pushed back against the scientific community and modernist ideas by doubling down on theological doctrines they deemed "fundamental" or traditionally core to the Christian faith.

The doctrines they doubled down on were ones that had been formed in direct opposition to liberal modernist theology. These became the main theological tenets of the fundamentalist movement. The five chosen fundamentals were: the historical accuracy and inerrancy of the Bible, the imminent and physical second coming of Jesus, the reality of Jesus's virgin birth, the bodily resurrection of Jesus, and the satisfaction theory of atonement (an early version of penal substitutionary theory of atonement, which is the idea that Jesus paid the penalty for our sins to satisfy the wrath of God).

Key to these fundamentals was the doctrine of inerrancy: the idea that the Bible has no errors and is true if it's interpreted correctly. This idea would come to dominate fundamentalist—and later evangelical—interpretation of Scripture. Although fundamentalism and evangelicalism are not synonymous, evangelical churches in the United States have been heavily influenced by fundamentalist doctrines.

While believers of inerrancy claim that they read the Bible literally, or pursue a plain sense reading of Scripture, they are actually applying their own theological lenses to their reading of Scripture. (You may recall that we touched upon this in part I of this book.) The doctrines that fundamentalists believe in, which include but are not limited to the five fundamentals, powerfully shape their interpretation of Scripture. For example, there are only a few verses in the New Testament letters that could be interpreted to support the penal substitutionary atonement theory. Yet fundamentalists prioritize a doctrinally influenced emphasis on, and interpretation of, those verses and downplay other passages that describe salvation in terms of God's love or God's defeat of evil.

Mainstream Christian universities and seminaries in the twentieth century rejected fundamentalist ideology, favoring modernist thought and critical biblical interpretation instead. In reaction to this rejection, fundamentalists and evangelicals began to form their own Bible colleges and seminaries, such as Moody Bible Institute, Liberty University, and Bob Jones University. Eventually, fundamentalists also started political groups like the Moral Majority and took over schools and even whole church denominations. (One example of this is the fundamentalist takeover of the Southern Baptist Convention in the 1980s.)

The result of this expansion of fundamentalism and evangelical doctrines was the widespread adoption of the doctrine of inerrancy and literalist interpretation of Scripture in churches across the United States. Today, the selective, literalist interpretation method that evangelicals favor—the kind that should be described as fundamentalist theological interpretation—is the dominant form of hermeneutics practiced by pastors and Christians in the church.

This popular interpretive practice is, however, a far cry from the interpretive approach that most Bible scholars and theologians employ.

The ideological gap between these two explains why the most recent work being done by scholars seems so distant from the biblical views set forth by people in the pews and by Christian content creators on social media.

When I (Jennifer) teach the Bible in evangelical settings, my students display no familiarity with even the basic biblical research I mention; in fact, they often feel threatened or upset by it. However, when I explain that the way they look at the Bible is part of a history of interpretation influenced by fundamentalist ideas, some of them can accept that there might be more than one way to read the Bible. And sometimes they can admit that listening to contemporary Bible scholars, those master chefs of interpretation, could help them uncover more depth and complexity in the Scriptures they love so much.

Conclusion

Just as we can learn much about cooking from reading about the history of food and famous chefs from the past, we as interpreters can benefit from studying the history of biblical interpretation. Readers have not always approached the Bible in the same way; there are a variety of influences, methods, and techniques that have evolved our interpretation of Scripture. Some of these methods serve as helpful examples (like looking at historical context) and others as cautionary examples (like ignoring literary context). But they are all instructive, encouraging us grow in our skills so that we might become better interpreters.

Now that we have laid out the basics of cooking, presenting the main ingredients of the biblical literature and interpretive history, we can move to the preparation stage. In the next section, we will introduce you to different ways interpreters like you can prepare the main ingredients of the Bible to feed yourself and others.

Part III

Preparing the Ingredients

JUST AS A chef takes ingredients and prepares them to be eaten by themselves and others, an interpreter takes biblical passages and interprets them to be meaningful for themselves and others. In part I, we learned about the role of chefs and interpreters. In part II, we learned about the basic ingredients an interpreter uses: the Bible and its many voices. Now in part III, we'll discuss how biblical passages are prepared—that is, made meaningful for people—through the use of interpretive questions.

In the opening chapters we learned that meaning is created by asking interpretive questions of a text. An interpretive question is a question that prioritizes one of a text's many contexts over the others. The reason different people get different meanings from the same passage is because they are asking different interpretive questions. In the next four chapters, we'll discuss some of the most common interpretive questions that biblical scholars pose to biblical texts so that you can learn how to ask these questions of the text as well.

Historical questions, concerning a biblical passages composition, are your bread-and-butter questions. These are the heartiest questions: dense, protein-heavy, and good for filling you up. They also serve as the foundation for many other kinds of interpretive questions, since it's helpful to first know when and why a text was composed before we go on to ask other interpretive questions.

Literary questions—those concerning language, artistry, and theme—are like the savory sides of interpretive questions. You don't *have* to ask them, and sometimes they are an acquired taste, but they deeply enrich your eating (or reading) experience. By drawing out the color and texture of texts, literary questions allow us to appreciate what is often implicit in a text, in a more explicit way.

Ideological questions that concern the gender, race, and class interests of both ourselves and biblical authors are the spiciest of questions. Some people might find ideological questions uncomfortable, in the same way that some people experience discomfort when eating any food with heat. But others find that there's a certain joy to be found in tasting and then enduring the hottest interpretive questions on offer.

Theological questions, those that concern what a passage says about a God we believe in, are like desserts. There's a certain self-indulgence in theological questions because they're less about investigating the text itself and more about using the text to help us construct a satisfying picture of God. That is to say, theological questions are about us. And you know what? You deserve it. From time to time we should set aside the labor of food and our nutritional and dietary concerns, and we should just playfully and sweetly enjoy food. Theological questions allow us to playfully and sweetly enjoy biblical texts for what they have to offer.

By the end of part III, just like a chef, you'll be able to take the same ingredients (biblical passages) and prepare them (interpret them) in delicious (meaningful) ways to suit your needs, your mood, and the occasion of your interpretation. No doubt a complex palate (a sophisticated Bible interpreter) will find time to enjoy a range of dishes (interpretive questions).

CHAPTER 11

Historical Questions

THE FIRST TYPES of interpretive questions we'll discuss are historical questions. Historical questions are often questions that ask when, where, why, or how a text is composed. For example:

- When and where was this text written?
- When and where is the story in this text set?
- Why was this text originally composed?
- Why might this text have been preserved by later communities?
- How did this text come together over time?

In biblical scholarship, historical questions are addressed by the *historical critical* method also known as historical criticism, which is an approach that prioritizes the setting and circumstances of a text's composition over other considerations. Historical criticism has been the dominant method of academic biblical scholarship from the eighteenth century through the first half of the twentieth century. Beginning in the sixties and seventies, literary and ideological methods become more popular among biblical scholars (and these will be discussed below), but historical criticism is still a very common approach for scholars to take.

Unfortunately, many historical questions are difficult, if not impossible, for lay people to answer. For example, the average person isn't going to be able to weigh in on debates about the precise historical dating of individual layers of the Pentateuch, answer technical questions about the grammar of Akkadian cognates (that is, words in Semitic languages that share a common origin and a similar meaning), or compare and contrast the pottery from Iron Age I and Iron Age II highland villages in Canaan. But that doesn't mean the average person can't be historically considerate as they interpret the Bible, and it doesn't mean that they won't benefit from the process of historical criticism. They just need to know the right questions to ask.

Below, I'll discuss four questions we all can consider when interpreting the Bible that allow us to be more conscientious in considering its history. Asking these questions will help us avoid imposing our own beliefs and the beliefs of contemporary religious communities on the text. This will in turn allow us to read the text in terms that more closely align with its original authors and audiences.

What does this passage mean in light of polytheism?

Historically and contemporarily, the majority of the Bible's readers have been, and are, Christians and Jews. Christianity and Judaism are monotheistic religions that affirm the existence of only a single God. While both religions have made space for other supernatural beings, such as angels and demons, members of both groups believe God to be in a distinct and unique category.

The Bible's original authors and audiences didn't exist in a monotheistic context, however. The great imperial powers that influenced ancient Israel were all polytheistic. The Roman Empire that dominated first-century Judea was polytheistic. The Canaanites that ancient Israel emerged from were polytheistic. Most Israelites throughout biblical history were probably polytheistic too.

Biblical authors do occasionally make gestures in the direction of monotheism, but strictly speaking, a lens of rigorous monotheism is something that was applied to the Bible after it was written. So when we encounter passages in the Bible where there are many divine beings, we shouldn't be quick to try to harmonize these beings with a monotheistic worldview and reduce them to angels or pretend they're parts of a Trinity that no human had conceived of yet. We can instead ask, "What does this passage mean in light of polytheism?"

Polytheism in the Old Testament

Consider, for example, the "sons of God" referenced in Genesis 6:2. Ancient Christians and Jews immediately saw these figures as angels or perhaps even human nobility. This early interpretation was then expanded upon and popularized in narrative form in the book of Enoch.

But to the text's first readers, living in a context in which the high god of a pantheon almost always had literal children who were themselves deities, it's likely these figures were seen as gods. This interpretation doesn't fit nicely into contemporary monotheistic theology, but when we're asking historical questions, whether or not something fits nicely into contemporary theology is irrelevant.

Let's look at another example. In Deuteronomy 32:8, in the middle of the Song of Moses, we're told that Elyon (which is a Canaanite name for a deity) gave the peoples of the earth to other gods as an inheritance. We then learn in verse 9 that one of these gods is Yahweh, who is given Jacob—that is, the people of Israel, as his inheritance.

In a polytheistic context, these verses make sense exactly as they're written: Yahweh received Israel from a higher deity, just like every other deity received their assigned people from a higher deity. This old piece of theology clashes with contemporary theology, but it would not have made ancient Israelites uncomfortable.

In later translations of Deuteronomy 32:8 in the Septuagint (an ancient Greek translation) and the Masoretic texts (medieval Jewish translations), we see attempts to make this verse compatible with Jewish and Christian theology by conflating Yahweh with Elyon and by demoting the gods who receive their inheritance first to angels and then to the Israelites. This indicates that as Christian and Jewish religion become more monotheistic, authors went back to older texts and attempted to align them with this new conviction. Still, evidence of the original wording persists.

As we discussed in chapter 5, introducing the Pentateuch, the "let us" language found in early creation stories is another example of a place where we miss the author's meaning if we immediately leap to make the verse fit with contemporary theology. The line in Genesis 1:26, "Let us make humans in our image," for example, is not the Trinity speaking to itself or God speaking to angels; it's God speaking to a divine council, which is an assembly of minor deities who attend a high deity in ancient pantheons.

We see references to this council in the text itself. In 1 Kings 22:19–22, the prophet Micaiah has a vision of this divine council, which includes among its company a lying spirit. In Psalm 82, God judges these other deities and condemns them to mortal death. In the opening chapters of Job, this divine council is again made up of the sons of God, and "the satan" is in attendance as part of that council (Job 1:6, 2:1).

In this story, "the satan" is used as a title, something like "the accuser" or "the prosecuting attorney," and it doesn't imply that the being who holds the title is evil. "The satan" only appears as a title twice in the Hebrew Bible: once in the opening of Job, and once in Zechariah 3, where "the satan" is supposed to act as a hostile witness. Strictly speaking, there's no reason to assume these two references to "the satan" refer to the same divine being. "Satan" as a name rather than a title only occurs once in the Hebrew Bible, and that's in 1 Chronicles 21:1, when Satan replaces God as the one who causes David to take a census.

Now, if we were to consider these passages in light of contemporary theology, we'd have to find some way to fit Satan into a monotheistic schema. But the original author and audience would have felt no such pressure. "The satan" or Satan, like every other divine being and son of God, would simply have been seen as a minor deity in its own right.

"But no," you might respond. "You can't be a god if you're not all powerful and if you didn't create the world." And while this statement sounds true from a Christian and Jewish perspective, once again, it would not have been true to the people who authored and first read these texts.

Most pantheons the world over are chock-full of deities that aren't all powerful, many of whom didn't even exist until long after the creation of the world. This is especially true of those in ancient Southwest Asia. Perhaps you're familiar with Greek mythology, for example. How many gods of Olympus are all powerful? How many of them created the world? That's right, not a single one. Are they still gods? The people who wrote about them certainly thought so, and the people who wrote about these minor deities in the Hebrew Bible probably thought of them in the same way. Again, when we're asking the historical question of what a passage means in light of polytheism, we have to let go of our own biases in order to answer with any degree of accuracy.

Polytheism in the New Testament

All of these examples have been from the Hebrew Bible or Old Testament. But polytheism is also relevant to the New Testament.

John 12:31 mentions the "ruler of this world" as a being who is antagonistic toward Jesus and God. John 14:30 and 16:11 echo this same idea. Second Corinthians 4:4 speaks about a "god of this world" who is similarly hostile. Ephesians 2:2 and 6:12 speak about cosmic powers that engage humanity in spiritual warfare. And Romans 8:38 assures that neither death, nor angels, nor divine rulers can separate us from the love of God in Jesus.

If the Gospel authors or Paul (or whoever the author was) simply thought these beings were all angels or demons, they could have written that. They didn't. Instead they chose to speak about divine beings that don't neatly fit into a monotheistic worldview. In a polytheistic environment, where the category of the divine can accommodate all sorts of beings, many of these beings would be gods, too, or something that's so much like a god that to say they aren't becomes a distinction without a difference.

Now you might say that these beings don't seem very personal. Their titles are all generic. They don't have names or descriptions, so maybe they aren't gods but rather abstract ideas. It's true, they do sound like abstract ideas, but it wasn't uncommon in the greater Greco-Roman world for abstract ideas to be deities. Mammon, from the Sermon on the Mount in Matthew 6:24, is both a word for wealth and a deity of wealth. Death (Greek *thanatos*) is an abstract idea, but also a god. Hades is both a god and the idea of the underworld. It makes sense, then, that when death and Hades are judged in Revelation 20:13, it isn't just abstract ideas that are judged; it's also the deities who embody and exercise sovereignty over these ideas.

A great diversity of divine beings is a problem for a contemporary monotheistic worldview, but it's no problem at all for the ancient polytheistic world in which biblical texts are composed. Remember, when we're asking historical questions, it's the world of the text's composition that we're prioritizing.

In addition to aiding us in understanding the Bible's references to divine beings, the interpretive question "What does this mean in light of polytheism?" is also helpful when we're trying to understand the ways the New Testament speaks about Jesus. Most contemporary New Testament readers are operating in a religious environment in which God is believed to be a Trinity of three consubstantial and coeternal divine persons, Father, Son, and Holy Spirit. So whenever these readers see verses speaking about Jesus as divine, they simply interpret the verses in light of this doctrine. But "the Trinity" as a term would not exist for more than a century after Jesus's death, and it would not become a codified doctrine until three centuries after Jesus's death.

Jesus's divinity is a complicated topic that's done a disservice when we simply rush past the relevant verses with the presumption of monotheism and Trinitarianism. You might say, "But Jesus forgives sins, so he must be God!", as if that settles it. But the angel sent to accompany the people of Israel in Exodus 23:21 also forgave sins. You might say, "But John says that Jesus preexists the creation of the world, so he must be God!" Yet Woman Wisdom of Proverbs 8 also preexisted the world. You might say, "But Jesus and the Father are one, so he must be God!" But John 17:21–23, 1 Corinthians 6:17 and 15:28, Romans 4:1–6, and Colossians 3:11 all speak of humanity, too, as experiencing unity with God.

While there are a plethora of passages in the New Testament that attribute divinity of *some kind* to Jesus, there are few if any passages that explicitly claim Jesus *is* God in the way Christians would eventually come to believe to be true. Even the famous opening in the Gospel of John, "and the Word was God," uses the word "god" in a way that doesn't necessarily mean "God with a capital *G*" but rather "god" in the sense of a divine being.

From an ancient standpoint that's more deeply in tune with polytheism, there's nothing wrong with the idea of Jesus being divine and like God in many ways but not identical with God. That understanding leaves open the question "Well how then is Jesus divine?" Answering this is where the hard work of theology comes in. But doing that theological work while presuming our much later answers to that question were in the minds of the authors who wrote the biblical stories, is anachronistic and egotistical.

The question "What does this passage mean in light of polytheism?" frees us from having to bring our own doctrines and dogmas to the text and allows us to better perceive the original author and audience's imagination and intent. You don't need to know anything about ancient Israelite or Greco-Roman religion to ask this question, beyond that these religions existed in polytheistic cultures, and you can ask this question on nearly every occasion where a divine being appears in the text.

It's possible that this question will make you or other Bible readers uncomfortable. But that's okay. That discomfort is simply the feeling of having our own biases decentered so another culture's perspective can take its place.

Is God really *X* in this story?

A second historical question we can ask concerns the attributes of divine beings. Again, in our contemporary landscape, Christians, Jews, Muslims, some Hindus, and members of many other religions believe that the god they worship is the greatest conceivable being. People often believe their god is all powerful (omnipotent), all knowing (omniscient), and perfectly good (omnibenevolent). And when Bible readers with these beliefs encounter biblical stories, they often interpret those stories in support of these classical divine attributes.

In principle, there's nothing wrong with that. But if we're interested in historical questions about what original authors and audiences believed, then it's worth asking, "Is God really *X* in this story?"—where *X* is an attribute people today commonly assume God must have.

Why is this a historical question and not, say, a theological one? Because doctrines related to divine power, knowledge, and goodness have long histories that developed into their current forms over time. In the ancient world, especially in the first millennium BCE in Southwest Asia, deities did not commonly have these classical divine attributes. So when we ask a question like "Is God really all powerful in this story?" we're taking a second, closer look to see if God really is all powerful in a story or if we've merely assumed that God is so out of unconscious habit.

Take, for example, the question "Is God really all knowing in the Garden of Eden?" To many Bible readers, the answer to the question is automatically *yes*, not because of anything they read in Genesis 2–3, but simply because they believe God is all knowing everywhere and at all times, so God must be all knowing in these stories too. But if we take a closer look at these chapters and ask this historical interpretive question, we might get a very different answer. Let's try it and see.

As soon as God creates Adam and gives him his instructions, God realizes that Adam is lonely and so sets about making a helper for him (Genesis 2:18). There are several things that are strange about this situation. For one, Adam isn't actually alone, God's there, but apparently God isn't able to satisfy Adam's loneliness. There's also the question of why God didn't predict this situation in advance and make Adam alongside a companion. Adam's loneliness does not seem difficult to predict, given that he is the only living creature on the planet. But God doesn't predict this. Adam's loneliness comes as something of a surprise.

God next creates animals, hoping one of those will be Adam's helper, but none of them satisfy him (Genesis 2:19–20). Again, this development is strange. Why is God going through this trial and error process? God eventually does create a satisfying helper for Adam in the form of Eve (Genesis 2:21–23), but this action is not portrayed as the inevitable result of divine wisdom but rather as the eventual result of repeated failed experiments.

Things look even worse for God in the following chapter. God apparently does not know about the snake's entrance into the Garden of Eden, and God does not know where Adam and Eve are or what they've done until he stumbles upon them, sees them hiding, and then interrogates them. God then has to take drastic steps to prevent Adam and Eve from becoming immortal by kicking them out of the garden.

This pattern continues even into the next stories. God doesn't seem to know about Cain's intentions to murder Abel (Genesis 4:6–9). God doesn't seem to know about "the sons of God" sleeping with human women at the beginning of the flood story (Genesis 6:2). God doesn't seem to know about all the people building the Tower of Babel until he takes a stroll and happens upon it (Genesis 11:5).

In all of these stories, bad things happen on God's watch, and God only reacts to them belatedly, after the fact, at which point nothing can be done except for him to punish everyone involved. The evidence of these stories points to a deity that doesn't necessarily know everything. Indeed, in several of these stories, God may even come off to some readers as incompetent.

If we're reading these stories through the lens of contemporary theology, we then have the unenviable task of having to invent reasons, in a manner not dissimilar to midrash, for why God merely looks incompetent but is actually all knowing. Reasons like: Maybe God wanted Adam to realize his own loneliness and how animals can't satisfy it before creating Eve. Maybe God knew what Adam and Eve were doing all along but asked them questions just to force them to realize the enormity of their own mistakes. Maybe God knew Cain was going to kill Abel and didn't intervene so the brothers could serve as an object lesson to future generations.

The problem with these explanations is that they're not in the Bible. Not a shred of textual evidence exists in support of them. We've made these explanations up so that we can feel more comfortable with these stories. But asking the historical question "Is God really omniscient in the Garden of Eden?" cuts through all that invention. If we search the text for an answer, without presupposing our own theology, the answer is *no*.

We can ask similar questions about other divine attributes in other stories. Is God really omnipotent in Judges 1:19, when God is with the people of Judah but they lose a battle to the Canaanites regardless? What about in 2 Kings 3:27, when God is with the people of Israel but they lose a battle to the Moabites regardless? Can God really be omnibenevolent when God commands slavery (Exodus 21:1–11 Leviticus 25:44–46, Ephesians 6:5–8, Colossians 3:22–25, 1 Peter 2:18–25), genocide (1 Samuel 15:1–3), or mass sexual assault (Numbers 31:1–18)?

Consider also the questions raised by Matthew 7:7–11, which says "Ask, and it will be given to you." Jesus's words here imply that God gives anything that's asked of God to people who pray. Yet clearly, people have prayed for all sorts of things and never gotten them. Terrible people have prayed for terrible things, and thankfully, haven't gotten them. But starving children have prayed for food, abused people have prayed for safety, and desperate parents have prayed for their child's life but haven't gotten it. Does that mean that there is a lack of power here?

Interestingly, Luke 11:13 clarifies this saying of Jesus's, specifying that God will always give the Holy Spirit, not "anything," when asked. But even that doesn't seem to be true. Haven't people prayed to be given knowledge of God, to experience God's presence, to know God is there but haven't received these things? Luke's version of this claim might be modest, but it still leaves something to be desired.

We're not asking these questions in order to disprove God's attributes, although a person can attempt to use them in that way if they want. Rather we ask them in an effort to clarify how the original author and audiences of these stories understood God. Biblical authors often thought God was powerful, wise, and good in certain ways, but they did not necessarily believe that God was omnipotent, omniscient, and omnibenevolent. You're of course free to believe that God is these things. You're free to justify that belief using passages where God is legitimately omnipotent, omniscient, or omnibenevolent, of which there are several. But that belief is a theological question, not a historical question.

What use would this prophecy have had to its first hearers?

There are many prophecies in the Hebrew Bible, and the New Testament authors often refer to these prophecies to explain the significance of Jesus's life, death, and resurrection to their audiences. Contemporary Christian Bible readers tend to follow suit when reading the prophets, unconsciously asking, "How can I relate this text to Jesus?"

Like we've said in so many other instances, there's nothing inherently wrong with this question. The problem comes when people answer this question and then presume the answer is the only *real* answer, the one answer God cares about, and the answer the original author intended to communicate to his audience. This presumption leads to a theology of Christian supersessionism, in which Christianity's validity requires the invalidation of Judaism. At worst, supersessionism leads to antisemitism, crusades of forced conversion, and genocide of Jewish populations. At best, supersessionism leads to mild prejudice against contemporary Jews and an inability to appreciate the Jewishness of Jesus.

To counter this error, we can ask the historical question "What use would this prophecy have had to its first hearers?" We might have to speculate a little bit, but even if we don't arrive at a single clear answer, close attention to texts can get us a long way.

Consider for example Isaiah 7:14, famously cited by Matthew 1:23: "Look, the virgin shall become pregnant and give birth to a son, and they shall name him Emmanuel." In quoting this verse, Matthew is appropriating its language to help him understand the significance of Jesus and the claims made about his birth in the first century CE. Isaiah was, however, speaking to an audience in the middle of the eighth century BCE, almost a millennium earlier. At the risk of stating the obvious, not a single soul in Isaiah's time cared about what was going to happen eight hundred years later. It would have been of no use *at all* to anyone in Isaiah's time to tell them that centuries later, people living entirely different lives in entirely different circumstances would find a lot of comfort in the birth of a special child. And if it was no use at all, then no one would have bothered to write the prophecy down and preserve it at great expense for the next many hundred years.

So, what use would this prophecy have to its first hearers? That's not difficult to see with a close reading. Isaiah 7 describes the beginnings of the Syro-Ephraimite War, in which northern powers align against King Ahaz of Judah. Ahaz is distraught, but Isaiah offers him comfort in the form of a prophecy. He says that a young woman will give birth to a son, that God will be with this son, and by the time the son comes of age the threat of these northern powers will be destroyed by Assyria at God's (really Ahaz's) invitation. That is to say, Ahaz doesn't need to worry. And if we go on to read 2 Kings 16:1–9, it turns out that Isaiah was more or less correct. In 2 Kings 18:7, we're told of King Hezekiah, "The Lord is with him." Emmanuel, from Isaiah 7:14, means "God is with us." Hezekiah, then, represents the immediate fulfillment of Isaiah's words.

This isn't originally a prophecy about what will happen eight hundred years later. It's comfort and political strategy that's immediately relevant to Ahaz's situation. That's its use for its first hearers. That's why people preserved the story.

The fact that neither Isaiah 7:14 nor any other verse in the Hebrew Bible or Old Testament originally had anything to do with Jesus doesn't mean later religious communities can't use older verses to help them make sense of their present. There's nothing illegal or incorrect about saying, "These older verses help me understand Jesus." This is what we do any time we come to the Bible for devotional purposes to build up our faith. Any time you find comfort in a psalm that originally had nothing to do with your situation, or any time you find wisdom in a teaching of Jesus that was originally addressed to his disciples, you're doing the same thing. That's fine, as long as you understand what you're doing. That's fine as long as you're not pretending an old verse was always about you and your situation to begin with.

How can we make sense of this passage in light of imperial oppression?

Though the Bible narrates more than a thousand years of history, nearly all of that history sees the people of Israel and Judah subjugated by foreign imperial powers. The Hebrew Bible's most famous story, the exodus from Egypt, is in fact a story of escaping an imperial power. After Egypt, there's Assyria, then Babylon, Persia, Greece, and Rome.

It's an old and generally true maxim that history is written by the winners. The Bible, however, is the opposite. It's written by the losers, losers who have been remarkably successful in preserving their unique religious identity despite all their losses. Many stories in the Hebrew Bible and New Testament are tinged with an awareness of this subjugated state, and so to get ourselves closer to the mindset of the biblical authors, it can be helpful to ask, "What does this passage mean in light of imperial oppression?" Some obvious places we might ask this question are passages in which explicit capitulation to imperial powers is advised.

Consider a trio of chapters in Jeremiah: 27, 29, and 50. Jeremiah is writing at a time when the Babylonian Empire is on the warpath. In 589 BCE, toward the end of Jeremiah, they destroy Jerusalem and the First Temple, capture most of the city's elites, and bring an end to the line of Davidic kings.

In Jeremiah 27:5–11, Jeremiah proposes a theology that says it's actually God who's behind the emerging power of the Babylonian Empire, and it's really God who's given the king of Babylon the power to subjugate all these different nations. Jeremiah indicates that if the people of Judah don't bow to this foreign invader, then God will see this as disobedience and destroy the nation. At a time when elites are contemplating whether to resist or capitulate, Jeremiah's theology is deeply political and clearly advocates for the latter while still preserving a sense of God's ultimate sovereignty over history.

Next, in Jeremiah 29:4–9, Jeremiah tells people in exile in Babylon after the destruction of Jerusalem to put down roots, intermarry, and ultimately pray for the prosperity of Babylon, who is oppressing them. Then, in a violent change of tone, Jeremiah 50:18–32 prophesies the brutal and complete destruction of Babylon by God for its violence against Jerusalem.

This theological whiplash could be difficult to understand when we're reading these passages far removed from their original historical context. The question "What does this passage mean in light of imperial oppression?" reminds us of that original context and helps us make sense of it. The experience of oppression, and the sentiments of the oppressed for their oppressors, is a complex phenomenon that cannot be understood in simple terms. That is, however, the appropriate frame of mind to be in when looking at these passages. Some days, the oppressed might feel it's best to accommodate their oppressors—not because oppression is good, but because people have limited time and resources to resist. But other days, the oppressed might feel it's best to desire and even work toward the destruction of their oppressors' power. These realities can produce contradictory theology, but that's simply a reflection of the very real experiences that the theology comes from.

Romans 13:1–5 provides a similar example in the New Testament. There, Paul advises the reader to submit to human authority figures, reasoning that anyone who exists as an authority does so only because God has made it so. Paul's context is Rome, a notoriously oppressive empire that not only persecuted Christians generally but also executed Jesus. The dynamic here is complicated. There's capitulation in Romans 13, but by the end of the chapter there's also something else. Paul reminds his audience in verses 11–14 that the end of history is at hand, an end that we know from his other writings (as in 1 Corinthians 15:28) will result in the subjugation of all people to Jesus. So this is less an instance of permanent advice and more a stopgap measure to tide his audience over until God's judgment sets everything right.

On the opposite side of the coin—defiance instead of capitulation—the question of how to make sense of a passage in light of imperial oppression shows us places where evidence of resistance can be seen. Consider two famous prayers in the Bible: Hannah's and Mary's.

Hannah's prayer in 1 Samuel 2, especially vv. 4–8, speaks of a dramatic reversal of social fortunes. In the words of this prayer, the rich and powerful will be humbled, while the humble will be raised to riches and power. Mary's prayer in Luke 1:46–55 speaks of the same reversal.

On a surface level, these women are celebrating miraculous births, events that primarily affect them. But when we ask the historical question "What does this passage mean in light of imperial oppression?", we see defiance in these prayers. After all, while births are private affairs, the content of the prayers is not. The prayers speak about widespread social and political upheaval.

These women see heralds of global change in their own intimate circumstances. In a context where the status quo is one of imperial oppression, this change is necessarily an end of this oppression. When we ask the right interpretive questions, Hannah and Mary's prayers aren't just pieces of pious praise but cries of resistance against an unjust world.

Conclusion

The historical interpretive questions discussed in this chapter aren't the only ones you can bring to bear on biblical texts. It's also important to ask who wrote a text, as well as when, where, why, and how did the text come together over time. These questions can be difficult for lay readers to answer, but they're still important to keep in mind. If you're the kind of person who enjoys memorizing facts about biblical texts, these would be good topics to zoom in on.

You can freely switch between different kinds of interpretive questions as well. You can ask historical questions one moment, then ask theological questions the next. Just like it's up to you what dishes to cook and how, it's up to you how to use these interpretive tools. Each one can help in different ways.

Historical questions help us to overcome our own biases and refocus on the issues that would be near and dear to the hearts of the people who originally wrote and read biblical texts. While we can't escape our biases entirely, we can protect ourselves from the worst excesses of those biases by keeping historical questions like these in mind.

CHAPTER 12

Literary Questions

IN THE LAST chapter, we saw that the historical questions we ask of a passage address the issues behind the text—that is, the situation of the author and audience, and the cultural background that we need to know in order to understand the text well. Literary questions, by contrast, center around the text itself.

In this chapter, we will be introducing questions that can be answered simply by paying careful attention to a passage in its literary contexts and using skills one might learn in English or literature classes. In other words, an interpreter can address most of these questions without looking at outside sources.

However, it is always a good idea to investigate what other people have said about a passage because their skills and perspectives can fill in our own gaps in knowledge and our analytical limitations. Biblical commentaries are a great place to go to look for how scholars have answered some of these questions in the past. We will provide a resource list with solid commentary options in the list at the end of this book. With that caveat, let's get to our literary questions.

What kind of literature is this? What literary devices does the author use?

Before an interpreter can analyze the literary features of a passage, they must determine the genre of a passage. That's because genre gives us clues about how to read a passage and about what literary features might show up in it.

We have talked quite a bit about genre already in our chapters on main ingredients from the Bible and provided tips for interpreting various literary types. (Remember what we learned about legends, law, poetry, and wisdom literature? And about gospels, epistles, and apocalyptic literature?)

Identifying genre can be a two-step process, though. This is because books of the Bible can be classified as certain genres and specific passages within those books can have subgenres. For example, if we were interpreting 1 Peter 2:18–3:7, we would notice that those verses are part of an epistle but the passage itself falls within the subgenre of household code. We would need to keep the features of epistle in mind as we analyze the passage (for example, remembering that occasional literature is specific to a particular time and people) as well as the features of household codes (such as that they tell us more about Roman family structure than they do about Christian ideals).

After looking at the big picture of genre, we can get down to the nitty gritty work of literary interpretation: closely observing the literary elements of a passage. In keeping with the theme of cooking, we can think of these elements as spices that the author used to season the passage. Below, we've listed some of the common spices that biblical authors use to cook up their literary masterpieces, along with some highlights of why and how they may be important. (Attention, all you English majors and lovers of literature: This is your time to shine!)

Literary elements (you may think of them as spices) to look for in biblical passages:

- **Repetition**: If a word, phrase, or concept is repeated, it is likely to be important to the main idea of the passage. An interpreter should pay attention wherever this occurs.
- **Key terms**: Key terms are concepts or words that need further study to be understood in the passage's context.
- **Figures of speech**: A passage's author will often use figurative language to communicate that an idea is important to that passage. Common figures of speech include similes ("It's easy as pie" or "Life is like a box of chocolates"), metaphors (the Lord is my Shepherd—or dare we say Chef?), personification ("That cheesecake was calling to me"), and hyperbole ("I was about to die from hunger").
- **Cause and effect**: Biblical literature often communicates results or consequences using literary formulas such as cause/effect statements, if/then statements, and purpose/results statements, including using key words like "so that" and "with the result that."
- **Comparisons and contrasts**: Two ideas or people or circumstances are set parallel to each other to emphasize their similarities (comparisons) or their differences (contrasts).

- **Dialogue and Questions**: The key message in a passage is often communicated via direct address or dialogue, and sometimes the biblical authors employ questions, rhetorical or otherwise, for emphasis.
- **Emotive terms**: Words that provoke emotion sometimes point to the pieces of a passage that are most important to the author. Emotional terms might include words about family, feeling words, and extreme/exaggerative words or commands.
- **Change in verb tense**: Verbs in a passage get at the heart of the action, so it's a good idea to notice when the tense of verbs change. Imperative verbs, or commands, such as "Be kind to one another" (Ephesians 4:32), are also important to pay attention to.
- **Quotes or allusions to other literature**: It is especially important to notice when the New Testament authors quote from or make allusions to the Hebrew Bible. A study Bible could help you identify such allusions, which are sometimes called "cross references."
- **Structural elements**: Ancient authors often utilized literary structure instead of direct, propositional statements to communicate important ideas. Common structural elements include a literary device called *inclusio* or bookends (that is: starting and ending a section with similar words or themes), chiasm (a parallel structure), and the inclusion of climactic phrases and turning points in their writing.

Reading a passage closely with an eye toward its literary elements doesn't come naturally to most people, so let's practice a little.

An Example from the Old Testament

The first example is poetry, although there are also elements of wisdom literature in it, as it gives advice on the wisdom of meditating on Scripture. The passage is Psalm 1:1–6.

When we scrutinize a passage's literary elements, the main ideas communicated by the author rise to the top. Notice in Psalm 1 that the whole psalm is contrasting the wicked and the righteous (repetition) and using comparison/contrast (signaled by the word "but" in

1 **Happy** are those
who do not follow the advice of the **wicked**
or take the path that **sinners** tread
or sit in the seat of **scoffers**,
2 *but their **delight** is in the* law of the Lord,
and on his law they meditate day and night. (the righteous)
3 They are like trees
planted by streams of water,
which yield their fruit in its season,
and their leaves do not wither.
In all that they do, they prosper. [C/E]
4 The **wicked** are not so
but are like chaff that the wind drives away.
5 Therefore the **wicked** will not stand in the **judgment**
nor **sinners** in the congregation of the righteous,
6 *for the Lord watches over the way of the righteous,*
*but the way of the wicked will **perish**.*

Literary Elements in Psalm 1

Repetition (wicked, righteous)

Key terms

figures of speech

Cause and effect— C/E

Comparison or *Contrast*

Emotional terms (in bold)

Verbs and their tenses:
follow, take the path, sit, meditate, planted, yield, do not wither, prosper, drives away, will not stand, watches over, will perish (all present tense except the ending phrases "the wicked will not stand" and "the wicked will perish")

verses 2, 4, and 6) to make us aware of this. The main difference between the two groups becomes apparent in the key action of meditating on the law of the Lord, which is a central idea because it is what separates the wicked and the righteous.

The author uses rich figures of speech like similes and metaphors (such as "like trees" in v. 3 and "like chaff" in v. 4) to emphasize the differences between the two groups and employs emotional terms like "wicked," "perish," "happy," and "prosper" to drive home that point to the readers. The switch from present tense to future tense ("will not stand in the judgment" and "will perish" in verses 5 and 6) casts a sense of foreboding over the fate of the wicked, emphasizing that there are future consequences to disregarding God's law. When we identify the literary features in this example (repetition, comparison and contrast, similes and metaphors, and a shift from present tense to future tense), we can see that they all point to the central idea that meditating on the law of the Lord separates the righteous from the wicked.

An Example from the New Testament

Now let's practice finding the literary elements in a narrative New Testament passage, Mark 1:1–8.

[1]The beginning of the good news of Jesus Christ.

[2] As it is written in the prophet Isaiah,
"See, I am sending my messenger ahead of you,
who will prepare your way,
[3] the voice of one **crying out** in the wilderness:
'Prepare the way of the Lord;
make his paths straight,' " **(D)**

[4] so John the baptizer appeared in the wilderness,
proclaiming a baptism of repentance for the **forgiveness**
of sins. [C/E] [5] And the whole Judean region and all the
people of Jerusalem were going out to him and were
baptized by him in the River Jordan, **confessing their**
sins. [6] Now John was clothed with camel's hair, with a
leather belt around his waist, and he ate locusts and wild
honey. [7] He proclaimed, *"The one who is more powerful*
*than I is coming after me; I am not **worthy** to stoop down*
and untie the strap of his sandals. [8] *I have baptized you*
with water, but he will baptize you with the Holy Spirit."
(D)

Literary Elements in Mark 1

1. Repetition: good news/voice/ messenger/crying out/proclaiming, prepare, in the wilderness, confessing/forgiving of sins, baptized)
2. Key terms – good news and baptize
3. figures of speech
4. Cause and effect— C/E
5. *Comparison/Contrast (italics)*
6. Dialogue or Direct Address **(D)** and Questions **(Q)**
6. **Emotional terms (in bold)**
7. Verbs and their tenses: Written, sending, will prepare, crying out, prepare!, make straight!, appeared, proclaiming, were going out, were baptized, confessing, clothed, ate, proclaimed, baptized, will baptize. Notice the past tense, future tenses, ongoing present tenses, commands (!), and passive tenses
8. Allusions or Quotes

A close look at this opening passage in Mark reveals strong connections to the past and the future of his audience. The narrative action is straightforward, depicting John baptizing people for their repentance, but the author is also placing the action in a historical and literary context by using the quote/allusion to Isaiah.

Allusions and quotes from the Old Testament appear frequently in the New Testament. If you want to understand a passage in its literary and historical context, it is a good idea to chase down where those allusions come from. A study Bible that lists cross references or a cross-reference website can help you with that task. The author implies that the allusion in Mark 1:2–3 is from Isaiah, and that is partly true; verse 3 quotes from Isaiah 40:3. However, verse 2 is a citation of Malachi 3:1, so it seems that the author has combined two different prophetic references in this quote, summarizing by saying "as it is written in the prophet Isaiah."

Remember, paraphrasing or loosely citing passages was a common practice of New Testament writers. For interpretive purposes, however, it is not accuracy of citation that is important but the general message and context of the quote's original source. If you read Isaiah 40:3 in its literary context, for example, you will see that the prophet is giving a message to the people about God's faithfulness and power, with an eye toward the end of their exile and suffering. Isaiah 40 is a chapter that's filled with rousing reminders of God's role as creator and shepherd, as the one who brings comfort and a hopeful future to the people. Malachi 3:1, which speaks of a messenger preparing the way for the Lord, is the beginning of a section that warns of God returning to the temple in judgment and mercy, offering the people a chance for repentance before the Day of the Lord.

Mark seems to have included these two prophetic allusions as a way to introduce John the Baptist's role as a messenger who heralds a shift between God and God's people, as well as to hint at what the "good news of Jesus Christ" in verse 1 might refer to. Instead of saying explicitly that Jesus has come as a divine presence to kick off an important moment in history, one that requires people to turn to God for a future salvation, Mark *alludes* to these ideas by connecting John's ministry and message to the prophets' messages. This approach is quite brilliant. Mark also uses hyperbole or exaggeration (the *whole* Judean region, *all* the people of Jerusalem!) as well as emotional terms and contrast (I have baptized you with water but he will baptize you with the Holy Spirit) to further enforce the significance of the divine moment John announces and sees on the horizon.

As you can see from these last two examples, asking the question "What literary elements (or spices) are central in this passage?" opens multiple interpretive paths up for consideration. This kind of close reading helps readers better grasp a passage's communicative goals and emotional tone as well as its main ideas. Asking this literary question is also a first step toward knowing what historical questions to ask.

For example, we saw in our Mark 1 passage that baptism and the good news were key concepts. Historical questions that arise from these concepts could include "What was the significance of baptism in a first-century Jewish context?" and "What is the social and cultural background of the phrase 'the good news'?" When we read a text closely, we can learn much from our own observational skills. But that reading will also eventually lead us to more inquiry and to other interpretative paths we may choose to follow.

A Note on Word Studies and Translations

Identifying the meaning of key words is a necessary part of studying the literary features of any literary passage. This task is especially tricky when we are working with texts that were written millennia ago in languages different from our own. Translation is more of an art than a science because there is rarely a word-for-word equivalent from one language to another. Plus, the work of translation is subject to the same kind of biases and preconceptions that interpretation is. In fact, all translations *are* interpretations. That's why it's important for us to be aware of the subjectivity and approximation involved in translation and to look at multiple translations when we're studying a passage.

There are several schools of thought on translation. First, there is the approach called *formal equivalence*, which stays close to a word-by-word replication but does not capture idioms or thoughts well. There is also *dynamic equivalence*, which attempts to balance faithfulness to the original words while also effectively communicating phrases and thoughts. And finally, there is *functional equivalence* or *paraphrase*, which focuses on communicating thoughts in a way that is natural to the contemporary audience rather than replicating the original text's exact words or word order. Often, in paraphrases, translators use multiple words to convey one Greek or Hebrew word.

Here's a list of popular Bible translations listed in order of greatest formal equivalence to least (that is, closest to paraphrase):

Interlinear
New American Standard Bible (NASB)
English Standard Version (ESV)
Revised Standard Version (RSV)
King James Version (KJV)
New King James Version (NKJV)
New Revised Standard Version, Updated Edition (NRSVue)
New International Version (NIV)
Common English Bible (CEB)
Christian Standard Bible (CSB)
New Living Translation (NLT)
Contemporary English Version (CEV)
The Message

So which approach is best? The answer isn't that simple, as each has its own strengths and weaknesses. Our advice is that interpreters—that's all of us—should use a translation in the dynamic equivalence range for everyday study. But for a more in-depth interpretation, we recommend a translation from the formal range not in the functional or paraphrase category. When you compare and contrast different translations, it becomes apparent which words are difficult to translate or don't have close equivalents in English. From there, it is a good idea to consult commentaries for scholars' opinions on what the key word you are studying could possibly mean.

How does this passage fit into the bigger picture?

Once we've explored the literary contours of a passage, we can zoom out to get a wider view of the passage in its context. The first level of zooming out involves looking at what comes right before and right after the main passage we're studying. The question we're asking here is "How does this passage fit into the bigger picture of this book?" Another way of putting this is "What is this passage's literary context?"

People often like to pretend that verses and passages in the Bible exist in a vacuum, especially when plucking them out to make a point or to use as quips for an Instagram post (a process known as "proof-texting" that involves selectively quoting verses out of context). But this is not the case. Rather, the biblical authors weave together words and sentences, sections and whole books, to communicate a web of persuasive ideas or practical narrations. That is why zooming out on a passage to explore its literary context is a key interpretative practice. Let's demonstrate this by using an example.

The Importance of Zooming Out on Literary Context

There is a short pericope in Luke 10:25–28 that expresses an idea that pops up all over the Jewish and Christian Scriptures—that love of God and love of neighbor should be central goals of those who follow God. But there is much more to this passage that we can see if we zoom out and look at its context. Let's start with the verses.

> An expert in the law stood up to test Jesus. "Teacher," he said, "what must I do to inherit eternal life?" He said to him, "What

> is written in the law? What do you read there?" He answered, "You shall love the Lord your God with all your heart and with all your soul and with all your strength and with all your mind and your neighbor as yourself." And he said to him, "You have given the right answer; do this, and you will live."
>
> Luke 10:25–28

Here, a crafty law expert asks Jesus a religious question in order to test him. Jesus, in typical rabbinic fashion, answers him with a question.

The man's response to Jesus contains two quotations from the Hebrew Bible. The first is from Deuteronomy 6:5, and the man cites it almost word for word ("Love the Lord your God with all your heart and with all your soul and with all your strength"), except he adds "with all your mind" to it. The second quotation comes from Leviticus 19:18 ("love your neighbor as yourself"), but in an abbreviated version.

If we're approaching the passage from a literary interpretation stance, then we want to understand how it fits into the passages that come before and after it. But first we need to interrogate the passage itself.

The passage is relatively straightforward, but there are some questions we can begin with. First, why is it significant that Jesus's partner in this conversation is an expert of the law, and why is Luke careful to communicate that he stood up to "test" Jesus? Second, what is the significance of Luke (or the law expert) adding "with all your mind" to the Deuteronomy quote?

Illustrating the Upside-Down Kingdom

Zooming out will help us answer those questions. Let's start with the first ones about the lawyer.

Right before our passage is a prayer from Jesus and an interaction with his disciples:

> At that very hour Jesus rejoiced in the Holy Spirit and said, "I thank you, Father, Lord of heaven and earth, because you have hidden these things from the wise and the intelligent and have revealed them to infants; yes, Father, for such was your gracious will. All things have been handed over to me by my

> Father, and no one knows who the Son is except the Father or who the Father is except the Son and anyone to whom the Son chooses to reveal him." Then turning to the disciples, Jesus said to them privately, "Blessed are the eyes that see what you see! For I tell you that many prophets and kings desired to see what you see but did not see it and to hear what you hear but did not hear it."
>
> Luke 10:21–24

The interaction between Jesus and a law expert appears after a passage in Luke that describes the upside-down nature of God's kingdom. Its placement here by the author of Luke is unlikely to be coincidental.

The theme of the upside-down kingdom can be found throughout the Gospels, and it demonstrates that under God's reign, the people considered intelligent, holy, wealthy, and powerful are at a disadvantage because of their position. On the contrary, those who are looked down on—the poor, weak, and ignored in society—will recognize the priorities of God because they are the heart of God's kingdom. In this passage, the disciples represent the ones who see and hear because of their disadvantaged position, and the expert in the law represents the "wise and the intelligent" (10:21) and the "prophets and kings" who did not hear (10:24).

This is the context of what appears just before the passage we're studying (Luke 10:25–28). But what about what comes after?

Directly after Jesus tells the law expert that he gave the correct answer, Jesus tells the famous parable of the good Samaritan (Luke 10:30–37). In doing so, he is giving an answer to the expert's disingenuous follow-up question "And who is my neighbor?" (Luke 10:29). Jesus's response shows that although the intelligent experts in the law have the so-called correct answers, they do not know (or care) what those answers look like in real life situations.

The parable shocks the law expert when it casts a Samaritan, the despised enemy of the Jewish people, as the hero of the story, rather than the religious, respected priest and Levite. But the parable is a perfect example of the upside-down kingdom. It also provides a practical example of how our enemy might be our neighbor—and how they might also provide the best example of neighborly love. The parable essentially says, "If you want to inherit the kingdom, you will have to love not just the neighbor who looks like you—the obvious, insider neighbor—but love your enemy, the one you despise."

By the end of the parable, we see that the respected expert may have given the right answer, but he is far from the kingdom if he thinks to test Jesus and resist the upside-down reign of God. The passage before the parable clues us in that this is all about the countercultural kingdom.

An Example of Loving God with All Our Minds

Now, let's go back to our second question about our original passage. Why does the law expert add the phrase "with all your mind" to the Leviticus passage about loving God with heart, soul, and strength? The passage that directly follows the parable of the good Samaritan provides some insight on that. This pericope is a famous but often misunderstood one—the story of Mary and Martha.

> Now as they went on their way, he entered a certain village where a woman named Martha welcomed him. She had a sister named Mary, who sat at Jesus's feet and listened to what he was saying. But Martha was distracted by her many tasks, so she came to him and asked, "Lord, do you not care that my sister has left me to do all the work by myself? Tell her, then, to help me." But the Lord answered her, "Martha, Martha, you are worried and distracted by many things, but few things are needed—indeed only one. Mary has chosen the better part, which will not be taken away from her."
>
> Luke 10:38–42

It is tempting to make this story about Martha's distraction and anxious activity or about her "inferior" devotion to Jesus (as many sermons in the past have done), but the literary context of this story purposefully draws our attention to Mary. Luke is giving us an example of what it looks like to love God with all our *minds.* The parable of the good Samaritan was a picture of what loving your neighbor (enemy) looks like; Mary learning at the feet of her rabbi exemplifies that love of God, not only with the heart, soul, and strength, but also with the mind, is paramount.

We can see the irony and beauty of the passage when we pay attention to its placement after Jesus and the law expert's interaction. Reading it in this context, we see that the phrase the law expert added ("with all your mind") does not describe his own actions—he is, after all, the negative example of one who does not see and hear. Instead, a woman, who typically could not have become an expert in the law or sat at a rabbi's feet as a disciple, becomes the exemplar of loving God with her mind. The upside-down kingdom strikes again. And we might have missed the interconnected messages in this section if we had not zoomed out to see how Luke arranged these passages to reveal deeper truths.

Exploring the Big Picture

Now that we have illustrated that studying the immediate literary context of a passage can unlock new interpretations, it's time to zoom out even further. This is the step that gets us to answering our original question: How does this passage fit into the bigger picture? (Or, What is the literary context?). Answers to this question can require study and a bit of research.

A first stage in this kind of study might look like an interpreter reading and outlining the entire book that a passage appears in. For books like the four-chapter Ruth, this step would not be labor intensive. However, outlining Acts or Romans could be a herculean task. As a shortcut, you could look up outlines of the book online or in Bible commentaries to get a feel for the book's movement and shape. Wherever you get your outlines, we recommend consulting more than one source. That's because outlines are as diverse as their interpreters are. An outline of a book will give you a better idea of how the passage you're studying functions in the overarching story or argument of a text. For an example from the Hebrew Bible, let's revisit a passage from Judges that we mentioned back in chapter 6: The Prophets.

In Judges 2, the author explains Israel's cycle of sin and redemption, in which the Israelites worship other gods, then God brings in a foreign people to oppress them, which results in the Israelites crying out to God for help and concludes with God sending a "judge" to defeat the foreign oppressors. If you outlined (or read an outline of) the book of Judges, you would notice that the pattern laid out in chapter 2 repeats itself in the later chapters. Each of the stories of the judges mimics the blueprint sketched there, following it as a narrative shape. Chapter 2, then, functions as a foundational model that sets the stage for the recurring theme of sin, punishment, repentance, and deliverance. It's a brilliant structure that gives the reader the impression that every time the cyclical pattern is repeated, the Israelites are sinking deeper into the spiral of disobedience. This continues until the end of Judges, when they hit rock bottom and are ready for a king to rescue them.

There is immeasurable interpretive value in the question "Where does this passage fit in the big picture?" Attempting to answer it opens countless new pathways for interpreters. When you engage in this work, you might discover how biblical authors used the structure of their books to communicate deeper truths or how passages fit together in order to make meaning in tandem with one another. At the very least, you may come to understand how connecting themes in books illustrate what is most important in both the small picture and the big picture. Either way, the point is clear: We should never underestimate the importance of literary context.

What is the author's primary message? What does the author want their audience to think, feel, or do in response to that message?

The first literary questions we introduced in this chapter—"What type of literature is this? What literary devices does the author use?" and "How does this passage fit into the bigger picture?"—can be answered by analyzing what we observe on the pages of the Bible. Tackling our last questions—"What is the author's primary message? What does the author want the audience to think, feel, or do in response to that message?"—will require a bit more imagination because their answers extend beyond the written pages. Another way to ask those two questions is: What are the communicative goals of the author in this passage? Since we are asking this of the implied author, all the evidence we will gather to answer these questions will come from within the text itself.

Biblical study that asks questions about the author's (probable) persuasive goals or communicative intent is called *rhetorical criticism*. The building blocks of rhetoric or rhetorical analysis have been around for thousands of years. Most famously, Aristotle discusses rhetoric in depth in his fourth-century BCE *The Art of Rhetoric*, and his categories have greatly influenced the study of rhetoric through interpretive history.

Most helpful for biblical interpretation are his three methods for persuasion: *pathos* (appealing to people's emotions), *ethos* (using the moral character or authority of the author to instill confidence), and *logos* (providing logical propositions or examples). All three of these methods, as well as other culturally specific techniques, can be found in biblical literature. As much as authors of the Bible tell stories or illustrate ideas, they also try to persuade their audiences to feel something (using *pathos*), think something (using *logos*), and do or be something or imitate someone (using *ethos*).

Five Questions

With this in mind, we have created a list of questions that can be asked of a passage to determine what and how an author might be communicating to an audience in a specific passage or text. These questions build upon the other literary questions we've already addressed in this chapter and can help us understand more about the message and goals of the author. They also require us to put ourselves in the minds of the original audience (implied readers) and imagine how they would answer.

Here are the five questions:

1. Are the characters in the story portrayed positively, negatively, neutrally, or as models of change? (This question works best with narratives, myths, parables, and apocalyptic literature.)
2. Are the claims in the passage presented as true or worthy of imitation, as false, as a warning, or as conditional? (This question works best with prophetic literature, poetry, wisdom literature, and epistles.)
3. Is the author evoking or appealing to any emotions in the passage?
4. Is the author promoting a certain principle or way of looking at the world?
5. Is the author trying to inspire an action or a change of perspective in their audience?

Some of these questions work better with certain types of literature than with others, but the example we will use—Jonah—is a rare text because it can be illuminated by all of these. The book of Jonah is unique among the prophets because it operates as an ironic narrative, or a satire. You could learn that tidbit by reading commentaries on Jonah, or you could figure it out yourself by asking questions about what the author is doing.

Now, let's ask the five questions of the book of Jonah.

Question 1: "Are the characters in the story portrayed positively, negatively, neutrally, or as agents of change?" In Jonah, the main character is portrayed negatively; he disobeys God, he runs like a coward from his job as a prophet of God, he shows arrogance on his escape boat, he tells sailors to kill him, he gives the worst prophetic message ever in Nineveh, he complains to God, he accuses God of being too merciful, and he asks God to kill him. But then the characters you would expect to be negative examples—the pagan sailors and the ruler and people of the tyrannical Assyrian Empire—are the ones who repent and recognize God's authority. They are portrayed as positive characters. The world of this story is turned upside down, and the irony of everything that happens is part of the book's message.

Question 2: Are the claims in the passage presented as true or worthy of imitation, as false, as a warning, or as conditional? The book of Jonah is story, not poetry or persuasive essay, but some explicit claims do appear in the text. First, there is Jonah's rambling prayer from the belly of the fish, whose final line claims this: "Deliverance belongs to the Lord!" (Jonah 2:9). The truth of this statement is demonstrated several times in the narrative, as when God delivers the ship from the storm, when God delivers Jonah from the fish belly, when God spares Nineveh from destruction, and when God saves Jonah from the sun by providing a bush for shade. All of this provides strong evidence that the author is presenting this claim about deliverance belonging to the Lord as being true, perhaps even as a main idea in the text.

The second claim takes the form of a rhetorical question, but it, too, invites readers to adopt a definitive answer. After God takes away Jonah's shade and Jonah gets angry, God says, "You are concerned about the bush, for which you did not labor and which you did not grow; it came into being in a night and perished in a night. Should I not be concerned about Nineveh, that great city, in which there are more than a hundred and twenty thousand persons who do not know their right hand from their left and also many animals?" (Jonah 4:10–11). This claim is the last verse of the book, and it is the line that causes the ancient audience to think over the whole story. If they had been asked at the beginning of Jonah, "Should God be concerned about Nineveh and its people?", they would have answered with a resounding *no*. Nineveh was the enemy who had invaded and tortured them, barbarians who did not worship the God of Israel. But after seeing that the Ninevites were the positive examples in the story and realizing that the momentum of the story villainized Jonah's hatred and disobedience, their opinion would likely have shifted.

The final claim in Jonah, then, is a true claim, worthy of imitation—God should be concerned about human beings, no matter where they live or whose enemy they have become. And so should the people of Israel.

Question 3: Is the author evoking or appealing to any emotions in the passage? The author of Jonah has crafted an action-packed, irony-driven narrative full of fantasy elements. The story was likely to have evoked disapproval, confusion, fear, amusement, anticipation, judgment, and finally compassion in the ancient audience. The story is a wild ride of emotions, and that's because it needed to take its reader (or hearers) on a journey of discovery before it hit them with the perspective-altering finale. The author is pulling out all the emotional stops because the main message of the story is so countercultural that it requires a catalytic force.

Question 4: Is the author promoting a certain principle or way of looking at the world? This question is easy to answer after responding to the other questions. Yes, the author seems to be promoting a principle of radical mercy, mercy even to our enemies, as modeled by the character of God in the story. The tale promotes a way of looking at the world that does not correspond to the typical human ethos.

In the mindset of the empire-driven world, revenge and anger are acceptable and even expected responses to our enemies. But when Israel is made to consider their enemies as people made in the image of God, with vulnerabilities and remorse and repentant animals (people and animals fast and wear sackcloth for repentance in 3:7–8!), their way of looking at the world is called into question.

Question 5: Is the author trying to inspire an action or a change of perspective for their audience? The topsy-turvy reality portrayed in this narrative, in which the prophet of God is a selfish, whiny schmuck and the murderous oppressors are penitent exemplars, certainly inspires a change of perspective for its audience. But, what kind of change might that entail?

Hebrew Bible scholars who attempt to date the book of Jonah tell us that it was not written in the time period during which it is set. It was likely composed post-exile, when the people of Israel were trying to resettle the land and had decided how to interact with the foreign and pagan people in the lands around them. This story would have provoked the people to reconsider how they might relate to their neighbor-enemies. It suggests that if God could have mercy on the Ninevites and their animals, then perhaps Israel could have mercy on the Samaritans or the Persians, and even welcome them into their midst.

Pursuing rhetorical questions about emotions, persuasive goals, and perspective changes led us naturally to the main point of Jonah. We had to use information gleaned from other literary questions and historical questions, but in the end, when we asked what the author wanted the audience to feel, think, or do, it brilliantly highlighted the message of the ancient satire of Jonah.

Conclusion

We have explored a lot of literary questions in this chapter. We hope that the main ones will solidify in your mind so well that they arise every time you interpret Scripture:

- What type of literature is this? What literary devices does the author use?
- How does this passage fit in the bigger picture? (What is the literary context?)
- What is the author's primary message? What does the author want the audience to think, feel, or do in response to that message?

Biblical literature is, at its core, literature. When we ask questions that acquaint us more deeply with the text or put us in the mind of the original author and audience, then we are opening ourselves up to new and more meaningful interactions with our Scriptures.

CHAPTER 13

Ideological Questions

THE THIRD TYPE of interpretive questions we'll discuss is ideological questions. "Ideology" can be a slippery term to define, but broadly speaking, it refers to all the beliefs to which people are committed, both consciously and unconsciously. For example, among biblical scholars who draw on the social sciences to aid their interpretations of the Bible, "ideology" usually refers to a narrow set of beliefs people have that affect how they think of their social identity, made up of such factors as their gender, race, class, and sexual orientation. And in the tradition of Marxist thought, "ideology" refers to the beliefs a wealthy upper class creates and imposes on a poorer lower class, which justifies the upper class's position in the world. Each of these different ways of defining ideology is important, and you'll see each reflected in our discussion below.

Ideological questions of biblical interpretation, then, focus on the way that social identity is constructed both in the biblical text and in the life of the person interpreting the biblical text. Among the four different kinds of interpretive questions discussed in this book (historical, literary, ideological, and theological), ideological questions are the newest ones to which biblical scholars have dedicated time in an academic environment.

Let's talk about some of the most common ideological approaches biblical scholars take.

Feminist hermeneutics began as part of the wider second-wave feminist movement with figures like Mary Daly and Rosemary Radford Ruether—Catholic theologians who critically examined Christian theology and biblical narratives from a feminist perspective. But it was the scholar Phyllis Trible who combined feminist thought with academic biblical studies and set the goal of translating biblical faith without the blinders of male theologians. Feminist hermeneutics examines the way beliefs about gender are enacted in biblical narratives, idealized in biblical poetry, and institutionalized in biblical law.

Queer hermeneutics, like feminist hermeneutics, focuses on how beliefs are enacted, idealized, and institutionalized in biblical texts, but in this case the beliefs are those about sexual orientation. Queer hermeneutics covers a wide array of goals and approaches. One goal is for queer readers to describe their understanding of biblical texts as read from their lived experiences. Queer hermeneutics can also include "queering the Bible," which means questioning what has been considered normative, natural, or dominant in interpretation. In this kind of reading, being queer is different in a good way, and a queer reading of the text can help readers to see how the Bible and its interpreters may be complicit with injustice. Queer hermeneutics can also seek to trouble our assumptions about gender and sexuality and show how artificial and often superficial these concepts are.

Liberation theology focuses on issues of economic class and the experiences of the poor and marginalized. The two most common strands of liberation theology you'll likely encounter in the United States are *Black liberation theology*, which found its roots in the work of American theologian James Cone, and *Latin American liberation theology*, which arose from the work of Peruvian philosopher, theologian, and Dominican priest Gustavo Guitierrez, both in the early 1970s. Both strands of liberation theology argue that God identifies with the poor, and so they read biblical texts in search of language that can be used to combat the poor's exploitation. For example, the Mexican theologian and philosopher Jose Miranda defines "idolatry" as anything a person does to step outside of a relationship where God's commands bear on them, and further understands God's commands to require economic justice. Combining these ideas, all failures to enact economic justice are idolatrous.

Womanist theology and *mujerista theology* are intersectional approaches to biblical interpretation. What does it mean to be "intersectional"? American biblical scholar Gale Yee explains it this way:

> "Intersectionality" was a term coined in 1989 by the African American lawyer Kimberlé Crenshaw to theorize the complex interconnections between gender, race, and class that have marginalized black and nonwhite women in the subjugation they routinely experienced. Rich white men experience "oppression" different from poor women of color, because both occupy different but intersected and often conflicted locations on gender, race, and class continuums.

That is to say, not all men experience privilege and oppression the same way. Their race and class also affect how they experience them. Similarly, not all white people experience privilege and oppression the same. Their gender and class affect how they experience them. Not all poor people experience privilege and oppression the same. Their gender and race affect how they experience them. The same can be said of every constituent element of our identity. When speaking of people's experiences of privilege and oppression, we can't accurately consider their experience in light of only a single element of their identity—for example, we can't consider someone's oppression in light of their race alone. We need to consider their experience at the intersection of every element of their identity. For example, we should consider someone's oppression in light of their race, gender, and class together.

Womanist and mujerista theology recognize that feminist hermeneutics cannot speak adequately for all women because feminist hermeneutics tend to focus on the perspectives and concerns of middle-class white women. Womanist and mujerista theology seek to broaden the conversation. In womanist and mujerista readings of Scripture, the race and class consciousness of liberation theology combines with the lived experiences and wisdom of women of color.

Womanist theology, coined by biblical scholar Katie Cannon, focuses on the experiences of Black women, while mujerista theology, coined by theologian Ada Maria Isasi-Diaz, focuses on the experiences of Latina women. Both theologies are quite autobiographical approaches to interpretation, finding resources for combating contemporary oppression by identifying with characters and situations in the biblical text.

Asian theology is an expansive term used to denote ideological approaches to thinking about the Bible and other sacred texts from the perspective of Asian people. Because Asia is so large, its peoples so diverse, and its boundaries sometimes so difficult to define, part of the task of Asian theology is simply understanding what Asian experience is. Asian interpreters often compare and contrast ideas in the Bible to similar ideas in Eastern thought. Asian interpreters in the Western world reflect on their experiences of living in a diaspora—that is, as ethnic minorities dispersed outside their homeland—which is something that's relevant to many parts of the Hebrew Bible, which were composed while the Israelites were in captivity in Babylon. And many Asian interpreters think about the effect colonialism has on biblical interpretation.

These are just a sampling of the types of identity-focused theology and biblical interpretation scholars have brought to bear on the biblical text and we're not implying that the list here is exhaustive. There are types of Black, Hispanic, and Latin American theology that aren't necessarily liberationist in their goals, and types based on the experience of First Nations peoples or peoples from other parts of the world. There are types of theology based on disability status or other conditions that affect people's social experience.

That's a lot to take in and remember, so we've combined many of these concerns into four easy-to-remember interpretive questions. Each question helps us to become more conscientious of the Bible's ideologies and how those ideologies might be at work in our lives today. By asking these questions, we're able to delve into the often unstated beliefs of the Bible's original authors while finding new ways to utilize the text in conversations about morality and politics.

Are there characters with social experience I can identify with?

It's often the case when religious folks read the Bible that they find themselves identifying with its major characters, but this way of relating tends to revolve around spiritual and existential themes, such as faith and doubt, calling and hesitation, and temptation and atonement. Ideological questions help us to identify with characters for different reasons.

In her book *Sisters in the Wilderness*, womanist scholar Delores Williams talks about identifying with the character of Hagar from the early chapters of Genesis. Hagar is Black, enslaved, and forced to bear and raise a child on behalf of her enslavers, a horrific experience that was shared by generations of Black women in the United States. Hagar is sometimes overlooked by Bible readers because, while she does have some significant scenes, she's not part of the main family line that Genesis is so interested in, and she's not a character that later texts call back to.

Despite this lack of appreciation, Hagar deserves to be remembered not only for her plight but because she is the first and one of the very few characters in all biblical texts who gives God a name. In Genesis 16:13, Hagar calls God *El Roi*, "the God who sees me." This deeply personal name, given at one of the lowest points in Hagar's life, is a testament to both her resilience and her theological imagination. Delores Williams uses Hagar's naming of God as a model for other women in similar circumstances to do theological work as well. Black women doing theology is biblical.

That might not seem like an enormous revelation for you, depending on your own background, but for people who have traditionally been excluded from making substantial contributions to mainstream academic biblical and theological study (to say nothing of other marginalizations), it's a big deal.

Are there characters in the Bible whose social experience you can identify with? Asking the question requires us to be aware not only of our own social identity but the social identity of biblical characters. You can of course identify with anyone in the Bible simply because you want to. But it's a special experience to be able to identify with someone who might be in a similar place as you. It's a way of feeling seen.

Such identifications don't need to be complicated. You don't need to match a character in every respect. For example, you might identify with Jacob not because he defrauds his brother of his inheritance or labors for a decade and a half to get multiple wives, but simply because he limps (Genesis 32:31), and you, too, have a disability that affects your movement. Similarly, you might identify with Moses not because of his supernatural conflict with Egypt or his direct encounters with God, but rather because you, too, find it difficult to speak (Exodus 4:10). You might identify with the main character of the Song of Songs simply because you, too, are Black and beautiful (Song of Songs 1:5a). Or maybe you identify with Jonathan because of his deep and passionate love for another man (1Samuel 18:1–4, 20:41–42), or with Ruth for her deep and passionate love of another woman (Ruth 1:16–17), or with the disciple Jesus loved because of his physical closeness with someone he admired (John 13:22–25).

The more creative you allow yourself to be with your cooking, the more you will enjoy your meal. Similarly, the more creative you allow yourself to be with your identifications, the more you'll enjoy what the Bible has to offer.

Different people identifying with different biblical characters because of their diverse social identities is one part of what makes reading the Bible in a community such an interesting experience.

Characters that don't resonate with you might resonate with someone else; when this happens, the other person can share with you why and how. In listening to them, you not only learn more about biblical characters but about the people in your community. The more diverse your community of Bible readers is, the more characters in the biblical text you can identify with as a community, and therefore the more sharing you can do with one another.

Identifying with characters in the text is part of the way we read the Bible for the depth of its worth. Such deep reading is not something that we're required to do, but it's always available to be done. Variety is the spice of life, both with food and biblical interpretation.

What does this passage have to say about gender, race, and class?

Our second ideological question might seem like a simple one, but it's not. The question "What does this passage say about gender, race, and class?" has infinite answers for us to explore. The reason for this is obvious once we really understand how complex these pieces of our identity are.

The Elements of Social Identity

Because our social identity affects so many of our experiences of the world, it's easy to forget that in some ways, it's all made up. Gender, race, and class are very real, but they're only real because we make them real. As a society, we create the terms of what it means to have a gender, to be a race, to live in an economic class. This is called "social construction." The makeup of these categories varies from place to place. Fitting in as a man in the contemporary world is different from fitting in as a man three thousand years ago. Being wealthy in the West is different from being wealthy on the other side of the planet. And on and on. Let's look at these pieces in more detail.

Gender isn't merely a physiological fact or even a simple psychological fact. It's rather a wide range of beliefs and practices that concern the way we relate to our bodies, as well as the expansive and often unconscious social expectations that are placed on us on account of our bodies. Gender is the way we style and present ourselves to the world. It's the way we feel at home, or not, in our own skin. It's the way other people respond to us, evaluate us, enter into relationships with us, and express desire for us. It affects the way we touch and enjoy being touched. Laws are made about it. Stories are told about it. We're bombarded by advertisements telling us about it and what we need to do to live up to it. Because the fabric of gender saturates so many human ideas and experiences, it is not surprising that many stories in the Bible have something to say about it.

Many of us think of *class* as the measure of a level of income, and it is that, but it is also a relationship between a person, labor, and material goods. For instance, does a person need to work every day of their lives to the point of exhaustion just to secure basic necessities? Or do they freely engage in intellectual and artistic labors and live in relative extravagance? Does a person suffer from a constant economic anxiety about where their next meal will come from? Or can they leisurely buy anything that suits them without really having to consider the cost?

Next in our list of factors in social identity is *race*. Ostensibly, a person's race is the group they fall in on account of physical traits they've inherited, such as skin and eye color, facial features, and physical proportions. It should be mentioned that, strictly speaking, there was no such thing as "race" in the ancient world. The concept of race as we think about it today was invented by white Western scientists during the Enlightenment as a way to hierarchically classify human beings, unsurprisingly with White people on top and people of color beneath. The invention of race justified the conquest and colonization of native populations all over the world on the grounds that those people were inherently inferior to their colonizers. The concept of race has over time evolved to have less obviously supremacist overtones, and generally speaking, when people talk about their race or the race of other people, it doesn't carry a connotation of superiority. Nevertheless, the relatively recent nature of the invention of race is important to keep in mind, because race is not something we see in the Bible.

To be sure, there are different empires, kingdoms, countries, provinces, cities, tribes, clans, families, kinship relations, and other ways that people groups relate to one another. But "race" is not one of them. No one in the Bible thinks of themselves as having a race, least of all one determined by skin color, and any claim about a biblical character's race is anachronistic by definition.

Nevertheless, we can still speak of characters' ethnicities. Ethnicity is a group a person falls into on account of cultural traits they've inherited, including language, religion, social norms, foods and arts, and self-stylization through clothing and mannerisms. There are some ways in which ethnicities function similarly to race. They can both affect the way a person appears, and they are both used to categorize and relate to different people.

People take pride in their ethnicity and share culture with people of the same ethnicity. Boundaries often exist between different ethnic groups, geographic, economic, legal, religious, and so on, and so there is frequently an ideology of ethnic insiders versus ethnic outsiders in biblical texts. There are prejudices, stereotypes, and slurs used by one ethnic group against another. Laws make distinctions on the basis of people's ethnicity, and there are a few laws that require ethnic segregation or forbid ancient Israelites from interethnic marriage.

Let's look at some examples where considering social identity can enliven our reading of biblical texts. First, in Ezra 10, Ezra the scribe forces more than one hundred married couples to divorce because the women in those marriages were ethnic outsiders. The fate of the divorced women is a matter of scholarly speculation, with some scholars believing that they were sent back to live with comfortable families and others believing they were executed shortly after. Even assuming the best circumstances, the event is a sad one—and a testament to how deadly serious the book of Ezra is about rhetorically maintaining a rigid distinction between people of different ethnicities.

The book of Ruth represents the other side of the coin. In it, Ruth is identified over and over again as a Moabite woman, an ethnicity the ancient Israelites weren't supposed to intermarry with. Yet through what appears to be an act of seduction, Ruth is able to secure a marriage to an Israelite man and thereby secure a viable life for herself and the vulnerable mother-in-law she dearly loves. Ruth's interethnic marriage to Boaz is then celebrated in the text, and the genealogy at the end of the book informs us that she's an ancestor of King David. The rhetorical point of the book is quite blunt: Without interethnic marriage, we wouldn't have one of the most famous people in ancient Israelite history.

These two stories offer very different perspectives on the significance of a person's ethnicity, with one taking a stance that is painfully exclusive and the other being optimistically inclusive.

Now let's consider how ethnicity works together with other elements of social identity. Rahab from Joshua 2 is a great example of a passage in which issues of gender, ethnicity, and class converge in one story. The character Rahab was a Canaanite prostitute who owned a home built into the wall of Jericho before the Israelites conquered the city and killed its inhabitants. Her social identity (female, Canaanite, prostitute) is exactly the opposite of the two men (male, Israelite, spies) who come to scout out the city and end up in her house, and that fact creates the narrative drama of the scene.

Since the ethnic difference between Rahab and the spies is also a religious difference, and since the war Joshua is fighting is a religious war, there's initially the implied question of whether or not Rahab is genuinely going to help the spies. That tension is heightened when Rahab lies to her own king about where the spies are, and it is only later that her true motivations are revealed.

Though the tension of ethnic/religious difference is resolved, gender and class create tension of a different kind. In other circumstances, the presence of these two men in such an intimate space with Rahab would be threatening to her, but in this situation, they are the ones who are hiding from the city's authorities. Prostitutes are a socially marginalized group, yet Rahab has managed to afford a home that proves vital for sheltering the Israelite spies. Therefore, there is a reversal of gender- and class-based expectations in the story.

The story concludes with a strange combination of violent xenophobia and ethnic inclusion, as on the one hand, Joshua's army annihilates the city's entire population of Jericho because they are Canaanite, while on the other hand, Rahab and her family are integrated into the Israelite people. Whatever ethnic boundary exists between Canaanites and Israelites is simultaneously depicted as something worth killing over and something that one sympathetic deed can overcome.

Another story where social identity is vital for understanding what's happening is Jesus and the Samaritan woman in John 4. Again, social identity creates the drama. The fact of the Samaritan woman's gender and ethnicity gives both characters two reasons not to publicly associate with each other. The fact that their conversation turns to the woman's sexual history provides a gender-based reason why their conversation would be considered inappropriate.

Just as the story of the good Samaritan in the Gospel of Luke demonstrates that our moral obligations for the charitable treatment of others extends even to those with whom we have ethnic animosity, the story of the Samaritan woman at the well demonstrates that theology, evangelism, and the very person of Jesus himself extends equally far.

As the above examples show, paying attention to social identity in biblical stories can be critical for understanding the tension of scenes and the expectations of audiences. When we are attentive to social identity, whole new interpretive questions become available to us.

How can this passage be used to aid the oppressed?

Ideological approaches to biblical interpretation almost always draw on the experience of historically oppressed groups, in part because groups that haven't historically experienced oppression already have their interests represented by mainstream academia and religious institutions. There's no category called "upper-class white male theology" because for a long time, in many places, that was the only group that studied the Bible formally and wrote commentaries and taught at seminaries. All theology was upper-class white male theology because that was the theology passed down, written, and studied. I (Jennifer) was educated in evangelical seminaries, and 98 percent of the biblical interpreters I read and the theologians I studied were upper-class white males. I've had to catch up on my reading since then, and doing so has opened up a better and more expansive interpretive world for me.

One question interpreters frequently ask and have a vested interest in when they're drawing on the experience of historically oppressed groups is how a passage can be used to aid the oppressed. Black theologians and biblical scholars give us prime examples of this approach. For example, the American author and philosopher Howard Thurman saw Jesus's nonviolent resistance as a survival technique that Black Americans could apply in their context. Martin Luther King Jr. quoted the words of the prophet Amos: "Let justice roll down like waters and righteousness like an ever-flowing stream" (verse 24). American theologian James Cone saw the exodus as a quintessential example of God's desire and power to free the enslaved, while womanist scholar Delores Williams saw the period of communal wilderness travel with God in their midst as more applicable to her experience as a Black woman.

Passages like Isaiah 56:1–8 center the experiences of traditionally marginalized groups. Whereas Deuteronomy 23:1–6 prohibited eunuchs and several groups of foreigners from participating in important Israelite rituals, Isaiah 56 reverses this, imagining their full inclusion in the religious life of the community. The opening verses in Isaiah 56 also imagine giving eunuchs and foreigners the things they traditionally lacked in ancient life: respectively, an enduring name via descendants and permission to minister to God like native Israelite priests.

> Do not let the foreigner joined to the Lord say, "The Lord will surely separate me from his people," and do not let the eunuch say, "I am just a dry tree." For thus says the Lord: To the eunuchs who keep my Sabbaths, who choose the things that please me and hold fast my covenant, I will give, in my house and within my walls, a monument and a name better than sons and daughters; I will give them an everlasting name that shall not be cut off. And the foreigners who join themselves to the Lord, to minister to him, to love the name of the Lord, and to be his servants, all who keep the Sabbath and do not profane it and hold fast my covenant—these I will bring to my holy mountain and make them joyful in my house of prayer; their burnt offerings and their sacrifices will be accepted on my altar, for my house shall be called a house of prayer for all peoples. Thus says the Lord God, who gathers the outcasts of Israel: I will gather others to them besides those already gathered.
>
> Isaiah 56:3–8

This passage is, in part, why Acts 8:26–40 will later prove to be so significant: It narrates the fulfillment of Isaiah 56's inclusive dream when an Ethiopian eunuch, who would normally be doubly excluded from full religious participation, is instead taught to read Scripture so he can understand Jesus and then is baptized into the emerging Christian church.

Passages like these do nothing on their own to change us, just like raw chicken that goes unprepared cannot be eaten. But passages like these become socially and politically powerful when we ask the question "How can this passage be used to aid the oppressed?" You can start a movement with this question. You can motivate legislative reform with this question. You can change the world with this question. We know this because it's been done before.

It's not uncommon to find stories that have an interest in uplifting the oppressed in the Bible, since the Bible itself was so often written by oppressed people. This is not to say that the biblical texts never condone oppression. They do. But as we've said before, the Bible is a multivocal text, and different voices stand on different sides of nearly every issue, this one included.

Who benefits from reading this passage prescriptively?

A powerful and almost universally applicable interpretive question to have at your disposal is this: "Who benefits from reading this passage prescriptively?" A prescriptive reading of a passage is one that *prescribes* what we should do or think based on the content of the passage. A prescriptive reading might tell us that we ought to be like a character in this passage, or we ought to do what's being done in this passage, or we ought to bring about what happens in this passage. A prescriptive reading of a passage contrasts with a descriptive reading of a passage, in which we read the passage as though it's merely *describing* a character, action, or event. In descriptive readings, we don't look for a message (either overt or implied) about our own behavior. We say the passage is telling a story and leave it at that.

Let's look at a couple of examples. If we chose to read Exodus 20:7 prescriptively ("You shall not make wrongful use of the name of the Lord your God"), we'd likely refrain from taking God's name in vain today. If we chose to read Exodus 21:7 prescriptively ("If a man sells his daughter as a servant, she is not to go free as male servants do"), we'd sell our daughters into slavery. So, what we choose to read as descriptive versus prescriptive is kind of a big deal.

Asking who benefits from a prescriptive reading of a biblical passage is the interpretive equivalent of "Follow the money." It can also be asked in a couple different ways: Who originally benefited from a prescriptive reading of this passage, and who might benefit from a prescriptive reading of it today? There's almost always a specific answer to these questions, and the answers are almost always specific social groups. With the answers in hand, we can decide if we want to support or push back against prescriptive reading. If it's benefiting someone to the harm of someone else, that might be cause for concern. But if it's benefiting someone in need of recognition or help, then perhaps we'd be inclined to join in on the interpretation.

Prescriptive Readings That Favor (or Don't Favor) Men

Consider the example of 1 Timothy 2:12, in which the apostle Paul states "I do not permit a woman to teach or to have authority over a man; she is to keep silent." A feminist approach to this verse might point out that "woman" here could mean "wife," and the term "wife" could have specific, non-Christian wives in mind. Interpreting the text this way defangs it, taking away much of its power to restrict contemporary women from positions of religious leadership.

But even without engaging that analysis, we can ask ourselves: Who benefits from a prescriptive reading of this passage? The answer is pretty easy to see: religious men, both ancient and contemporary. When read prescriptively, men gain the unearned advantage of being the only ones allowed to speak in religious gatherings, teach, and hold institutional power. But when read descriptively, this is simply a biblical author's position.

On the other side of the coin we have Romans 16, in which Phoebe is a deacon (v. 1), Prisca is a coworker in Christ and leader of a house church (v. 3), and Junia is an apostle (v. 7). Who benefits from reading these passages prescriptively? Religious women, again both ancient and contemporary. In a prescriptive reading of it, men *and women* should hold leadership positions and institutional authority.

Prescriptive Readings That Advocate Prejudice

Unfortunately there's a history of prescriptively reading verses in the Bible as a justification for prejudice against LGBTQ+ people. For example, Leviticus 18:22 and 20:13 are often taken to be straightforward and comprehensive condemnations of homosexuality. But neither verse says anything like this. Instead, both condemn a specific action: "You (a male) shall not lie with a man as with a woman." The "as with a woman" part of this sentence comes from the ambiguous Hebrew phrase *mishkaveh isha*. Literally, this phrase means "the lyings of women," or even more simply, "a woman's bed." Serious linguistic analysis of this phrase has only been ongoing for thirty years, but biblical scholars today generally believe this is either a prohibition against forms of male/male incest or against the supposed feminization of the receptive partner in a sexual act. Either way, it only concerns men, and specific acts men might do, not all gay people.

Elsewhere, 1 Corinthians 6:9 and 1st Timothy 1:10 condemn *arsenokoites*, a Greek word that's sometimes irresponsibly translated as "homosexual." Not only does this Greek word not mean homosexual, it *can't* mean homosexual, since the word *homosexual* wasn't invented until the late nineteenth century. People in the ancient world didn't think of themselves as having a sexual orientation. Instead, they adopted a sexual role that was largely determined by their social status. Higher status people (wealthy free men) adopted a penetrative role, and lower status people (women and the enslaved of all genders) adopted a receptive role.

In Christian history, *aresenokoites* has been understood to refer to a male concubine, male rape, anal sex between a man and his wife, and pedophilia. It's only in the twentieth century that it also came to be understood as homosexuality. Since the word is a compound of "man" and "bed," what's certain is that, again, it only concerns men and specific acts men might do, not all gay people.

Having said that, we must point out that a prohibition against men engaging in a specific sexual act with other men is no more a prohibition against homosexuality than a prohibition against a specific kind of person eating a specific kind of food is a prohibition against all eating. Lactose intolerant people probably shouldn't eat a bucket of ice cream, but that doesn't mean no one else can, and it certainly doesn't mean that ice cream can't be the treat people prefer most.

So who benefits from reading passages like these verses prescriptively? It doesn't take a scholar to see that the answer is straight people—in particular, straight people with a desire to leverage heteronormativity and family values against others in order to center themselves and marginalize others.

Because the Bible is a multivocal text, anyone who wants to read it prescriptively is always doing so by elevating some of the Bible's voices over others. We're all picking and choosing. The question is, are we picking and choosing well? Are we picking and choosing morally? Faithfully? Sustainably?

Everyone who goes to the grocery store picks and chooses what food to purchase and all the ingredients they need to prepare that food. But you can pick healthy food or unhealthy food. Sometimes you pick foods only you like. Sometimes you pick food everyone in your house likes. Sometimes you stick to your list and your budget, and sometimes you don't. Not all picking and choosing is equal.

The Bible is like a grocery store in that way, and while we're not saying that people shouldn't shop for prescriptive readings at all, we are saying that we all should shop for them responsibly.

Conclusion

Ideological questions turn our attention to social experience and the way social experience is constructed both in the text and in our lives today. Like historical questions, ideological questions deal with biases. But while historical questions help us escape our personal biases by focusing our attention on the world of the original author and audience, ideological questions help us get the most value out of our personal biases through identifying with the text. Ideological questions also open up the possibility of liberating readings that benefit the poor and oppressed, which can fuel social transformation in the contemporary world or push back against those who would read the text to benefit oppressors.

CHAPTER 14

Theological Questions

THUS FAR, WE have suggested historical, literary, and ideological questions that readers can ask of an individual text to prepare different interpretive dishes. We have shared these different parts of the meal with you so they can help you read like a Bible scholar and become a master chef of biblical interpretation. But there is a final category of interpretive questions that we want to introduce you to, one that serves as the dessert, the final dish of our meal: theological questions.

When scholars began to study the historical-critical questions of the Bible, they inadvertently (but sometimes purposefully) began to suppress the spiritual and religious aspects of biblical study. Perhaps they could not envision how critical study of the Bible might work hand in hand with the more practical and religious studies of the church. But it does not have to be an either/or scenario. We can be responsible interpreters of the Bible when it comes to critical study and we can ask the questions that matter for the practical concerns of the church.

In this chapter we are offering three theological questions that you can ask when you want to press beyond the history and the text to ask the big *why* questions—the ones that shape people's worldviews and affect the way they think about God, faith, and the Bible.

How does this passage fit into the big picture of the Bible?

It can be tempting for people who study the Bible academically to think about the passages and books of the Bible they study as separate units, unrelated to other books and ideas in the Bible. Dealing with singular passages is more manageable, and it requires less emotional intelligence than navigating the connectedness and complexity of the diverse books of the Bible to work for the practical needs of the church. Most of the time, critical study of the Bible (especially the types of modern criticism we talked about in Chapter 10: The History of Biblical Interpretation) ignores that the books of the Bible do not stand alone, that they are part of a larger collection called the canon, and are useful for people of faith as a whole and not just as separate units.

We've talked already about how the Hebrew canon was shaped into sections called the Torah (the Pentateuch), the Prophets, and the Writings. The faith communities that chose these books and adopted them into their canon cared about how they fit together. Jewish and Christian communities have interpreted and interacted with the biblical texts as pieces of a larger discussion (probably the best word to use for Jewish communities) or a larger story (this is the way Christian communities often phrase it) throughout history. Since churches try to use the whole Bible as their guiding text, it is important that we think about how these texts fit together in a theological way—or a way that fits the diverse themes and messages together coherently.

If contemporary interpreters want to take seriously the communal nature of the Bible and heed the way our ancestors in the faith have read the Bible, then we should keep asking this question of individual passages and books: "How does this fit into the big picture of the Bible?" (Or, How does this fit into the larger discussion that is happening in Scripture and history?) This is not a literary question because it does not focus on one book and its structure or features. It is not a historical question because it cannot be limited to one time period or culture. It is also not an ideological question because it encompasses a collaborative interpretation rather than a specific community's approach to the Bible. It is a theological question because it requires that we have some sort of overarching framework that guides our interpretation.

Here's what we mean by that: The shape and story of the canon can provide that framework. But while the shape of the Bible is fixed, the story plotline or big picture is something that is open to interpretation. The Bible does not offer a statement about what big picture it is telling because the authors who wrote the books didn't know it would eventually be a part of a bigger story, part of a community's canon.

This openness means there are multiple big pictures that interpreters could use as their theological framework, since, as we have already established, the Bible is a multivocal text written by the people of God in various times. Put another way: There is more than one possible "big picture of the Bible" that a passage could be fitting into.

Three Big Pictures

For example, one story the Bible might be telling is that of how the people of God have related to God throughout history. This particular story appreciates the diverse voices in the biblical canon; it also has its ups and downs, and it is still being written. When we read a passage with this story as our framework, then we can see ourselves in the stories of the Israelites or the first Christians. We can learn from their mistakes and their successes because we tend to have similar victories and make similar mistakes in the cyclical pattern that is human history.

Another big-picture framework might be the story of how God redeems creation. This story revolves around the themes of salvation, wholeness, and hope for a better world. It is an appropriate narrative for a collection of books that starts with two creation stories, traces how the goodness of creation unravels from the questionable choices that humans make, and ends in Revelation with God bringing about a new heaven, a renewed earth, and a redeemed humanity.

This way to explain the story of the Bible has been articulated by theologians throughout church history, from Augustine to N. T. Wright, and it is often described as a four-act play: Creation, Fall, Redemption, and Restoration. When we interpret with this story in mind, it is important that we pay attention to Israel's role in the redemption part of the story and not skip over the stories and themes of the Hebrew Bible in our rush to get to Jesus. Many Christian churches throughout history have distanced themselves from the Jewish roots of the faith and separated Jesus from the bigger picture of the story of Israel.

There are, of course, many possible ways to articulate the big picture of the Bible, but we will mention just one more: the story of God's love and presence. This simplistic sounding story focuses on how the Bible's stories and poems and prophecies depict the many different ways God shows up among God's people and how God's love for humanity endures. The questions that become important in this story framework are: "Where does God show up in this passage?" and "What does this passage demonstrate about God's love?"

Jesus in the Three Stories

Let's look at a key story in Scripture—the death of Jesus—and see how it fits it into each of the three-story frameworks discussed above. The execution of Jesus is of course narrated in all four Gospels, but let's refer to Mark's account, since it is the first one written.

Our first big-picture framework is how the people of God have related to God. The events leading up to Jesus's death and his death itself fit within this big picture the way several other biblical stories do—as an example of God's people missing and even rejecting the work of God. This happens all throughout the prophetic literature, and it happens here, too, when the religious authorities, then Judas, and then the people around the cross fail to recognize Jesus as a messenger of God and accept his works and teachings as God's work.

Our second big-picture framework, the story of how God redeems creation, gives Jesus's death a central role in the story. The crucifixion, as interpreted by later Christians, is the salvific event by which God begins the redemption of all creation. The details of how this works are sketchy in Mark and the other Gospels—we do not get a clear picture of exactly *how* Jesus's death brings salvation. It is, however, clear that something important happens between God and humanity at the cross. The crucifixion (along with resurrection) is the event from which the restoration and flourishing of God and humanity's relationship move forward.

And what about our third big-picture framework, the story of God's love and presence? Mark reports hints of a divine presence at the cross when Jesus dies—darkness, a torn temple curtain, a centurion's exclamation about Jesus being God's son. Later Christian theology will claim that Jesus himself was the presence of God on earth. Jesus preaching about the kingdom, healing the sick, loving all sorts of people, and then submitting to a Roman execution, all teach us about the love of God for humanity and show us what it looks like when God's presence comes to be among the people. That Jesus suffered and endured the death of a lowly criminal at the hands of an oppressive empire gives us a picture of God's solidarity and love for those who suffer and experience oppression.

When we situate our questions about the Bible within a big-picture framework, then we can answer for ourselves the big questions that come up in life. *Who is God? Who are we? And how does God relate to us in the world?* are some of the most important questions humans ask. The Bible lays a foundation for us to answer those questions for ourselves, and we can use its stories (and its big story) to help us wrestle with the deepest parts of human existence.

How does this passage relate to the doctrines or traditions of my faith community?

Theological convictions can provide us with a sense of unity and cohesion regarding our diverse collection of biblical texts. The theological convictions shared by faith communities are sometimes called creeds, doctrines, or dogmas. If you were to visit the website of a nondenominational American church, these convictions would frequently be found under a tab that says something like "what we believe."

The earliest creeds represent the answers that church leaders came up with to settle the intense theological debates from the first centuries of the church. The Catholic Church and Protestant mainline denominations often recite these ancient creedal statements in their church services even today. The most common creed is probably the Apostle's Creed, which may date back to the third century in its earliest forms. Its final version reads:

I believe in God,
the Father almighty,
Creator of heaven and earth,
and in Jesus Christ, his only Son, our Lord,
who was conceived by the Holy Spirit,
born of the Virgin Mary,
suffered under Pontius Pilate,
was crucified, died and was buried;
he descended into hell;
on the third day he rose again from the dead;
he ascended into heaven,
and is seated at the right hand of God the Father
almighty;
from there he will come to judge the living and the dead.

I believe in the Holy Spirit,
the holy catholic Church,
the communion of saints,
the forgiveness of sins,
the resurrection of the body,
and life everlasting.

Congregations commonly use creeds like this as a way of uniting its people in similar beliefs, but these statements can also be used as a lens through which to interpret Scripture. In the scholarly world, this is called *theological interpretation*. Creeds, or the traditional beliefs of a denomination, can serve as guardrails for interpreting the Bible; they might even work as molds that help the church shape biblical content into practical doctrines for everyday use.

For example, naming the Holy Spirit as a separate person from Jesus and the Creator could help interpreters notice more clearly when and where the Spirit shows up as a character in the Bible and could motivate Christians to notice the work of the Spirit in their own lives. The same phrase, "I believe in the Holy Spirit," might also compel a reader to find descriptions of the Trinity (which is an early church doctrine, not a clearly articulated biblical concept) in places that it does not actually appear.

Clearly, then, there are pros and cons to reading Scripture through the lens of the creeds. One positive is that doing so helps the people of a faith community unify around core beliefs, guiding them toward what they may consider most important or applicable within the biblical text. There are limits to this, however.

For instance, you might have noticed that the Apostle's Creed doesn't cover many subjects. It is New Testament–focused, and although it makes several statements about Jesus, it doesn't mention anything about his life and teachings. It also highlights some ideas from the Bible that are not included in all the Gospels or that seem almost trivial to the big picture. How important is it that Jesus was born of a virgin, for example? Only two of the four Gospels report this detail, so it must not be key to the narrative. We need to be careful not to treat the creeds as biblical statements or central ideas of Scripture.

All of this still applies if you come from a church tradition that does not use the creeds. I (Jennifer) was raised Southern Baptist and have been one form of Baptist or another for most of my life. Few Baptist groups value the creeds, but we do have strong traditions and doctrines that shape church life. Remember the fundamentalist beliefs that arose as a response to modern scholarship and science? Several of those convictions—especially about the inerrancy of the Bible and the penal substitutionary atonement theory—strongly influence conservative Baptist churches to read the Bible in a certain way.

The same is true of other evangelical churches. If you asked someone from an evangelical-leaning nondenominational church what the Bible says about Jesus's death and salvation, they would likely explain that Jesus paid the legal debt or price of sin that we owed by substituting his life for ours and appeasing the wrath of God. That interpretation (penal substitution) is supported by only a few passages in the New Testament. There are many other ways that the biblical authors talk about salvation and Jesus's death, but this one doctrine dominates evangelical theology because a particular tradition dictates their interpretation of Scripture, whether they recognize it or not.

This brings up the point that the theological question of how a passage relates to the doctrines or traditions of a particular faith community may or may not be a conscious question we ask when we interpret the Bible. Our traditional theology may in fact operate as an unrecognized lens.

This is exactly why it is important to ask the question, not just so we can align ourselves with our faith community and its convictions if we so choose, but so we can make sure that we aren't imposing tradition onto the passages we study and thus hindering the text from speaking on its own terms.

How does this passage affirm or challenge my view of God or my view of humanity?

Our last theological question has the potential to both affect a person's worldview and become a guiding factor in one's biblical interpretation and life of faith. Humanity has been concerned with two profound questions for most of our history: Who are we, and who is God? Those of us who value the wisdom and witness of the Bible turn to its literature to help find answers to those questions. But such answers are complex and certainly not straightforward.

Affirming and Challenging Our Views of God

It should be clear by now that when we ask what the Bible says about God, we will find a cacophony of answers spread across the various genres and eras represented in Scripture. The Bible presents a prismatic picture of God, an image that's mediated through the experiences and perspectives of its authors. Similarly, our own views of God are multifaceted and forged in the fires of what we have read, experienced, and learned in life.

Given all that, perhaps the best way to ask the divine theological question (who is God?) is to ask how what we read in a particular passage affirms or challenges our current view of God. In this way, we acknowledge that we already come to the text with preconceived views and that what we read in Scripture might affirm, enhance, or challenge our views of who God is.

As we go about our questioning, it's important to recognize that some of the pictures the Bible paints of God are metaphorical and some are rhetorical devices used to make a point. In addition, its pictures of God are sometimes distorted by trauma or influenced by the nations that surround or dominate Israel. Views of God are complicated, mysterious, and subject to our own perspectives.

That is why the Bible's diversity and multivocality is a blessing in disguise. We can place a passage like 2 Samuel 6:67, where God strikes down Uzzah for accidentally touching the Ark of the Covenant, next to the picture of God that Jesus gives us in the parable of the prodigal son. While 2 Samuel portrays a God that is holy and powerful, one that seems to value reverence over mercy, Luke 15:11–32 gives us a God who is a loving and forgiving parent, willing to give people second chances, valuing relationships over honor.

When I (Jennifer) read these two passages, the first one clashes with the view of God that I've developed from my experience of life with God and my study of Jesus. One of my theological convictions is that Jesus embodies the character of God in his life and ministry. I can see how portraying a God who is to be revered and feared makes sense in the context of the story of Samuel, when gods and kings demanded respect and awe. But because that view of divine character challenges my view of the God who forgives an errant people and loves faithfully, I lean more into the theology of the parable of the prodigal son. This passage affirms my view of God likely because the teachings of Jesus have deeply shaped my view of God. Herein lies the beauty and complexity of a multivocal Bible: We cannot with honesty or consistency affirm everything in the Bible equally. We must decide which voices hold the most sway over our theologies and practices and why. Once we do, we can truly appreciate the diversity in the Bible and learn to apply its truths in our lives in authentic and transformative ways.

Affirming and Challenging Our Views of Humanity

The question "How does the passage affirm, challenge, or shape my view of humanity?" is a more answerable question than the God one. We have all seen human nature play out as we have interacted with people and read books of fiction and history. The nature of humanity is written all around us. This is how we can read the stories of the Bible and relate so well to them even though they were written millennia before we were born. The nature of humanity has not changed much over the course of civilization.

This is why the character of David still holds such sway over us. In the story of his rape of Bathsheba, we see many of the common ugly cracks in human nature. We recognize how prone people are to objectifying and devaluing women. We come to understand better how humans are corrupted by lust and power, how those in power often control and abuse those with no power. As we follow David's story, we realize that the urge to lie and cheat to cover our mistakes is a strong human impulse. We see how arrogant people who think they are above everything, even the law, are the most destructive among us. Finally, we see that human hubris and destructive behavior have dire consequences for the offender and everyone around him. The David and Bathsheba story affirms our worst fears about humanity, but it also challenges those fears because we read about the resilience of Bathsheba, the loyalty of Uriah, the repentance of David, and the courageous speaking-truth-to-power exemplified by Nathan.

When we come to the Bible with humility and curiosity, we can witness how humans behave in constructive and destructive ways in history and thus gain wisdom about what it means to be human. The Bible warns us about humanity's common character pitfalls—selfishness, lust for power, unfaithfulness, and fear, to name a few. But it also models traits to emulate—self-sacrifice, humility, love, and the pursuit of justice. If we want to grow in our understanding of the world and of ourselves, we should recognize what and how the Bible teaches us about ourselves. Some of its stories affirm what we hope to be true about people, some challenge our simple analysis of people, and some shape our journeys of self-understanding. All of it is a record of humans interacting with God and each other and can give us insight into one of the most profound subjects we ponder: Who is God, and who are we as beings made in the image of God?

Conclusion

The theological questions we have discussed in this chapter can help us build bridges between the ancient text that is the Bible and the everyday circumstances of our contemporary world. When we ask big picture questions—like *What is the overarching story Song of Solomon here? How does the Bible fit with my faith or faith tradition? How do the teachings of the Bible help us understand God and humanity?*—we are participating in a purposeful task that has ultimate value.

Our theological reflection serves as the final dish in the multicourse meal prep we demonstrated in this section. Recall that from the beginning of part III ("Preparing the Ingredients"), we have presented you with multiple ways to prepare interpretive dishes for yourself and others. Historical questions (chapter 11) served as the hearty and foundational first course, literary questions (chapter 12) were the savory sides of our interpretive meal, and ideological questions (chapter 13) provided us some spicy fare. Now, we have finished preparing our dessert dish of theological questions, and the full meal is ready to be served.

In part IV, "Feeding People," we will discuss the ways in which we might serve the interpretive meals we have cooked when we are feeding ourselves and when we are feeding others.

Part IV

Feeding People

If we were to ask, “What is the purpose of making food?”, you’d probably assume it was a trick question because the answer seems so obvious. The purpose of making food is to eat it. To be sure, we can make food with additional reasons in mind. Making food can be a good way to spend time with family, to celebrate a holiday or other special occasion, to entertain guests, to provide charity, or to impress someone on a date. We may make food because it’s our job, because someone depends on us, or for any other number of reasons. But even these extra reasons relate back to the main reason: to eat.

When we ask, “What’s the purpose of interpreting the Bible?”, the answer might not seem as obvious. There doesn’t seem to be a main reason like there was with food, only extra reasons. But we’d like to suggest that there *is* a main reason we interpret the Bible, and that reason is very similar to the main reason we make food: to eat. Not literally, of course, but rather to feed the cultural and spiritual imaginations of ourselves and others. That’s a kind of eating, too, and just like the traditional kind of eating, it can be delicious, nutritious, bland, poisonous, and anything in between.

Now that you’ve learned about identity in part I, about the Bible in part II, and about different interpretive questions in part III, you have all the tools you need to interpret the Bible in a great diversity of ways. The only question that remains to be answered is this: Why read the Bible at all? There are basically two answers: for yourself and for others. These final chapters will look to expand on these answers so that you can go out and interpret confidently.

CHAPTER 15

Interpreting for Yourself

LET'S RETURN TO our original metaphor of cooking. One thing that's very obvious about food is that we simply don't have to consume all of it. This is also true of the Bible, though that fact is less obvious.

Some people will take issue with that statement. Some will even argue, at great length if they're allowed, that we must choose between believing in every word of the Bible or believing in none of it. It's either all true or all false, they'll say. It's either all precious or all worthless, they'll insist. This is as absurd as saying all food is delicious or all food is gross.

Why do people argue this point? It's difficult to say for sure, but our sneaking suspicion is that people know there are life-giving things in the Bible, but they have been taught (whether they realize it or not) to gatekeep access to these beautiful things. "You can have these beautiful things," they'll essentially say, "but only if you agree with our theology, our ideology, our institution, et cetera."

Imagine a young child growing up in a church environment that celebrates prejudice, or commits and covers up abuse, or is anti-intellectual to the point of ignorance, or something else of the sort. Imagine this child reading the Bible, feeling captivated by the imagery of the psalms or the teachings of Jesus. Now imagine someone saying to this child, directly or indirectly, "You can have the psalms and Jesus, but only if you believe the same things we believe about all the rest of it." The child is told that they can have what they want, but only if they commit to interpreting the Bible the way the church interprets the Bible. "Yes, you can have the psalms, but you must hate the people we hate. Yes, you can have Jesus, but you have to vote the way we vote. Yes, you can have the Bible, but only if you ask the questions we want you to ask."

Young children are impressionable. They believe it when adults tell them the alleged cost of a thing, and so the child agrees. Years later, that former young child—now all grown up—might tell another young child what they were told, and so the cycle continues. Or perhaps, years later and upon more reflection, that once young child will realize that the adults in their life lied to them about the Bible, and they'll understandably feel betrayed.

Such a church only manufactures two kinds of people: those who are willing to toe an ideological line no matter who is hurt, and those who leave, brokenhearted.

The fact of the matter is, there are bad things in the Bible: bad people, bad actions, bad events, bad laws, bad advice, even bad pictures of God (or pictures of a bad god, depending on how a person looks at it). But it's equally true that there are good things in the Bible. Gloriously good, exquisitely good. How do we handle this variety in a healthier way than the hypothetical toxic church above? With a discerning palate.

Trying New Things

If you've ever raised a picky eater (or been one or are a partner to one), you're probably aware that the most common advice for helping a person to eat a greater variety of foods is to expose them to diversity often and in small amounts alongside food they already feel comfortable with. Does your child only eat chicken nuggets and mac and cheese? Cool, mine (Aaron's) too. How are we supposed to fix this? Put a little bit of something else on their plate, over and over and over and over again. Pediatricians say it takes seven positive exposures to a new food to acclimate a child to it. I think it's closer to seventy, but that's not my field. Regardless, the idea is that in small, experimental amounts over a long period of time, our tastes can broaden.

Now let's apply this reasoning to the Bible. Maybe you grew up interpreting the Bible by asking nothing but dogmatic, Protestant theological questions: *How does this passage support sola scriptura? How does this passage support salvation by faith? How does this passage help my personal relationship with my Lord and Savior Jesus Christ?* These were your chicken nuggets and mac and cheese. How do we broaden our tastes? Exposure to small, experimental amounts of something else over a long period of time.

Look back at the dozen or more interpretive questions detailed in part III of this book and try them out in small ways. Ask one new question of a passage. Then ask another question of the same passage. That's like making fried chicken versus making teriyaki chicken; the main ingredient is the same, but the preparation, seasoning, and sides are all different.

Next, ask yourself the same kinds of questions you'd ask after eating a new kind of food. How'd it taste going down? What'd you like and not like? Would you get the same food again? Is it a healthy food you could see yourself eating as a staple, or maybe a sweeter treat you'll only have on special occasions? Maybe it's a food you'll only eat when certain family or friends are around. Maybe it's a comfort food that you can turn to when everything else in life feels stressful.

Whatever your experience, be patient with yourself. Like with a picky toddler with a wedge of sweet potato, it might take more than one exposure to acclimate yourself to something new. But just as a picky toddler eventually gains favorite foods, if you're patient, you'll be rewarded with the capacity to appreciate brand new things and get more enjoyment out of life.

Don't Make Yourself Sick

On the other side of the coin, if you sincerely try something a few times and it keeps making you sick, stop. Please. While it may take a while to learn, there is a genuine difference between "This is making me uncomfortable because it's new and I'm not used to it" and "This is making me uncomfortable because it's bad for me." And once you learn the difference, trust yourself. For example, maybe asking certain kinds of theological questions makes you feel ill. At that point, forcing yourself to continue is self-harm, and it's far healthier to stop.

You may even be at a point in your life where asking *any* interpretive question of any part of the Bible makes you ill. Let me assure you that you're not alone in that feeling. There's nothing wrong with you, and it's not your fault. Let me say it one more time in case you're reading quickly and the last sentence is still processing. There's nothing wrong with you, and it's not your fault. Just like a bad experience with a food (or the people serving the food) can turn you off to it for years, or even the rest of your life, bad experiences with the Bible can do the same.

It's a little late in this book to say it, but it's worth saying just the same: You don't need to read the Bible at all. You can walk away from it, temporarily or permanently, for serious reasons or no reason whatsoever. Some religious folks might say, "Without the Bible, you'll suffer eternal consequences." But, to be frank, a god who requires us to love the favorite book of the people who mistreated us doesn't seem like a god worth worshipping. It takes courage to walk away from something that's hurting you when the people around you are trying to make you stay, and if you're a person who's walked away from a religious community or the Bible because you knew you'd be better off, we sincerely compliment you for your bravery.

If you've ever walked away from the Bible, or simply wanted to, here's a fun fact: Most people throughout history never had a Bible, and their faith was just fine. The Bible didn't even exist in its complete form until long after both Judaism and Christianity existed, and even then, most people couldn't read, so they didn't really engage with it. You can be a good and faithful person without interacting with the Bible at all, if that's what you need to do. Most theology doesn't come from the Bible anyway. It comes from religious tradition, reason, and the spiritual experiences of religious people in prayer, worship, and fellowship.

But assuming you're committed, for one reason or another, to reading the Bible, and assuming you've been patient with yourself, tried new interpretive questions, and expanded your interpretive palate, you're in a good position to deal with the bad and the good of the Bible.

When we're picky interpreters, and we can only interpret in a limited number of ways, we don't have many options for how to deal with the best and worst the Bible has to offer. We have to read it all the same way. But once we have a variety of interpretive questions that we feel comfortable asking, we can interpret difficult, immoral, or prejudicial passages in ways that mitigate the harm they can do, and good passages in ways that maximize the good they can do.

Enjoying Your New Palate

Here's another food analogy. Imagine that when you were young, your parents made you eat steamed and unseasoned broccoli. (This may or may not have actually happened.) You hated it as a kid, and you still can't eat it to this day.

But then let's say you learn a new way to prepare broccoli. Maybe you steam it and then flatten it onto a baking sheet with olive oil, seasoned salt, and a mix of parmesan and mozzarella cheese. Then you bake it until it's a bit crispy, and you enjoy eating broccoli for the first time in your life. Because of the way you were raised, broccoli was never going to be in the cards for you. But because you explored and experimented, now you can enjoy (or at least tolerate) the same main ingredient prepared in a different way.

We can apply the same principles of exploration and experimentation to the Bible. Let me give you an example. Deuteronomy 24 opens with a rather sexist law concerning divorce. This law of divorce is entirely unilateral, with only men being able to initiate it, and it appears as though they can initiate it for rather vague and flippant reasons. The law further bars remarriage to a divorced woman, presuming that such a woman is "defiled" after having been with another man. There are no parallel consequences for men and no condition under which they become "defiled." This is bad. Sexism is bad, and laws which reinforce sexist conditions like this are bad.

But there are also more positive things found in the rest of Deuteronomy 24, many of them related to social justice. Verses 6 and 10–15 prohibit taking advantage of poor laborers. Verses 17–22 establish a rudimentary social safety net for poor and marginalized people, securing them a basic degree of legal representation and food. All of this is good and represents values that continue to be relevant in the contemporary world.

If we were picky and inflexible interpreters, then we'd have no choice but to read these different parts of Deuteronomy 24 in the same way. If we wanted to say one passage should influence our moral thinking, then we'd need to say the same for the other. If we wanted to say one genuinely represents the desire of a good God, then we'd need to say the same for the other. But now that we've expanded our interpretive palate, we are no longer constrained in this way.

If we chose to ask standard theological questions of these verses, we'd end up asking something like "What does this tell us about God?" And we'd either have to conclude that God is sexist and sexism is good, or that since sexism is evil, this God must be evil, or, since sexism is evil but God is supposed to be good, that this God is incoherent and can't exist.

But instead, we can choose to ask historical, literary, or ideological questions of Deuteronomy 24's opening verses. Historically, who benefits from a law like this? What's the broader literary significance of the word "defile"? Ideologically, what does this say about the intersection of gender and class and how they contribute to the oppression of women? We can get interesting answers to the questions without having to affirm, teach, or theologize the sexism in these verses.

For the latter verses in Deuteronomy 24—the ones that do not portray evils like sexism—we can safely rush to ask the same theological question we avoided asking before: "What does this tell us about God?"

We find that the passage says that God is sympathetic to the plight of the poor and marginalized, and we should be too. This bit of theology is healthy, almost nutritious.

We can repeat this same strategy all throughout the Bible. When we encounter bad things, we can avoid prescriptive interpretations that would have us legitimize and repeat the bad thing in question. When we encounter good things, we can embrace prescriptive interpretations knowing that legitimizing and repeating them will benefit ourselves and those around us.

Now, a person might argue with this approach and say something like "Who are *you* to judge what is good or bad in the Bible?" And the answer is that literally anyone—any reader of the Bible—can judge what we find there. If people aren't allowed to judge what's good or bad in the Bible, then we have no basis for saying that God is good and that sin is bad. A person who says "Who are *you* to judge?" is also judging the text as they're reading it. They just don't like that you're judging it differently because that implies that their judgment isn't the only possible way to interpret the text. But as we have learned time and time again throughout this book, there are always other ways of interpreting texts. Now you have the power to interpret how you want. You may choose to judge things good that you were raised to see as bad, and you may choose to judge things bad that you were raised to see as good. Perhaps at the end of this book, you haven't changed any of your judgments at all. That's fine, too, but at least you have the tools to change them if you want to.

Conclusion

Growing up, I (Aaron) loved the TV show *Iron Chef*, originally a competitive Japanese cooking show from the 1990s in which two chefs were tasked with creating multiple courses out of a surprise main ingredient. The ingredient could be as conventional as rice or as exceptional as a cactus, a deep-sea urchin, or a softshell turtle. In sixty minutes, these chefs made all sorts of dishes: soups out of fruits, desserts out of seafood, salads out of meats, pastas out of vegetables. All of the spontaneous creativity was astounding, but as impressive as that creativity was, it wasn't the primary goal. In the end, if the judges didn't find the chef's dishes to be delicious, they couldn't win.

Your mission, should you choose to accept it, is to become an Iron Chef of the Bible, someone who's so fluent in interpretative questions that they can turn any passage in the Bible into something that satisfies them and the people they might be interpreting for. It'll take practice, and you'll have to stretch the bounds of your imagination, but the prize will nourish you for the rest of your life. The same is true for all of us. That's a very good reason to interpret for ourselves.

But perhaps the best reason to interpret for ourselves is also the simplest. Interpreting the Bible for ourselves emancipates us from having to rely on the interpretations of others. Think of it this way: If you lived in a house with a fully stocked kitchen—filled to the brim with good ingredients, dishes, and appliances—but you didn't know how to cook a thing, you wouldn't do very well for yourself. You might not starve, but your options would definitely be limited. You could graze and nibble, but you wouldn't be able to partake of a meal unless you called someone else in to cook for you. At which point, you'd be subject to their tastes. Their biases. Their preferences. Their judgments about what's good and bad. Their choice of meal—even if their choice of what to cook was dramatically different from what you'd cook if you could.

Similarly, relying on someone else's interpretation of the Bible leaves you subject to their biases and beliefs and all the other factors we've talked about that go into biblical interpretation. When someone else is interpreting, you have no power over how good your interpretation—your meal—is. You get what you get, and that's it.

When you interpret for yourself, though, you're the one asking the questions, making discoveries, making interpretive choices. Working with the ingredients. Making the meal. You have the opportunity to learn and to grow. You stand to gain a precious and empowering freedom. And who doesn't want to be freer?

You may still be asking "where is God in all of this?" Different people have different theologies, but let me be transparent with you and share mine. Maybe you'll find it helpful.

I think God is a bit like Anthony Bourdain, content to travel the world, meet people where they're at, and enjoy any food made for him that's prepared in good faith. That's biblical, by the way. When the prophet Micah rhetorically asks what foods ought to be presented to God, he considers a list of foods conventionally offered to deities by religious people. "Shall I come before him with burnt offerings, with calves a year old? Will the Lord be pleased with thousands of rams, with ten thousands of rivers of oil? Shall I give my firstborn for my transgression, the fruit of my body for the sin of my soul?" Micah 6:6b-7. But those foods don't impress God. What does? The next verse says: justice, kindness, and a humble walk with God. Are we interpreting justly, kindly, and humbly? Then you're interpreting in a theologically faithful way and God is pleased.

CHAPTER 16

Interpreting for Others

INTERPRETING THE BIBLE can be a fulfilling individual exercise, and in the last chapter we suggested some helpful ways and good reasons you might do that. But ever since the beginning of the Christian movement, even since before there was a New Testament canon, God's people have also interpreted Scripture *for* one another and *with* one another—a practice that, like cooking for others, can also be extremely fulfilling.

For example, at the end of Luke's Gospel, Jesus sits down to eat with his disciples and proceeds to open their minds and teach them about the Scriptures (Luke 24:44–45). The earliest Jesus followers in Acts study the Scriptures when they come together, and the first sermons attributed to Peter and Paul interpret passages from the Hebrew Bible for their listening crowds (Acts 2:14–36, 42; 13:13–41; 17:11). These are just a few examples of someone interpreting Scripture for (and with) someone else.

Christians have, in fact, always interpreted the Bible in communities, and it is wonderful that they do, because there is great strength in that collective endeavor. When people from different walks of life, as well as from varied ethnic, socioeconomic, gender, and cultural backgrounds, read the Bible together, a much larger world of possible interpretations opens up. In this book, we have established that the Bible was written in a way that reflects a multiplicity of voices and stories; it makes sense, then, that interpreting Scripture with a diverse community can help readers gain perspective on that multivocality.

How does all this relate to you? That—much like what and when you cook something, and for whom (and why) you cook—is up to you. There are a wide range of situations you might find yourself in when it comes to interpreting the Bible with and for others.

As an enthusiastic amateur chef, you might cook for a friend or partner as a way to demonstrate your love, or you might make a meal for your children to nourish them. You could invite a family member or friend over to cook with you so they can learn how to make a special dish of yours or simply so you can spend time together. You might serve as the chef for a celebration or a special event, cooking in order to entertain or to create a community experience. You might even cook to change the world for the better, embodying your love of God and neighbor by feeding a people in need or bringing a meal to someone who is sick.

Interpreting the Bible for others is much the same. There are many people and groups you can do this for and many reasons to do it. Below we have suggested several situations in which you might interpret the Bible with and for others. We have tried to also match each occasion with the kinds of interpretive questions that would fit best, though the list of possibilities is not exhaustive. And it doesn't need to be. The truth is, we have equipped you to be among the next generation of Iron Chefs of the Bible. That means that with practice, you can decide for yourselves which questions to ask when you are interpreting the Bible with and for other people. These ideas can help get you started.

Interpreting the Bible with and for Kids

At my (Jennifer's) church in North Carolina, our children's Sunday school class has a unique and effective way of teaching the Bible. Instead of using the cookie-cutter curriculum widely available from many evangelical Christian publishers (the kind that prescribes "truths" from Bible stories and uses them to shape kids' theology and behavior), our children's ministers write their own curriculum that promotes curiosity and wonder. Rather than tell kids what a passage means, the teachers encourage them to ask questions of the passage or imagine themselves as characters in the story world. Every week, this teaching practice produces creative and helpful interpretations from the kids, who are often more skilled readers of stories than adults are because they are open and inquisitive and bring way less interpretive baggage to the Bible.

In addition to encouraging children's questions, teachers or parents might pose adapted versions of our literary questions from chapter 12 when they read the Bible with their children. They could ask questions like: What words or images stand out to you when you hear this story? Do the characters in this story show us a good example of how to act, or do they show us an example of how *not* to act? What does this passage make you think or feel? Such questions can encourage children to treat the Bible as literature, which is what it is, and can help them grow as readers in general.

Interpreting the Bible with and for a Congregation

Not everyone has the opportunity or desire to preach in a church, but those of us who do have a responsibility to interpret the Bible for others well. Even if you don't ever preach a sermon, it is helpful to think about how the sermons you hear deal with Scripture. There is no specific set of questions that everyone who is interpreting Scripture for the purpose of preaching should ask, and that's because sermons should be tailored to the congregation and its needs. It is often the case, however, that preachers—at least those who are responsible interpreters—use the four types of questions we've covered in this book (historical, literary, ideological, and theological) when they are interpreting a passage.

It is as important to ask historical questions of a text (to provide background to a passage) as it is to ask literary questions (to understand its genre, structure, and context). A preacher might not include all their historical and literary findings in the sermon. But understanding the background knowledge and literary detail still aids in good interpretation.

Most congregations seem to expect sermons to address the theological questions of text; they trust that their pastor will explore many avenues of questions but in the end will deliver an interpretation that is helpful, practical, and applicable for their lives. That is why preachers might want to ask some of the theological questions we discussed in chapter 14, such as "How might this passage shape our view of God or humanity?" or "What does this passage demonstrate about God's love?"

When I (Jennifer) took preaching classes at seminary, we students were taught to focus our attention on the Gospel-centered question "What is the message (or the good news) in this passage for the people of God in this time and place?" Answering this question requires a well-researched understanding of the passage in question, as well as a healthy dose of congregational and cultural awareness. No one said that interpreting with and for a congregation is a simple task.

A pastor interprets *for* their people, but also *alongside* them, with an understanding of what the congregation already knows or may need to know and what questions they want to or should ask of a text. With this in mind, a preacher could determine that their congregation needs to look at a passage with new eyes and through diverse perspectives. If that is the case, then the ideological questions we discussed in chapter 13 would definitely come in handy.

The interpretive questions a preacher asks on behalf of a congregation must also extend beyond the pulpit and sanctuary into their everyday lives. This aspect of applicability usually finds its response in the invitation aspect of a sermon. The term "invitation" here does not mean playing a hymn at the end of a service and calling people to ask Jesus into their hearts (although it could mean that too). Rather, we are referring to the invitation part of a sermon that answers the most practical of interpretive questions: "Is there a response or action that this passage is calling people to take?"

Interpreting the Bible with and for a Small Group

We American Christians love our small groups. They are the backbone of congregational life in many churches, the means by which people connect to one another, support one another, and walk through life together. Small groups don't have to revolve around the Bible—they can be book club groups or craft circles or yoga classes, for example—but a large enough percentage of small groups in churches do study the Bible, so we should talk about interpreting the Bible in this context.

One of the greatest strengths of a small group is that it can function as its own interpretive community. When there are ten people in a group, there will be at least ten different perspectives represented in the conversation and even more interpretive questions asked. This is a good thing because it exposes us to others' experiences and ideas. It is also a risky thing, because as we established in chapters 2 and 3, people in a group will each have their own social locations, biases, and preunderstandings as well.

Because of this, having conversations about the interpretive process, the interpreter, and the nature of the Bible can be an important first step in getting a small group on the same page. Doing this can help everyone to get the most benefit from the diverse interpretive perspectives each person brings to the Bible. (It may be helpful to use this book as primer for any small groups you are a part of that want to study the Bible.)

Once a small group has established their interpretive foundations, the people in it face a smorgasbord of possibilities for how they can interpret together. They might choose to focus on one line of interpretive questions—such as studying the historical aspects of a text, prioritizing literary elements, or opening up fresh ideological questions. Or they may prefer to combine approaches. Whatever they choose, the key benefit to interpreting the Bible in a community is that it sparks new interpretive possibilities, opens people's minds to other people's viewpoints, and produces focal points for study according to the priorities and concerns of the particular group.

Interpreting the Bible with and for Hurting People

There are countless ways to interpret the Bible with and for others, but we will mention just one more. It is an important one because it has the potential to cause harm to those who are vulnerable. Scripture has long been a source of comfort to people who are grieving or people who find themselves in dark and difficult places. But for just as long, people have also interpreted the Bible in ways that cause injury to hurting people.

How many well-meaning Christians have tried to comfort a grieving spouse or parent with Romans 8:28: "We know that all things work together for good for those who love God, who are called according to his purpose"? They might also tack on the phrase that the writer Kate Bowler warns us about: "Everything happens for a reason, after all."

When it comes to interpreting Scripture with and for people who are sick and suffering, who have lost loved ones, or who may be in a place of doubt or pain, we do not approve of applying Bible verses or passages to reason or explain away suffering. This use of them can cause more pain than comfort. Instead, we recommend thinking of the Bible as a companion for sufferers.

So much of the Hebrew Bible was written during times of exile and famine and war; it was written by people who cried out to God in anguish, in frustration, and in fear. The psalms of lament demonstrate this kind of honesty in suffering; Ecclesiastes express the pain of people who don't understand why the world is the way it is. Offer passages like these as sustenance for the sorrowful instead of feeding those who grieve the pithy sayings of the proverbs or the pastoral optimism of the Pauline letters. In this way, you can meet hurting people where they are and sit with them there instead of using the Bible to make them feel like they need to rush through their grief and move on.

Interpretations that Nourish

Our warning about interpreting the Bible with and for people who are hurting demonstrates that not all interpretations of Scripture are helpful and life-giving. In fact, just as there are foods that are bad for us and for others, some interpretations of the Bible can be bad or even toxic.

Sometimes it's a mild kind of bad, like when we get historical facts from the Bible wrong. Did the exodus really happen as described in the Bible? People often say *yes*, but the answer is *no*. But believing that the exodus account is historically accurate is not overtly damaging.

Sometimes our interpretations of the Bible can cause great destruction, like the kind of interpretations that justify crusades, inquisitions, colonialism, slavery, the subjugation of women, or just the kind that keep us up at night afraid of the fires of hell. Bad habits of interpretation lead to bad social, psychological, and political health, and these can have, and have had, long-term negative repercussions.

Fortunately, though, there is an answer to bad habits of interpretation: good habits of interpretation. That's what this whole book is about. Good habits of interpretation work against such harm. Good interpretation can provide nourishment, sustenance, and health, much in the way good foods do.

It is our hope that the instruction we have provided in these pages has helped you to start good habits that, with practice, will make you into a cook whose interpretations nourish you and others. Once you know yourself as an interpreter, you'll be able to open yourself up to the Bible's multivocal flavor and ask good questions. Then, you can whip up interpretive masterpieces—the kind of dishes that feed our love for God and love for others.

DISCUSSION QUESTIONS

CHAPTER 1: WHAT DOES IT MEAN TO INTERPRET?

1. Of the four types of interpretive questions discussed in the chapter—historical, literary, ideological, and theological—which one do you think about the most when you read the Bible? Why do you think those questions are central to your study of the Bible?
2. Have you often encountered people who insist they are "simply" reading the text and not interpreting it, that the Bible speaks and they passively receive it? How have you responded to this claim in the past? How might you respond after reading this chapter?

CHAPTER 2: THE CHEF MATTERS: THE INTERPRETER AND THEIR CONTEXT

1. In appendix 1, we have provided a Social Location Inventory. Take the time to fill out this inventory and then continue to the next discussion question.
2. Reread the passage we discussed in this chapter: John 2:1–11. Which parts of your cultural history might affect the questions you ask or what you notice in these passages?
3. What kinds of assumptions, biases, or emotional reactions rise to the surface when you read the following poetic passage from the Song of Songs (8:6–7)? How might these influence your interpretation of the verses?

> *Set me as a seal upon your heart,*
> *as a seal upon your arm,*
> *for love is strong as death,*
> *passion fierce as the grave.*

Its flashes are flashes of fire,
a raging flame.
Many waters cannot quench love,
neither can floods drown it.
If one offered for love
all the wealth of one's house,
it would be utterly scorned.

CHAPTER 3: NAVIGATING BIASES

1. Have you ever seen someone in power deny their interpretive biases, perhaps to convince people that their reading of the Bible is objectively correct? Describe that experience.
2. What are some good ways to handle biases?
3. How have you seen your biases change over time? Why do you think this has happened and how has it changed your interpretation of the Bible?

CHAPTER 4: THE BIBLE IN GENERAL

1. Did you think of the Bible as a multivocal text before reading this chapter? If so, how did you come to that conclusion, and how has it shaped the way you interpret the Bible? If not, what might change in your reading of Scripture if you start to appreciate its multivocality more?
2. How do you feel when someone talks about the contradictions in the Bible? What influences or events in your religious journey might contribute to those feelings?
3. Some people believe that the Bible is univocal because they believe it was ultimately authored by God and has one voice. How would you describe the authorship of the Bible?

CHAPTER 5: THE PENTATEUCH

1. What do the two different accounts of creation in Genesis tell us about the nature of the Bible? How would you explain why there are two creation stories in the Pentateuch?

2. Why do you think the Exodus is one of the most referenced events in the Bible?
3. Scholars say that it is better to look at the laws in the Hebrew Bible as theological (as an idealized picture of God's will for Israel) rather than legal (as rules to be enforced). How might this view change your approach to interpreting books like Exodus and Leviticus?

CHAPTER 6: THE PROPHETS

1. First and Second Samuel present conflicting portraits of David, with some negative and some positive assessments of his character and actions. What kind of portrayal of David have you encountered in contemporary church and pop culture? Why do you think that has become the central view of David?
2. Some of the early prophets, like Amos and Micah, focus their prophetic critique on wealth and idolatry, calling the people of God to the pursuit of social justice. Has this message been central, peripheral, or ignored in your faith community? Why do you think this is?
3. One of the major goals of the prophets is to bring about change in their people. What do you think is a modern-day equivalent for the message and literature of the prophets? What brings about change in the people of God today?

CHAPTER 7: THE WRITINGS

1. What is your response to this assessment from the chapter: "In a canon that generally ignores women's agency in general and sexual agency in particular, Song of Songs is truly a standout piece of literature"?
2. In the Psalms, we read about human emotions poured out to God in poetic form. How would thinking about the psalms as human messages rather than divine instructions change the way you interpret them?
3. We encounter the phenomenon of revisioning history in the stories of 1 and 2 Chronicles. What does this retelling of history teach us about human tendencies and about the nature of the Bible?

CHAPTER 8: THE GOSPELS AND ACTS

1. What is the advantage of having four accounts of the life and ministry of Jesus? How do the unique perspectives help us understand Jesus better?
2. After reading about the specific emphases and themes of Matthew, Mark, Luke, and John, which one do you connect with the most? Why?
3. How might acknowledging Acts as a limited and purposeful account of the early church affect the way we interpret and apply it today?

CHAPTER 9: NEW TESTAMENT EPISTLES AND REVELATION

1. If we acknowledge how Paul's letters in the New Testament typically address problems specific to a particular church or individual, how might that change the way we read them in our context today?
2. Have you encountered people who read the patriarchal household codes in the New Testament and assume that they lay out God's will for families for all time? How would you respond to this interpretation?
3. What has been your experience with the book of Revelation and the interpretation of its symbolism? How might situating the book in its first-century context help you combat some of the more harmful readings of this piece of apocalyptic literature?

CHAPTER 10: THE HISTORY OF BIBLICAL INTERPRETATION

1. What can we learn from the earliest interpretations of Scripture, both Jewish and Christian?
2. The spiritual and mystical interpretation of Scripture was popular in the Middle Ages. Have you benefited from a more spiritual approach to reading Scripture? If so, how?
3. What experience, if any, do you have with the fundamentalist interpretation of Scripture? How do you think fundamentalist doctrines have impacted our society?

CHAPTER 11: HISTORICAL QUESTIONS

1. What is polytheism, and why might it be relevant for the interpretation of the Bible?
2. What is the relationship between God's attributes and the Bible?

CHAPTER 12: LITERARY QUESTIONS

1. Have you ever studied biblical literature in the same way you study other literature? If so, how has it opened new meaning to you? If not, how might it affect your interpretation if you did consider the literary context and elements of a text?
2. How did the chapter's analysis of Jonah demonstrate how paying attention to characters can illuminate important themes of a story?

CHAPTER 13: IDEOLOGICAL QUESTIONS

1. Why is gender a complicated topic when it comes to the Bible and our contemporary context?
2. How can it be valuable to identify with characters in the Bible? Give an example.

CHAPTER 14: THEOLOGICAL QUESTIONS

1. What would you or your faith community say is the big-picture story of the Bible? Did the story frameworks from the chapter resonate with you, or would you pick another one?
2. How has your view of God evolved over the course of your faith journey? What has influenced that change, if there has been one?

CHAPTER 15: INTERPRETING FOR YOURSELF

1. Why might a person gatekeep access to the best the Bible has to offer?
2. Why is it important to be patient with yourself as you interpret with the Bible?

CHAPTER 16: INTERPRETING FOR OTHERS

1. Have you ever tried to interpret the Bible with children? What were the challenges you faced? How might you do it differently after having read this book?
2. When you hear sermons that change your thinking or make an impact on you, what questions is the preacher usually addressing—historical, literary, ideological, or theological?
3. Has anyone tried to comfort you with Scripture when you were hurting or suffering? How did they do it, and how did you respond?

APPENDIX 1

Social Location Inventory

Exploring Who I Am and What I Bring to the Text

In chapter 2, we discussed the importance of social location as an important starting point for those who want to learn to interpret well. The following questions can help you understand better your culture, preconceptions, and position in society and raise your awareness of the role social location plays in the interpretive work you do. It's a good exercise to return to again and again, as all interpreters—and their work of interpretation—benefit greatly from keeping their social location at the front of their minds.

1. UNDERSTANDING MY CULTURE

Describe the various aspects of the culture or cultures you grew up in. What kind of values or behaviors did they encourage? What kinds of values and behaviors did they discourage?

Would you say the culture of your family was more individualistic or more collectivist? Did they instill independence in you, or did they model reliance on family and community help?

How has your ethnic/national heritage impacted you? How might the geographical region you come from have affected you as a person?

2. ACKNOWLEDGING MY PRECONCEPTIONS

Describe the *spiritual or religious environments* that have shaped you. What foundational values did you learn from these environments (e.g., characteristics like generosity, honesty, and concern for the poor, or commitments like following the rules or reading the Bible as inerrant)?

What are some of the *moral teachings* that have been handed down to you? Are there proverbs or sayings that were important in your upbringing? (For example, my dad loves to say, "Don't sweat the small stuff.")

How have the *intellectual or academic environments* in your history affected your priorities in life? Do you come from a family that values education or not? How has that molded you?

Would you say that you are aware of your *emotional responses* and can express emotions well? How has your history aided your emotional intelligence or hindered it?

3. EXPLORING MY DEMOGRAPHICS

For each of the following categories, describe yourself and your demographic and write a sentence about how that characteristic might influence or bias your interpretation of the Bible:

- Age and generation (Boomer, Gen X, Millennial, Gen Z, etc.)
- Gender and sexual orientation
- Race, ethnicity, or nationality
- Social class
- Marital status and history
- Political association or ideology
- Social groups or clubs that are central in your life (like CrossFit or PETA)

ACKNOWLEDGING SOCIAL LOCATION IN BIBLICAL INTERPRETATION

Reread Romans 13:1–7, which we discussed briefly in chapter 2. How might your *cultural influences*, your *preconceptions*, and the various *demographic groups* you belong to influence your interpretation of this passage, either by prompting you to read something into the passage's meaning or to overlook details in it?

ROMANS 13:1–7

Let every person be subject to the governing authorities, for there is no authority except from God, and those authorities that exist have been instituted by God. Therefore whoever resists authority resists what God has appointed, and those who resist will incur judgment. For rulers are not a terror to good conduct but to bad. Do you wish to have no fear of the authority? Then do what is good, and you will receive its approval, for it is God's agent for your good. But if you do what is wrong, you should be afraid, for the authority does not bear the sword in vain! It is the agent of God to execute wrath on the wrongdoer. Therefore one must be subject, not only because of wrath but also because of conscience. For the same reason you also pay taxes, for the authorities are God's agents, busy with this very thing. Pay to all what is due them: taxes to whom taxes are due, revenue to whom revenue is due, respect to whom respect is due, honor to whom honor is due.

APPENDIX 2

Resources for Further Study

The Bible is probably the most complicated book the average person will ever get their hands on, but that doesn't mean there isn't great information out there for how to navigate that complexity. If you're interested in learning more about the Bible and the kind of work that mainstream biblical scholars do, check out some of the resources below.

HEBREW BIBLE

For studying its cultural and historical contexts:

Amy-Jill Levine and Marc Zvi Brettler, *The Bible With and Without Jesus: How Jews and Christians Read the Same Stories Differently* (HarperOne, 2023).

A lovely book that goes back and forth between understanding the books of the Hebrew Bible in their original context and understanding those same books in light of their usage in the New Testament. With a charitable eye toward interfaith understanding, this book can help Christians, Jews, and other readers better understand how the Bible is read by people in different times and places.

Richard Elliot Friedman, *Who Wrote the Bible?* (Simon & Schuster, 2019).

Like a detective piecing together clues, Friedman shows how biblical scholars have begun to uncover the real authors of the first five books of the Bible. Easy to read and with insights that will change the way you look at some of the Bible's most famous early stories, this book is a great introduction to what academic biblical scholarship can do.

To go more in depth on the content and background of the Hebrew Bible/Old Testament, we recommend these introductions:

John J. Collins, *A Short Introduction to the Hebrew Bible*, 3d ed. (Fortress Press, 2018).

Collins's work represents a pretty standard historical-critical take on all things Hebrew Bible. It is a bit challenging, but there is great info in it. Since it's in its third edition, it's also current.

Walter Brueggemann and Tod Linafelt, *An Introduction to the Old Testament: The Canon and Christian Imagination*, 3d ed. (Westminster John Knox Press, 2021).

In this work, Brueggemann and Linafelt provide a more theological introduction to the Hebrew Bible, although they do cover history and content as well.

NEW TESTAMENT

For studying its cultural and historical contexts:

Bruce W. Longenecker, Elizabeth E. Shively, T. J. Lang, editors. *Behind the Scenes of the New Testament: Cultural, Social, and Historical Contexts* (Baker Academic Press, 2024).

This is a big book, but it is the most recent and thorough guide to the pertinent background issues for New Testament study. Some of the best scholars in the business contributed to this volume.

To go more in depth on the content and background of the New Testament, we recommend these introductions:

Raymond E. Brown, *An Introduction to the New Testament: The Abridged Edition* (Yale University Press, 2016).

This is a fairly accessible and abridged introduction to the New Testament that surveys historical and cultural background as well as other introductory matters of scholarship on the New Testament.

Eugene Boring, *An Introduction to the New Testament: History, Literature, Theology* (Westminster John Knox Press, 2012).

This is a longer introduction, but it is thorough in its investigation of the origin, importance, background, and content of the New Testament.

COMMENTARIES

If you want to use commentaries in your biblical study, we have some advice:

1. If a commentary is free online, it is probably not a solid academic commentary.
2. Good academic commentaries are expensive, but if you have access to a university library (especially a Christian one), you can find them there, either in the reference section or in the stacks, where you can check them out.
3. Commentaries on the whole Bible don't offer much depth. However, we do recommend these commentaries on the New Testament, the Old Testament, and Apocrypha because they provide multiple scholars' voices on the background and content of biblical books and they are not outrageously expensive:

Gale A. Yee, Hugh R. Page Jr., Matthew J. M. Coomber, editors. *Fortress Commentary on the Bible: The Old Testament and Apocrypha* (Fortress Press, 2014).

Margaret Aymer, Cynthia Briggs Kittredge, David A. Sanchez, editors, *Fortress Commentary on the Bible: The New Testament* (Fortress Press, 2014).

BIBLE TRANSLATIONS

Tim Wildsmith, *Bible Translations for Everyone: A Guide to Finding a Bible That's Right for You* (Zondervan, 2024).

This book helps people understand more about translation, details the different translations that are available and how they differ, and provides history for some of the translations.

OTHER BIBLE RESOURCES

Peter Enns's books and The Bible for Normal People:

Pete Enns often writes for more general audiences, and he addresses a lot of different interpretation topics. We recommend *The Bible Tells Me So*, *How the Bible Actually Works*, and *The Sin of Certainty*. *The Bible for Normal People (and Faith for Normal People)* podcast has years of episodes that focus on making the best in biblical scholarship accessible to the everyday interpreter.

Yale Lectures:

An entire Old Testament Intro course by Yale professor Christine Hayes is available on YouTube: https://www.youtube.com/watch?v=-mo-YL-lv3RY&list=PLh9mgdi4rNeyuvTEbD-Ei0JdMUujXfyWi.

An entire Old Testament Intro course by Yale professor Dale Martin is also available: https://www.youtube.com/watch?v=dtQ2TS1CiDY&list=PL279CFA55C51E75E0.

The Bible Project:

The Bible Project's YouTube channel offers a wealth of video resources on the literary structure of biblical books, key biblical themes, and biblical theology. The scholars who work on the Bible Project are more conservative in their theological commitments than Aaron and Jennifer are, but their work is solid and helpful.

https://www.youtube.com/@bibleproject

A Children's Storybook Bible:

God's Stories as Told by God's Children (The Bible for Normal People), 2025. https://www.godsstoriesbook.com/

Aaron and Jennifer both wrote for this collection and love it because its stories are written by a wide range of Bible scholars, pastors, and activists and the goal of the volume is to tell Bible stories from a scholarly perspective in a way that is accessible to children and useful for families.

NOTES

PART I: SETTING THE TABLE

9 ***It's inseparable from those from the get-go":*** Katheryn Schulz, "Eat Your Words: Anthony Bourdain on Being Wrong," *Slate*, May 31, 2010, https://slate.com/news-and-politics/2010/06/eat-your-words-anthony-bourdain-on-being-wrong.html.

CHAPTER 5: THE PENTATEUCH

75 ***As biblical scholar Robert Gnuse points out:*** Robert Karl Gnuse, *Trajectories of Justice: What the Bible Says About Slaves, Women, and Homosexuality* (Cascade Books, 2015), 25.

CHAPTER 6: THE PROPHETS

78 ***Unfortunately, Joshua and the Israelites:*** Israel Finkelstein and Neil Silberman refer to the conquest as a "classic literary expression of the yearnings and fantasies of a people at a certain time and place." Israel Finkelstein and Neil Silberman, *The Bible Unearthed: Archaeology's New Vision of Ancient Israel and the Origin of Its Sacred Texts* (Touchstone, 2002), 95.

79 ***Biblical scholars have known:*** John Collins says, "Of nearly twenty identifiable sites that were captured by Joshua or his immediate successors according to the biblical narrative, only two, Hazor and Bethel, have yielded archaeological evidence of destruction at the appropriate period." John J. Collins, *Introduction to the Hebrew Bible*, 3rd ed. (Fortress Press, 2018), 197.

91 ***According to the Jewish scholar:*** Abraham Joshua Heschel, *The Prophets* (Harper, 2001), 4.

CHAPTER 13: IDEOLOGICAL QUESTIONS

198 ***Jose Miranda defines "idolatry":*** Jose Miranda, *Marx and the Bible* (Wipf and Stock, 2004), 40.

198 ***"Intersectionality" was a term coined:*** Gale Yee, *The Hebrew Bible: Feminist and Intersectional Perspectives* (Fortress Press, 2018), 2.

201 ***Delores Williams uses Hagar's naming:*** Delores S. Williams, *Sisters in the Wilderness: The Challenge of Womanist God-Talk* (Orbis Books, 2013), 23.

206 ***American theologian James Cone:*** James Cone, *God of the Oppressed* (Orbis Books, 1997), 58.

207 ***womanist scholar Delores Williams:*** Williams, *Sisters in the Wilderness,* 160.

CHAPTER 16: INTERPRETING FOR OTHERS

237 ***They might also tack on the phrase:*** Kate Bowler, *Everything Happens for a Reason: And Other Lies I've Loved* (Penguin), 2018.